Building Micro-Frontends
Scaling Teams and Projects,
Empowering Developers

Luca Mezzalira
Foreword by Neal Ford

Beijing · Boston · Farnham · Sebastopol · Tokyo

Building Micro-Frontends

by Luca Mezzalira

Published by O'Reilly Media, Inc., 1005 Gravenstein Highway North, Sebastopol, CA 95472.

O'Reilly books may be purchased for educational, business, or sales promotional use. Online editions are also available for most titles (*http://oreilly.com*). For more information, contact our corporate/institutional sales department: 800-998-9938 or *corporate@oreilly.com*.

Acquisitions Editor: Jennifer Pollock	**Indexer:** Ellen Troutman-Zaig
Development Editor: Angela Rufino	**Interior Designer:** David Futato
Production Editor: Gregory Hyman	**Cover Designer:** Karen Montgomery
Copyeditor: nSight Inc.	**Illustrator:** O'Reilly Media, Inc.
Proofreader: Justin Billing	

November 2021:   First Edition

Revision History for the First Edition
2021-11-17:   First Release

See *http://oreilly.com/catalog/errata.csp?isbn=9781492082996* for release details.

978-1-492-08299-6

[LSI]

Table of Contents

Foreword

Named architecture styles (such as microservices) are like art periods in history—no one plans for them, no single person is responsible for the ideas, yet they suffuse through a community. For example, no group of artists gathered in France in the late 19th century and decided to create impressionism. Rather, forces in the art world (reacting to the introduction of primitive photography) drove artists toward representation rather than capturing reality.

The same is true for styles of architecture—regardless of what some developers may suspect, there is no ivory tower to which architects retreat to concoct the New Big Thing. Instead, clever architects notice new capabilities appearing within the ecosystem, and they identify ways to combine these emerging capabilities to solve old problems. For microservices, the advent of DevOps, programmatic control of machine configuration (which led to containerization), and the need for faster turnaround spawned this architecture style at several influential organizations.

In the past, the name of the architecture style would lag for several years as people figured out that a trend was underway and identified the distinguishing characteristics that would lead to a name. However, that story slightly differs for microservices. Architects have become clever about noticing the development of new trends and keep a keen eye out for them. In March 2014, Martin Fowler and James Lewis published an iconic essay on Fowler's website (*https://oreil.ly/mZEYB*) describing a new architecture style going by the name *microservices*. They didn't coin the term, but they certainly contributed to the popularity of the new style. And I suspect the authors did the industry a favor as well—their delineation of the characteristics of microservices quite early in their life cycle helped teams hone in on what *is* and *isn't* a microservice more quickly, avoiding months or years of churn trying to figure out their real uses.

Because they were describing a new phenomenon, Fowler and Lewis necessarily predicted a few things, including the impact microservices would have on user interface design. They observed that one of the defining features of microservices is the decoupling of services, and they predicted that architects would partition user interfaces to match the level of decoupling.

Alas, the real world interfered with their prediction…until now. It turns out that user interfaces are necessarily monolithic in nature: users expect to go to a single place to interact with an application, and they expect certain unified behaviors—all the parts of the user interface work in concert. While it is possible to create truly decoupled user interfaces, this has proved challenging for developers, who have awaited proper framework and tool support.

Fortunately, that support has finally arrived. You hold in your hand the definitive guide to this important aspect of microservice development. Luca Mezzalira has done an excellent job describing the problem in clear terms, following up with cutting-edge support to solve common roadblocks.

This well-organized book begins by covering the frontend issues that developers currently face, then delves into the various aspects of micro-frontends. Luca provides not only technical details but also critical ecosystem perspectives, including how to untangle a monolith into a more decoupled user interface, and how common engineering practices such as continuous integration can fit into teams' use of this new technology.

Every developer who builds microservices, regardless of whether they build user interfaces, will benefit from this enjoyable guide to a critical subject.

— *Neal Ford, Director/Software Architect/*
Meme Wrangler at Thoughtworks, Inc.

Preface

At the beginning of December 2016, I took my first trip to Tokyo. It lasted just a week but, as I would discover, I would need to travel to the Japanese capital many more times in the following weeks. I clearly remember walking to the airplane at London Heathrow and mentally preparing my to-do list for the impending 12-hour flight. By now I'd been traveling for a couple of weeks on the opposite side of the world: attending conferences in the San Francisco Bay Area and then another event in Las Vegas.

The project I was working on at that time was an over-the-top platform similar to Netflix, but dedicated to sports, with daily live and on-demand content available in multiple countries and on more than 30 different devices (web, mobile, consoles, set-top boxes, and smart TVs). It was near the end of the year, and as a software architect, I had to make a proposal for a new architecture that would allow the company to scale to hundreds of developers distributed in different locations, without reducing the current throughput and enhancing it as much as I could.

When I settled in my seat, I became relatively calm. I was still tired from the Vegas trip and a bit annoyed about the 12 hours I would have to spend on the airplane, but I was excited to see Japan for the first time. A few minutes later, I had my first glass of champagne. For the first time in my life, I was in business class, with a very comfortable seat and a lot of space for working.

At the end of the first hour, it was time to get my laptop out of my backpack and start working on "the big plan"; I still had more than 10 hours of flight time during which I could start on this huge project that would serve millions of customers around the world. I didn't know at that time that the following hours would deeply change the way I would architect cross-platform applications for frontend.

In this book, I want to share my journey into the micro-frontend world, all the lessons and tips for getting a solid micro-frontend architecture up and running, and, finally, the benefits and pitfalls of this approach. These lessons will allow you to evaluate whether this architecture would fit your current or next project.

Now it's time for your journey to begin.

Why I Wrote This Book

I started thinking about micro-frontends in 2015, and during the following years I had the opportunity to implement them in a large-scale organization with distributed teams composed of hundreds of developers and to explain their benefits and their pitfalls. During this time, I also had the opportunity to share this experience in conferences, webinars, and meetups, which gave me the possibility to engage with the community, listening to their stories, answering their questions, and engaging with other companies that embraced this paradigm in different ways.

More recently, I suggested several of the practices presented in this book to enterprise organizations all over the world, from Australia to North America. I was exposed to multiple challenges during the design and implementation phase. All the learnings are gathered in these pages as well.

This book represents my research, experiences, studies, and insights from the trenches collected over several years of work. I want to share real examples and topics that I believe are key for succeeding with micro-frontends. Finally, don't expect to find hundreds of lines of code: this book focuses on the architecture, mental models, and methodologies learned while implementing micro-frontends. In my humble opinion, it is by far more valuable to focus on multiple methods, understanding their benefits and pitfalls, rather than only a single way to implement an architecture. This is a book for everyone who is interested in learning how to use this architecture style end to end, despite the inevitable evolution we are going to see in the next few years. What you are going to learn in these pages will provide the North Star for creating successful micro-frontend projects.

Who This Book Is For

This book is for developers, architects, and CTOs who are looking to scale their organizations and frontend applications. It's a collection of mental models and experiences useful for approaching any micro-frontend architecture. In these pages, you can find the principles and the solutions applied for every approach implemented thus far. Following these practices, you will be able to achieve a micro-frontend project with the right mindset and overcome common challenges your teams are going to face during the journey.

In this book, you'll find technical architectures and implementation as well as end-to-end coverage of implementing micro-frontends, from the design phase to how to organize your teams for migrating existing or greenfield projects to micro-frontends.

How This Book Is Organized

The chapters in this book cover specific topics so a reader can jump from one to another without too many references across chapters. The best way to read this book is sequentially. However, it's also useful as a reference during working hours, so if you need to jump to a specific topic, you can pick the chapter and read just the part you are interested in.

The book covers the following:

Chapter 1, "The Frontend Landscape"
> This chapter covers the thought process for arriving at micro-frontends and provides an overview of the different architectures available for frontend development.

Chapter 2, "Micro-Frontend Principles"
> In this chapter, we analyze the principles behind microservices and how they are applicable to frontend development. In particular, we dive deep into the micro-frontend principles used as a North Star for our implementations.

Chapter 3, "Micro-Frontend Architectures and Challenges"
> This chapter is a cornerstone for understanding micro-frontends. I introduce the four key pillars for creating a successful micro-frontend architecture. The decisions framework covers how to identify, compose, orchestrate, and communicate the possibilities of micro-frontends. Once these decisions are made, we can easily design the rest of the system from any perspective, such as automation strategy, design system, and so on.

Chapter 4, "Discovering Micro-Frontend Architectures"
> There are many implementations of micro-frontends, and in this chapter we are going to explore all of them. I categorize and analyze the benefits and pitfalls of micro-frontends but, more importantly, I try to find the right use case for every architecture presented.

Chapter 5, "Micro-Frontend Technical Implementation"
> After the architecture analysis in Chapter 4, we use what we have learned so far to implement a micro-frontend project, using one of the many micro-frontend architectures available following the decisions framework.

Chapter 6, "Build and Deploy Micro-Frontends"
> This chapter covers the principles and the best practices for creating successful automation strategies for micro-frontends. Specifically, we will see different repository strategies, the key steps to include in a continuous integration pipeline, and how to deliver micro-frontends in production.

Chapter 7, "Automation Pipeline for Micro-Frontends: A Case Study"
After the theory shared in Chapter 6, this chapter discusses an example of automation strategy for micro-frontends. These are real insights from the trenches that can be immediately applicable in existing automation pipelines.

Chapter 8, "Backend Patterns for Micro-Frontends"
This chapter covers different patterns for integrating a micro-frontend architecture with a monolith API layer or with microservices. Backend for frontend (BFF), API gateways, and services dictionary are the patterns covered with examples and best practices.

Chapter 9, "From Monolith to Micro-Frontends: A Case Study"
In this chapter, we analyze a potential use case, looking at the journey to migrate a legacy frontend application to micro-frontends. We explore how ACME Inc. teams start their migration to a frontend-distributed architecture and which decisions they made for achieving their goals.

Chapter 10, "Introducing Micro-Frontends in Your Organization"
This chapter concludes the book by focusing on organization. Architecture is not only technical implementation and guidance but also, and more importantly, a mechanism for helping your teams to be successful.

Appendix, "What Does the Community Think About Micro-Frontends?"
There are plenty of stories and experiences that should be told. The community has a lot to share, and in these pages, I gathered great experiences and good suggestions from people who worked in the trenches developing micro-frontend projects at scale.

Conventions Used in This Book

The following typographical conventions are used in this book:

Italic
Indicates new terms, URLs, email addresses, filenames, and file extensions.

`Constant width`
Used for program listings, as well as within paragraphs to refer to program elements such as variable or function names, databases, data types, environment variables, statements, and keywords.

`Constant width italic`
Shows text that should be replaced with user-supplied values or by values determined by context.

This element signifies a tip or suggestion.

 This element signifies a general note.

O'Reilly Online Learning

 For more than 40 years, *O'Reilly Media* has provided technology and business training, knowledge, and insight to help companies succeed.

Our unique network of experts and innovators share their knowledge and expertise through books, articles, and our online learning platform. O'Reilly's online learning platform gives you on-demand access to live training courses, in-depth learning paths, interactive coding environments, and a vast collection of text and video from O'Reilly and 200+ other publishers. For more information, visit *http://oreilly.com*.

How to Contact Us

Please address comments and questions concerning this book to the publisher:

O'Reilly Media, Inc.
1005 Gravenstein Highway North
Sebastopol, CA 95472
800-998-9938 (in the United States or Canada)
707-829-0515 (international or local)
707-829-0104 (fax)

We have a web page for this book, where we list errata, examples, and any additional information. You can access this page at *https://oreil.ly/building-micro-frontends*.

Email *bookquestions@oreilly.com* to comment or ask technical questions about this book.

For news and information about our books and courses, visit *http://oreilly.com*.

Find us on Facebook: *http://facebook.com/oreilly*

Follow us on Twitter: *http://twitter.com/oreillymedia*

Watch us on YouTube: *http://youtube.com/oreillymedia*

Acknowledgments

First of all, I'd like to thank my family, my girlfriend Maela, and my daughters for everything they do and the strength I receive from them to move forward every single day. Thanks to all the people who inspire me on a daily basis in any shape or form of communication.

A huge thank-you to DAZN, who allowed me to apply a micro-frontends architecture and to explore the benefits of it end to end, and who trusted my ideas and judgment.

Thanks to O'Reilly for the opportunity to write about micro-frontends. In particular, thanks to Jennifer Pollock and Angela Rufino for all the support I had during these months of writing and the constant feedback for improving the book. And thanks also to Erin Brenner, my fantastic editor who spent a considerable amount of time unwinding my thoughts and translating them in what you are about to read.

To my "virtual mentor," Neal Ford, the person whom I called "the architect" for his incredible knowledge, who gently agreed to write the foreword to this book.

Finally, thanks to all the people who reviewed this manuscript and provided fundamental suggestions for improving the book. Thanks also to all the attendees of my talks and workshops who shared their experience and challenges that are probably now present in these pages.

CHAPTER 1

The Frontend Landscape

I remember a time when web applications were called rich internet applications (RIAs) to differentiate them from traditional, more static corporate websites. Today, we can find many RIAs, or web applications, across the World Wide Web. There is a proliferation of online services that allow us to print business cards on demand, watch our favorite movies or live events, order a pepperoni pizza, manage our bank accounts from our comfortable sofas, and do many, many other things that make our lives easier.

As CTOs, architects, tech leads, or developers, when we start a greenfield project, we can create a single-page application or an isomorphic one, whose code can run in both the server and the client, or even work with a bunch of static pages that run in our cloud or on-premises infrastructure. While we now have such a broad range of options, not all are fit for every job. To make the right decision for our projects, we need to understand the challenges we will face along the way.

Before we jump into the topic of this book, let's analyze the current architectures available to us when we work on a frontend application.

Micro-Frontend Applications

Micro-frontends are an emerging architecture inspired by microservices architecture. The main idea behind it is to break down a monolithic codebase into smaller parts, allowing an organization to spread out the work among autonomous teams, whether collocated or distributed, without the need to slow down their delivery throughput.

However, designing an API and encapsulating the logic into a microservice is actually the easiest part. When we realize there is significantly more to take care of, we will understand the complexity of the microservices architecture that adds not only high flexibility and good encapsulation between domains but also an overall complexity around the observability, automation, and discoverability of a system.

For instance, after creating the business logic of a service, we need to understand how a client should access our API. If it's an internal microservice that should communicate with other microservices, we need to identify a security model. Then we need to deal with the traffic that consumes our microservice, implementing techniques for spike traffic like autoscaling or caching. We also need to understand how our microservice may fail. It may fail gracefully without affecting the consumers and just hiding the functionality on the user interface. Otherwise, we need to have resilience across multiple availability zones or regions.

Working with microservices simplifies the business logic, but we need to handle an intrinsic complexity at different levels like networking, persistence layer, communication protocols, security, and many others. This is also true for micro-frontends. If the business logic and the code complexity are reduced drastically, the overhead on automation, governance, observability, and communication have to be taken into consideration.

As with other architectures, micro-frontends might not be suitable for all projects; existing architectures such as server-side rendering or Jamstack are still valid options. Nevertheless, micro-frontends can provide a new way to structure our frontend applications at scale, solving some key scalability challenges companies have encountered in the past from both a technical and organizational perspective.

Too often I have seen great architectures on paper that didn't translate well into the real world because the creator didn't take into account the environment and its context (company's structure, culture, developers' skills, timeline, etc.) where the project would have been built.

Melvin Conway's law put it best: "Any organization that designs a system (defined more broadly here than just information systems) will inevitably produce a design whose structure is a copy of the organization's communication structure."[1] Conway's law could be mitigated with the inverse Conway maneuver, which recommends that teams and organizations be structured according to our desired architecture and not vice versa. I truly believe that mastering different architectures and investing time in understanding how many systems work allow us to mitigate the impact of Conway's law, because it gives us enough tools in our belt to solve both technical and organizational challenges.

Micro-frontends, combined with microservices and a strong engineering culture where everyone is responsible for their own domain, may help achieve organizational

---

1 Melvin E. Conway, "How Do Committees Invent?" Thompson Publications, Inc., 1968. Mel Conway's Home Page, accessed October 4, 2021, *https://www.melconway.com/Home/Committees_Paper.html*.

agility and better time to market. This architecture can be used in combination with other backend architecture, such as a monolith backend or service-oriented architecture (SOA). However, micro-frontends are suited well when we can have a microservices architecture, allowing us to define slices of an application that are evolving together.

Single-Page Applications

Single-page applications (SPAs) consist of a single or a few JavaScript files that encapsulate the entire frontend application, usually downloaded up front. When the web servers or the content delivery network (CDN) serves the HTML index page, the SPA loads the JavaScript, CSS, and any additional files needed for displaying any part of our application. Using SPAs has many benefits. For instance, the client downloads the application code just once, at the beginning of its life cycle, and the entire application logic is then available up front for the entire user's session.

SPAs usually communicate with APIs by exchanging data with the persistent layer of the backend, also known as the server side. They also avoid multiple round trips to the server for loading additional application logic and render all the views instantaneously during the application life cycle.

Both features enhance the user experience and simulate what we usually have when we interact with a native application for mobile devices or desktop, where we can jump from one part of our application to another without waiting too long.

In addition, an SPA fully manages the routing mechanism on the client side. What this means is, every time the application changes a view, it rewrites the URL in a meaningful way to allow users to share the page link or bookmark the URL for starting the navigation from a specific page. SPAs also allow us to decide how we are going to split the application logic between server and client. We can have a "fat client" and a "thin server," where the client side mainly stores the logic and the server side is used as a persistence layer, or we can have a "thin client" and a "fat server," where the logic is mainly delegated to the backend and the client doesn't perform any smart logic but just reacts to the state provided by the APIs.

Over the past several decades, different schools of thought have prevailed on whether fat or thin clients are a better solution. Despite these arguments, however, both approaches have their pros and cons. The best choice always depends on the type of application we are creating. For example, I found it very valuable to have a thin client and a fat server when I was targeting cross-platform applications. It allowed me to design a feature once and have all the clients deployed on multiple targets react to the application state stored on the server.

When I had to create desktop applications in which storing some data offline was an essential feature, I often used a fat client and a thin server instead. Rather than managing the state logic in two places, I managed it in one place and used the server for data synchronization.

However, SPAs have some disadvantages for certain types of applications. The first load time may be longer than those of other architectures because we are downloading the entire application instead of only what the user needs to see. If the application isn't well designed, the download time could become a killer for our applications, especially when they are loaded with an unstable or unreliable connection on mobile devices such as smartphones and tablets.

Nowadays, we can cache the content directly on the client in several ways to mitigate the problem. On top of most consolidated techniques like code splitting or lazy-loading of JavaScript bundles, a technique worth a mention is using progressive web apps. Progressive web apps provide a set of new capabilities based on service workers. A service worker is a script that your browser runs in the background, separate from a web page, for providing functionality such as offline experience or push notifications.

Thanks to service workers, we can now create our caching strategy for a web application, with native APIs available inside the browsers. This pattern is called offline first, or cache first, and it's the most popular strategy for serving content to the user. If a resource is cached and available offline, return it first before trying to download it from the server. If it isn't in the cache already, download it and cache it for future usage. It's as simple as that but very powerful for enhancing the user experience in our web application, especially on mobile devices.

Another disadvantage relates to search engine optimization (SEO). When a crawler—a program that systematically browses the World Wide Web in order to create an index of data—is trying to understand how to navigate the application or website, it won't have an easy job indexing all the contents served by an SPA unless we prepare alternative ways for fetching it.

Usually, when we want to provide better indexing for an SPA, we tend to create a custom experience strictly for the crawler. For instance, Netflix lowers its geofencing mechanism when the user-agent requesting its web application is identified as a crawler rather than serving content similar to what a user would watch based on the country specified in the URL. This is a very handy mechanism, considering that the crawler's engine is often based in a single location from which it indexes a website all over the world.

Downloading all the application logic in one go can be a disadvantage as well because it can lead to potential memory leaks when the user is jumping from one view to another if the code is not well implemented and does not correctly dispose of the unused objects. This could be a serious problem in large applications, leading to several days or weeks of code refactoring and improvements in order to make the SPA code functional. It could be even worse if the device that loads the SPA doesn't have great hardware, like a smart TV or a set-top box. Too often I have seen applications run smoothly on a MacBook Pro quad-core and then fail miserably when running on a low-end device.

An SPA's last disadvantage is on the organizational side. When an SPA is a large application managed by distributed or colocated teams working on the same codebase, different areas of the same application could end up with a mix of approaches and decisions that could confuse team members. The communication that overhead teams use to coordinate between themselves is often a hidden cost of the application.

We often completely forget about calculating the inefficiency of our teams, not because they are not capable of developing an application but because the company structure or architecture doesn't enable them to express it in the best way possible, slowing down the operations, creating external dependencies, and overall generating friction during the development of a new feature. Also, the developers may feel a lack of ownership since many key decisions may not come from them and since the codebase of a large SPA may be started months, if not years, before they join the company.

All of these situations are not presented in the form of an invoice at the end of the month, but they might impact the teams' throughput since a complex codebase may slow down drastically the team's potential for delivery.

Isomorphic Applications

Isomorphic or universal applications are web applications where the code between server and client is shared and can run in both contexts. It is particularly beneficial for the time to interaction, A/B testing, and SEO. Thanks to the possibility of generating the page on the server side, we are in charge of optimizing our code for the key characteristics of our project.

These web applications share code between server and client, allowing the server, for instance, to render the page requested by the browser, retrieve the data to display from the database or from a microservice, aggregate it, and then prerender it with the template system used for generating the view in order to serve to the client a page that doesn't need additional round trips for requesting data to display.

Because the page requested is prerendered on the server side and is partially or fully interpreted on the backend, the time to interaction is enhanced. This avoids a lot of round trips on the frontend, so we won't need to load additional resources (vendors, application code, etc.), and the browser can interpret a static page with almost everything inside.

An SEO strategy can also be improved with isomorphic applications because the page is rendered server side without the need for additional server requests. When served, it provides the crawler an HTML page with all the information inside ready to be indexed immediately without additional round trips to the server.

Isomorphic applications share the code between contexts, but how much code is really shared? The answer depends on the context. For instance, we can use this technique in a hybrid approach, where we render part of the page on the server side to improve the time to interact and then lazy-load additional JavaScript files for the benefits of both the isomorphic application and the SPA. The files loaded within the HTML page served will add sophisticated behaviors to a static web page, transforming this page into an SPA.

With this approach, we can decide how much code is shared on the backend based on the project's requirements. For example, we can render just the views, inlining the CSS and the bare minimum JavaScript code to have an HTML skeleton that the browser can load very quickly, or we can completely delegate the rendering and data integration onto the server, perhaps because we have more static pages than heavy interactivity on the client side. We can also have a mixed approach, where we divide the application into multiple SPAs, with the first view rendered on the server side and then some additional JavaScript downloaded for managing the application behaviors, models, and routing inside the SPA.

Routing is another interesting part of an isomorphic application because we can decide to manage it on the server side, only serving a static page any time the user interacts with a link on the client.

Or we can have a mixed approach. We can use the benefits of server-side rendering for the first view and then load an SPA, where the server will do a global routing that serves different SPAs, each with its own routing system for navigating between views. With this approach, we aren't limited to template libraries; we can use virtual Document Object Model (DOM) implementations like React or Preact. Many other libraries and frameworks have started to offer server-side rendering out of the box, like Vue with Nuxt.js, Meteor, and Angular.

The last thing to mention about isomorphic applications is that we can integrate A/B testing platforms nicely without much effort. A/B testing is the act of running a simultaneous experiment between two or more variants of a page to see which one performs the best. In the past year or so, many A/B testing platforms had to catch up with the frontend technologies in not only supporting UI libraries like jQuery but also embracing virtual DOM libraries like React or Vue. Additionally, they had to make their platforms ready for hybrid mobile applications as well as native ones.

The strategy these companies adopted is to manage the experiments on the server side, leveraging the isomorphic characteristic of running on the server and client side. This is obviously a great advantage if you are working with an isomorphic application, because you can prerender on the server the specific experiment you want to serve to a specific user. Those solutions can also communicate with the clients via APIs with native mobile applications and SPAs for choosing the right experiment.

But isomorphic applications could suffer from scalability problems if a project is really successful and visited by millions of users. Because we are generating the HTML page prerendered on the server, we will need to create the right caching strategy to minimize the impact on the servers. In this case, if the responses are highly cacheable, CDNs like Akamai, Fastly, or Amazon CloudFront could definitely improve the scalability of our isomorphic applications by avoiding all the requests hitting origin servers. Organization-wise, an isomorphic application suffers similar problems as an SPA whose codebase is unique and maintained by one or multiple teams.

There are ways to mitigate the communication overhead if a team is working on a specific area of the application without any overlap with other teams. In this case, we can use architecture like backends for frontends (BFF) for decoupling the API implementation and allow each team to maintain their own layer of APIs specific to a target.

Static-Page Websites

Another option for your project is the static-page website, where every time the user clicks on a link, they are loading a new static page. This is fairly old school, but it's still in use—with some twists. A static-page website is useful for quick websites that are not meant to be online for a long period, such as ones that advertise a specific product or service we want to highlight without using the corporate website or that are meant to be simple and easier to build and maintain by the end user.

In the last few years, this type of website has mutated into a single page that expands vertically instead of loading different pages. Some of these sites also lazy-load the content, waiting until the user scrolls to a specific position to load the content. The same technique is used with hyperlinks, where all the links are anchored inside the same page and the user is browsing quickly between bits of information available on the website. These kinds of projects are usually created by small teams or individual contributors. The investment on the technical side is fairly low, and it's a good playground for developers to experiment with new technologies or new practices or to consolidate existing ones.

Jamstack

In recent years, a new frontend architecture called Jamstack (*https://jamstack.org*) (JavaScript, APIs, and Markup) emerged with great results.Jamstack is intended to be a modern architecture to help create fast and secure sites and dynamic apps with JavaScript/APIs and prerendered markup, served without web servers. In fact, the final output is a static artifact composed of HTML, CSS, and JavaScript, basically the holy trinity of frontend development. The artifact can be served directly by a CDN since the application doesn't require any server-side technology to work. One of the simplest ways for serving a Jamstack application is using GitHub pages (*https://pages.github.com*) for hosting the final result. In this category, we can find popular solutions like Gatsby.js (*https://www.gatsbyjs.org*), Next.js (*https://nextjs.org*), or Nuxt.js (*https://nuxtjs.org*).

The key advantages of these architectures are better performance and cheaper infrastructure and maintenance since they can be served directly by a CDN; great scalability because they serve static files; higher security due to the decrease of attack surface; and easy integration with headless CMS.

Jamstack is a great companion for many websites we have to create, especially considering the frictionless developer experience. In fact, frontend developers can focus only on the frontend development and debugging, and this usually means a more focused approach on the final result.

Summary

Over the years, the frontend ecosystem has evolved to include different architectures for solving different problems. A piece has been missing, though: a solution that would allow for the scaling of projects with tens or hundreds of developers working on the same project. Micro-frontends are that missing piece.

Micro-frontends will never be the only architecture available for frontend projects. Yet they provide us with multiple options for creating frontend projects at scale. Our journey in learning micro-frontends starts with their principles, analyzing how these principles should be leveraged inside an architecture and how much they resemble microservices.

CHAPTER 2

Micro-Frontend Principles

At the beginning of my career, I remember working on many software projects where small or medium-size teams were developing a monolithic application with all the functionalities of a platform available in a single artifact, and the product produced during the development of a software and deployed to a web server.

When we have a monolith, we write a lot of code that should harmoniously work together. In my experience, we tend to preoptimize or even over-engineer our application logic. Abstracting reusable parts of our code can create a more complex codebase, and sometimes the effort of maintaining a complex logic doesn't pay off in the long run. Unfortunately, something that looked straightforward at the time could look very unwieldy a few months later.

In the past decade, public cloud providers like Amazon Web Services (AWS) or Google Cloud started to gain traction. Nowadays they are popular for delegating what is increasingly becoming a commodity, freeing up organizations to focus on what really matters in a business: the services offered to the final users.

Although cloud systems allowed us to scale our projects in an easier way than before, monoliths, unfortunately, require us to scale not just a single part of our system but the entire system, causing many headaches if our system is not modularized or written with high standards.

Furthermore, working on a monolith codebase with distributed teams and colocated ones could be challenging, particularly after reaching medium or large team sizes because of the communication overhead and centralized decisions where a few people decide for everyone.

In the long run, organizations with large monoliths typically slow down all the operations necessary for advancing any new feature, losing the great momentum they had at the beginning of a project where everything was easier and smaller, with few complications and risks. Also, with monolith applications, we have to deploy the entire codebase every single time, which comes with a higher chance of breaking the APIs in production, introducing new bugs, and making more mistakes, especially when the codebase is not rock solid or extensively tested. Solving these and many other challenges its staff faces, a company might move from complex monolith codebases to multiple smaller codebases and scoped domains called *microservices*.

Nowadays, microservices architecture is a well-known, established pattern used by many organizations across the world. Microservices split a unique codebase into smaller parts, each of them with a subset of functionalities compared to a monolithic architecture, where every part is independent from each other, allowing teams full ownership and independent evolution of the codebase. This business logic is embraced by developers because the problem solved by a microservice is simpler than looking at thousands of lines of code. There is a concrete reduction of team cognitive load compared to handling a monolithic codebase.

Another significant advantage is that we can scale part of the application and use the right approach for a microservice instead of a one-size-fits-all approach similar to a monolith. However, there are also some pitfalls to working with microservices. The investment on automation, observability, and monitoring has to be completed to have a distributed system under control. Another pitfall is the wrong definition of a microservice's boundary, for instance, having a microservice that is too small for completing an action inside a system relying on other microservices, thereby causing a strong coupling between services and forcing them to be deployed together every time. When this phenomenon is extended across multiple services, we risk ending with a big ball of mud or a system that is hard to extend due to its complexity.

Microservices bring many benefits to the table but can bring many drawbacks as well. In particular, when we are embracing them in a project, the complexity of having a microservices architecture could become more painful than beneficial. Considering the amount of architecture available in software development, we should pick microservices only when needed and not choose them recklessly just because it is the latest and greatest approach.

Micro-frontends are an emerging approach to defining software deliveries along business and responsibility boundaries, in contrast to the monolithic approaches we have taken with web development in the past. Keep in mind, however, that neither microservices nor micro-frontends are a universal answer to all software decomposition. To understand where they fit in and even what they are, let's look at some of the forces that are pushing us in this direction.

Monolith to Microservices

When we start a new project or even a new business offering a service online, the first iteration should be used for understanding if our business could succeed or not. Usually, we start by identifying a *tech stack*—a list of tech services used to build and run a single app—that is familiar to our team. By minimizing the bells and whistles around the system and concentrating on the bare minimum, we're able to quickly gather information about our business idea directly from our users. This is also called an *MVP* or *minimum viable product*.

Often, we design our API layer as a unique codebase (monolith), so we need to set up one continuous integration or continuous delivery pipeline for the project. Integrating observability in a monolith application is quite easy; we just need to run an agent per virtual machine or container for retrieving the health status of our application servers. The deployment process is trivial, considering we need to handle one automation strategy for the entire API's layer and one deployment and release strategy, and when the traffic starts to increase, we can scale our machine horizontally, having as many application servers as needed to fulfill the users' requests. That's also why monolithic architectures are often a good choice for new projects since we can focus more on the business logic of an application instead of investing too much effort on other aspects, such as automation.

Where are we going to store our data? We have to decide which database better suits our project needs—a graph, a NoSQL, or a SQL database? Another decision that must be made is whether we want to host our database on a cloud service or on premises. We should select the database that will fit our business case better. For instance, if we need to create a concrete view of data to populate a user interface, probably having a NoSQL database would make more sense than any other database. At the same time, we can say that using a graph database for mapping relations between users, like in a social network application, would be a better fit for this kind of database.

Finally, we need to choose a technology for representing our data, such as within a browser or a mobile application. We can pick the best-known JavaScript framework available or our favorite programming language; we can decide to use server-side rendering or an SPA architecture; then we define our code conventions, linting, and CSS rules.

At the end, we should end up with what you can see in Figure 2-1.

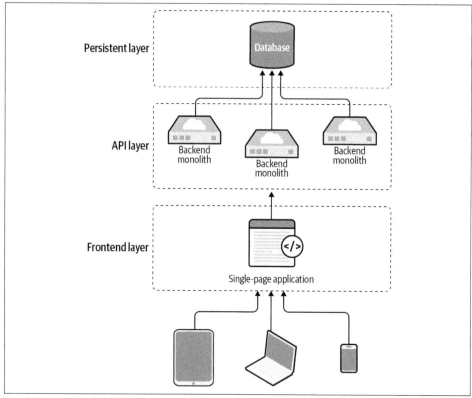

Figure 2-1. Monolith application with single-page application

Hopefully, the business ideas and goals behind our project will be validated and more users will subscribe to our online service or buy the products we sell.

Moving to Microservices

Now imagine that, thanks to the success of our system, our company decides to scale up the tech team, hiring more engineers, QAs, scrum masters, and so on. While monitoring our logs and dashboards, we realize not all our APIs are scaling organically. Some of them are highly cacheable, so the CDNs are serving the vast majority of the clients. Our origin servers are under pressure only when our APIs are not cacheable. Luckily enough, they're not all our APIs, just a small part of them.

Splitting our monolith starts to make more sense at this point, considering the internal growth and our better understanding of how the system works.

Embracing microservices also means reviewing our database strategy and, therefore, having multiple databases that are not shared across microservices; if needed, our data is partially replicated, so each microservice reduces the latency for returning the response. Suddenly, we are moving toward a consistent ecosystem with many moving parts that are providing more agility and less risk than before.

Each team is responsible for its set of microservices. Team members can make decisions on the best database to choose, the best way to structure the schemas, how to cache some information for making the response even faster, and which programming language to pick for the job. Basically, we are moving to a world where each team is entitled to make decisions and be responsible for the services they are running in production, where a generic solution for the entire system is not needed, except for the key decisions, like logging and monitoring, as we can see in Figure 2-2.

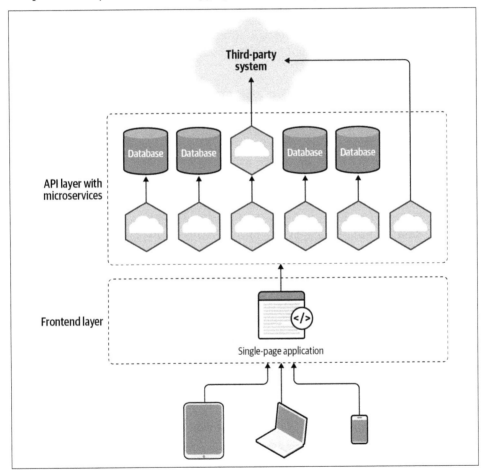

Figure 2-2. Microservices with single-page application

However, we are still missing something here. We are able to scale our API's layer and our persistent layers with well-defined patterns and best practices, but what happens when our business is growing and we need to scale our frontend teams, too?

Introducing Micro-Frontends

Historically, on the frontend we didn't have many options for scaling our applications, for several reasons. Until a few years ago, there wasn't a strong need to do so because having a fat server, where all the business logic runs, and a thin client, for displaying the result of the computation made available by the servers, was the standard approach.

This has changed a lot in the past few years. Our users are looking for a better experience when they navigate our web platforms, including more interactivity and better interactions. Companies have arisen that provide services with a subscription model, and many people are embracing those services. Now it's normal to watch videos on demand instead of on a linear channel, to listen to our favorite music inside an application instead of buying CDs, and to order food from a mobile app instead of calling a restaurant.

This shift of behaviors requires us to improve our users' experience and provide a frictionless path to accomplish what a user wants without forgetting quality content or services. In the past, we would have approached those problems by dividing parts of our application in a shared components library, abstracting some business logic in other libraries so they could be reused across different parts of the application. In general, we would have tried to reuse as much code as possible.

I'm not advocating against solutions that are still valid and fit perfectly with many projects, but we encounter quite a few challenges when embracing them. For instance, when we have a medium or large team of developers, all the rules applied to the codebase are often decided once, and we stick with them for months or even years because changing a single decision would require a lot of effort across the entire codebase and be a large investment for the organization. Also, many decisions made during the development could result in trade-offs due to lack of time, ideal consistency, or simply laziness. We must consider that a business, like technology, evolves at a certain pace and it's unavoidable.

Code abstraction is not a silver bullet either; prematurely abstracting code for reuse often causes more problems than benefits. I have frequently seen abstractions make code thousands of times more complicated than necessary, only to be reused just twice inside the same project. Many developers are prone to over-engineering some solutions, thinking they will reuse them tens if not hundreds of times, but in reality they use them far fewer times. Using libraries across multiple projects and teams could end up producing more complexity than benefits such as making the codebase more complex or requiring more effort on manual testing or adding overhead in communications.

We also need to consider the monolith approach on the frontend. Such an approach won't allow us to improve our architecture in the long run, particularly if we are working on platforms meant to be available for our users for many years or if we have distributed teams in different time zones.

Asking any business to extensively revise the tech it uses will cause a large investment up front before it gets any results. Now the question becomes quite obvious: do we have the opportunity to use a well-known pattern or architecture that offers the possibility of adding new features quickly, evolving with the business and delivering part of the application autonomously without big-bang releases?

I picture something like Figure 2-3.

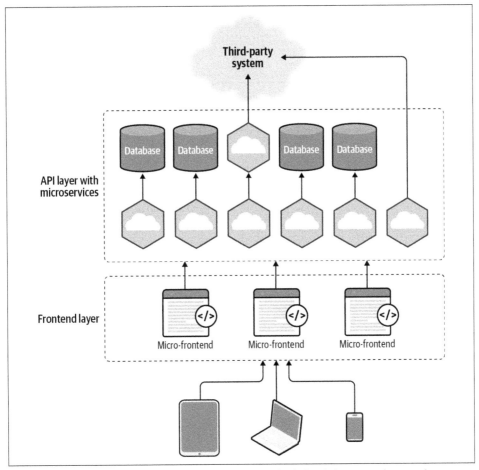

Figure 2-3. Microarchitectures combined. This is a high-level diagram showing how microservices and micro-frontends can live together.

The answer is yes, we can definitely do it, and this is where micro-frontends come to the rescue. This architecture makes more sense when we deal with mid-large companies, and during the following chapters, we are going to explore how to successfully structure our micro-frontend architectures. However, first we need to understand what the main principles behind micro-frontends are, to leverage as guidance during the development of our projects.

Microservices Principles

At the beginning of my journey into micro-frontends, I stepped back from the technical side and looked at the principles behind other architectures for scaling a software project. Would those principles be applicable to the frontend too? Microservices' principles offer quite a few useful concepts. Sam Newman has highlighted these ideas in his book *Building Microservices* (O'Reilly). I've summarized the theories in Figure 2-4.

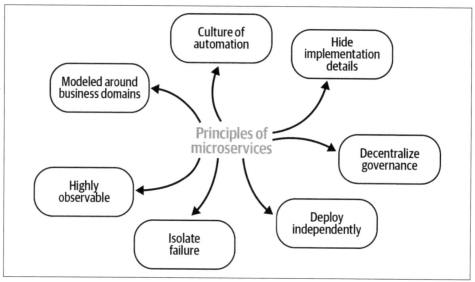

Figure 2-4. Microservices principles

Let's discuss these principles and see how they apply to the frontend.

Modeled Around Business Domains

Modeling around business domains is a key principle brought up by domain-driven design (DDD). It starts from the assumption that each piece of software should reflect what the organization does and that we should design our architectures based on domains and subdomains, leveraging ubiquitous languages shared across the business. When working from a business point of view, this provides several benefits, including a better understanding of the system, an easier definition of a technical representation of a business domain, and clear boundaries with which a team should operate. We will discuss this topic extensively in the next chapters.

Culture of Automation

Considering that microservices are a multitude of services that should be autonomous, we need a robust culture of automating the deployment of independent units in different environments. In my experience, this is a key process for leveraging microservices architecture; having a strong automation culture allows us to move faster and in a reliable way.

Hide Implementation Details

Hiding implementation details when releasing autonomously is crucial. If we are sharing a database between microservices, we won't be able to change the database schema without affecting all the microservices relying on the original schema. DDD teaches us how to encapsulate services inside the same business domain, exposing only what is needed via APIs and hiding the rest of the implementation. This allows us to change internal logic at our own pace without impacting the rest of the system.

Decentralize Governance

Decentralizing the governance empowers developers to make the right decision at the right stage to solve a problem. With a monolith, many key decisions are often made by the most experienced people in the organization. These decisions, however, frequently lead to trade-offs alongside the software life cycle. Decentralizing these decisions could have a positive impact on the entire system by allowing a team to take a technical direction based on the problems they are facing instead of creating compromises for the entire system.

Deploy Independently

Independent deployment is key for microservices. With monoliths, we are used to deploying the entire system every time, with a greater risk of live issues and longer times for deploying and rolling back our artifacts. With microservices, however, we can deploy autonomously without increasing the possibility of breaking our entire API layer. Furthermore, we have solid techniques, like blue-green deployment or canary releases (more on these in Chapter 6) that allow us to release a new version of a microservice with even less risk, which clears the path for new or updated APIs.

Isolate Failure

Because we are splitting a monolith into tens—if not hundreds—of services, if one or more microservices becomes unreachable due to network issues or service failures, the rest of the system should be available for our users. There are several patterns for providing graceful failures with microservices, and the fact that they are autonomous and independent just reinforces the concept of isolating failure.

Highly Observable

One reason that you would favor monolithic architecture in comparison to microservices is that it is easier to observe a single system than a system split into multiple services. Microservices provide a lot of freedom and flexibility, but this doesn't come for free; we need to have an eye on everything through logs, monitors, and so on. For example, we must be ready to follow a specific client request end to end inside our system. Keeping the system highly observable is one of the main challenges of microservices.

Embracing these principles in a microservices environment will require a shift in mindset not only for your software architecture but also for how your company is organized. It involves moving from a centralized to a decentralized paradigm, enabling cross-functional teams to own their business domains end to end. This can be a particularly huge change for medium to large organizations.

Applying Principles to Micro-Frontends

Now that we've grasped the principles behind microservices, let's find out how to apply them to a frontend application.

Modeled Around Business Domains

Modeling micro-frontends to follow DDD principles is not only possible but also very valuable. Investing time at the beginning of a project to identify the different business domains and how to divide the application will be useful when you add new functionalities or depart from the initial project vision in the future. DDD can provide a clear direction for managing backend projects, but we can also apply some of these techniques on the frontend. Granting teams full ownership of their business domain can be very powerful, especially when product teams are empowered to work with technology teams.

Culture of Automation

As for the microservices architecture, we cannot afford to have a poor automation culture inside our organization; otherwise, any micro-frontend approach we are going to take will end up a pure nightmare for all our teams. Considering that every micro-frontend project contains tens or hundreds of different parts, we must ensure that our continuous integration and deployment pipelines are solid and have a fast feedback loop for embracing this architecture. Investing time in getting our automation right will result in the smooth adoption of micro-frontends.

Hide Implementation Details

Hiding implementation details and working with contracts are two essential practices, especially when parts of our application need to communicate with each other. It's crucial to define up front a contract between teams and for all parties to respect that during the entire development process. In this way, each team will be able to change the implementation details without impacting other teams unless there is an API contract change. These practices allow a team to focus on the internal implementation details without disrupting the work of other teams. Each team can work at its own pace, without external dependencies, creating a more effective integration.

Decentralize Governance

Decentralizing a team's decisions finally moves us away from a one-size-fits-all approach that often ends up being the lowest common denominator. Instead, the team will use the right approach or tool for the job. As with microservices, the team is in the best position to make certain decisions when it becomes an expert in the business domain. This doesn't mean each team should take its own direction but rather that the tech leadership (architects, principal engineers, CTOs) should *provide some guardrails* between which teams can operate without needing to wait for a central decision. This leads to a sharing culture inside the organization becoming essential for introducing successful practices across teams.

Deploy Independently

Micro-frontends allow teams to deploy independent artifacts at their own speed. They don't need to wait for external dependencies to be resolved before deploying. When we combine this approach with microservices, a team can own a business domain end to end, with the ability to make technical decisions based on the challenges inside their business domain rather than finding a one-size-fits-all approach.

Isolate Failure

Isolating failure in SPAs isn't a huge problem due to their architecture, but it is with micro-frontends. In fact, micro-frontends may require composing a user interface at runtime, which may result in network failures or 404s for one or more files. To avoid impacting the user experience, we must provide alternative content or hide a specific part of the application.

Highly Observable

Frontend observability is becoming more prominent every day, with tools like Sentry and LogRocket providing great visibility for every developer. Using these tools is essential to understanding where our application is failing and why. For microservices, where anything can fail at any given point, being able to resolve the issue quickly is far more important than preventing problems. This moves us toward a paradigm where we can better invest our resources by remaining ready to address system failures than by trying to completely prevent them. As with all microservices principles, this is applicable to the frontend, too.

The exciting part of recognizing these principles on the frontend and backend is that, finally, we have a solution that will empower our development teams to own the entire range of a business domain, offering a simpler way to divide labor across the organization and iterate improvements swiftly in our system.

When we start this journey into the *microworld*, we need to be conscious of the level of complexity we are adding to a project, which may not be required for any other projects. There are plenty of companies that prefer using a monolith over microservices because of the intrinsic complexity they bring to the table. For the same reason, we must understand when and how to use micro-frontends properly, as not all projects are suitable for them.

Micro-Frontends Are Not a Silver Bullet

It's very important that we use the right tool for the right job. Too often I have seen projects failing or drastically delayed due to poor architectural decisions.

Micro-frontends are not appropriate for every application because of their nature and the potential complexity they add at the technical and organizational levels.

Micro-frontends are a sensible option when we are working on software that requires an iterative approach and long-term maintenance, when we have projects that require multiple teams to work on the same application, or when we want to replace a legacy project in an iterative way. However, they are not a silver bullet for all frontend applications, such as server-side rendering, SPAs, or even single HTML pages. Micro-frontend architecture has plenty of benefits but also has plenty of drawbacks and challenges. If the latter exceed the former, micro-frontends are not the right approach for a project. We will explore the pros and cons of this architecture later in the book.

Summary

In this chapter, we introduced what micro-frontends are, what their principles are, and how those principles are linked to the well-known, established microservices architecture. Next, we will explore how to structure a micro-frontend project from an architectural point of view and the key technical challenges to understand when we design our frontend applications using micro-frontends.

CHAPTER 3

Micro-Frontend Architectures and Challenges

A micro-frontend represents a business domain that is autonomous, independently deliverable, and owned by a single team. The key takeaways in this description, which will be discussed later, are closely linked to the principles behind micro-frontends:

- Business domain representation
- Autonomous codebase
- Independent deployment
- Single-team ownership

Micro-frontends offer many opportunities. Choosing the right one depends on the project requirements, the organization structure, and the developer's experience. In these architectures, we face some specific challenges to success bound by questions such as how we want to communicate between micro-frontends, how we want to route the user from one view to another, and, most importantly, how we identify the size of a micro-frontend.

In this chapter, we will cover the key decisions to make when we initiate a project with a micro-frontend architecture. We'll then discuss some of the companies using micro-frontends in production and their approaches.

Micro-Frontends Decisions Framework

There are different approaches for architecting a micro-frontend application. To choose the best approach for our project, we need to understand the context we'll be operating in. Some architectural decisions will need to be made up front because they will direct future decisions, like how to define a micro-frontend, how to orchestrate the different views, how to compose the final view for the user, and how micro-frontends will communicate and share data. These types of decisions are called the *micro-frontends decisions framework*. It is composed of four key areas:

- Defining what a micro-frontend is in your architecture
- Composing micro-frontends
- Routing micro-frontends
- Communicating between micro-frontends

Define Micro-Frontends

Let's start with the first key decision, which will have a heavy impact on the rest. We need to identify how we consider a micro-frontend from a technical point of view. We can decide to have multiple micro-frontends in the same view or have only one micro-frontend per view (Figure 3-1).

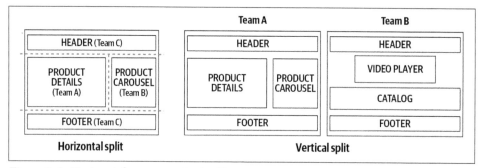

Figure 3-1. Horizontal versus vertical split

With the horizontal split, multiple micro-frontends will be on the same view. Multiple teams will be responsible for parts of the view and will need to coordinate their efforts. This approach provides greater flexibility considering we can even reuse some micro-frontends in different views, although it also requires more discipline and governance for not ending up with hundreds of micro-frontends in the same project.

In the vertical split scenario, each team is responsible for a business domain, like the authentication or the catalog experience. In this case, domain-driven design (DDD) comes to the rescue. It's not often that we apply DDD principles on frontend architectures, but in this case, we have a good reason to explore it.

DDD is an approach to software development that centers the development on programming a domain model that has a rich understanding of the processes and rules of a domain. Applying DDD for frontend is slightly different from what we can do on the backend. Certain concepts are definitely not applicable, although there are others that are fundamental for designing a successful micro-frontend architecture. For instance, Netflix's core domain is video streaming; the subdomains within that core domain are the catalog, the sign-up functionality, and the video player.

There are three subdomain types:

Core subdomains
These are the main reasons an application should exist. Core subdomains should be treated as premium citizens in our organizations because they are the ones that deliver value above everything else. The video catalog would be a core subdomain for Netflix.

Supporting subdomains
These subdomains are related to the core ones but are not key differentiators. They could support the core subdomains but aren't essential for delivering real value to users. One example would be the voting system on Netflix's videos.

Generic subdomains
These subdomains are used for completing the platform. Often companies decide to go with off-the-shelf software for them because they're not strictly related to their domain. With Netflix, for instance, the payments management is not related to the core subdomain (the catalog), but it is a key part of the platform because it has access to the authenticated section.

Let's break down Netflix with these categories (see Table 3-1).

Table 3-1. Subdomains examples

Subdomain type	Example
Core subdomain	Catalog
Supportive subdomain	Voting system
Generic subdomain	Sign-in or sign-up

Domain-Driven Design with Micro-Frontends

Another important term in DDD is the *bounded context*: a logical boundary that hides the implementation details, exposing an API contract to consume data from the model present in it.

Usually, the bounded context translates the business areas defined by domains and subdomains into logical areas where we define the model, our code structure, and, potentially, our teams. Bounded context defines the way different contexts are communicating with each other by creating a contract between them, often represented by APIs. This allows teams to work simultaneously on different subdomains while respecting the contract defined up front.

Often in a new project, subdomains overlap bounded context because we have the freedom to design our system in the best way possible. Therefore, we can assign a specific subdomain to a team for delivering a certain business value defining the contract. However, in legacy software, the bounded context can accommodate multiple subdomains because often the design of those systems was not thought of with DDD in mind.

The micro-frontend ecosystem offers many technical approaches. Some implementations are done with iframes, while others are done with components library or web components. Too often we spend our time identifying a technical solution without taking the business side into consideration.

Think about this scenario: three teams, distributed in three different locations, working on the same codebase. These teams may go for a horizontal split using iframes or web components for their micro-frontends. After a while, they realized that micro-frontends in the same view need to communicate somehow. One of those teams will then be responsible for aggregating the different parts inside the view. The team will spend more time aggregating different micro-frontends in the same view and debugging to make sure everything works properly.

Obviously, this is an oversimplification. It could be worse when taking into consideration the different time zones, cross-dependencies between teams, knowledge sharing, or distributed team structure. All those challenges could escalate very easily to low morale and frustration on top of delivery delays. Therefore, we need to be sure the path we are taking won't let our teams down.

Approaching the project from a business point of view, however, allows you to create an independent micro-frontend with less need to communicate across multiple subdomains. Let's reimagine our scenario. Instead of working with components and iframes, we are working with single page applications (SPAs) and single pages. This approach allows a full team to design all the APIs needed to compose a view and to create the infrastructure needed to scale the services according to the traffic. The combination of microarchitectures, microservices, and micro-frontends provides independent delivery without high risks for compromising the entire system for release in production.

The bounded context helps design our systems, but we need to have a good understanding of how the business works to identify the right boundaries inside our project. As architects or tech leads, our role is to invest enough time with the product team or the customers so we can identify the different domains and subdomains, working collaboratively with them.

After defining all the bounded contexts, we will have a map of our system representing the different areas that our system is composed of. In Figure 3-2, we can see a representation of bounded context. In this example, the bounded context contains the catalog micro-frontends that consume APIs from a microservices architecture via a unique entry point, a backend for frontend. We will investigate more about API integration in Chapter 8.

In DDD, the frontend is not taken into consideration, but when we work with micro-frontends with a vertical split, we can easily map the frontend and the backend together inside the same bounded context.

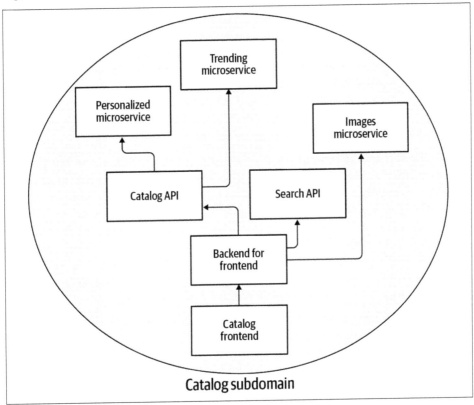

Figure 3-2. A representation of bounded context

I've often seen companies design systems in accordance with Conway's law, which states, "Organizations which design systems are constrained to produce designs which are copies of the communication structures of these organizations."[1] These companies needed their team structures to instead be flexible enough to adapt to the best possible solution for the organization in order to reduce friction and move faster toward the final goal: having a great product that satisfies customers! The inverse

---

1 Melvin E. Conway, "How Do Committees Invent?" Thompson Publications, Inc., 1968. Mel Conway's Home Page, accessed October 4, 2021, *https://www.melconway.com/Home/Committees_Paper.html.*

Conway maneuver recommends evolving your team and organizational structure to promote your desired architecture.

How to Define a Bounded Context

Premature optimization is always around the corner, which can lead to our subdomains decomposing where we split our bounded contexts to accommodate future integrations. Instead, we need to wait until we have enough information to make an educated decision.

Because our business evolves over time, we also need to review our decisions related to bounded contexts. Sometimes we start with a larger bounded context. Over time, the business evolves and eventually the bounded context becomes unmanageable or too complex. So we decide to split it. Deciding to split a bounded context could result in a large code refactor but could also simplify the codebase drastically, speeding up new functionalities and development in the future.

To avoid premature decomposition, we will make the decision at the last possible moment. This way, we have more information and clarity on which direction we need to follow. We must engage up front with the product team or the domain experts inside our organization as we define the subdomains. They can provide you with the context of where the system operates. Always begin with data and metrics. For instance, we can easily find out how our users are interacting with our application and what the user journey is when a user is authenticated and when they're not. Data provides powerful clarity when identifying a subdomain and can help create an initial baseline, from where we can see if we are improving the system or not.

If there isn't much observability inside our system, let's invest time to create it. Doing so will pay off the moment we start identifying our micro-frontends. Without dashboards and metrics, we are blind to how our users operate inside our applications. Let's assume we see a huge amount of traffic on the landing page, with 70% of those users moving to the authentication journey (sign-in, sign-up, payment, etc.). From here, only 40% of the traffic subscribes to a service or uses their credentials for accessing the service. These are good indications about our users' behaviors on our platform. Following DDD, we would start from our application's domain model, identifying the subdomains and their related bounded context and using behavioral data to guide us on how to slice the frontend applications.

Allowing users to download only the code related to the landing page will give them a faster experience because they won't have to download the entire application immediately, and the 40% of users who won't move forward to the authentication area will have just enough code downloaded to understand our service. Obviously, mobile devices with slow connections benefit from this approach for multiple reasons: less data is downloaded, less memory is used, and less JavaScript is parsed and executed, resulting in a faster first interaction of the page.

It's important to remember that not all user sessions contain all the URLs exposed by our platform. Therefore, a bit of research up front will help us provide a better user experience. Usually, the decision to pick horizontal instead of vertical depends on the type of project we have to build. In fact, horizontal split better serves static pages like catalogs or ecommerce instead of a more interactive project that would require a vertical split.

Another thing to consider is the skill sets of our teams. Usually, a vertical split is better suited for a more traditional client-side development experience, while the horizontal split requires a developer experience investment for creating a solid and fast feedback loop for the teams.

Micro-Frontends Composition

There are different approaches for composing a micro-frontends application (see Figure 3-3).

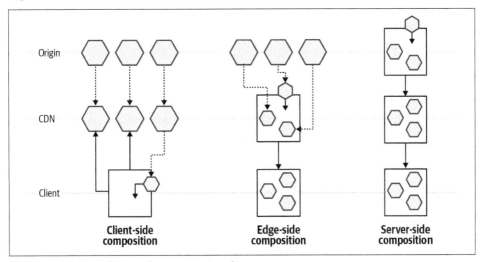

Figure 3-3. Micro-frontends composition diagram

In the diagram in Figure 3-3, we can see three different ways to compose a micro-frontends architecture:

- Client-side composition
- Edge-side composition
- Server-side composition

Starting from the left of our diagram, we have a client-side composition, where an application shell loads multiple micro-frontends directly from a content delivery network (CDN), or from the origin if the micro-frontend is not yet cached at the CDN level. In the middle of the diagram, we compose the final view at the CDN level, retrieving our micro-frontends from the origin and delivering the final result to the client. The right side of the diagram shows a micro-frontends composition at the origin level where our micro-frontends are composed inside a view, cached at the CDN level, and finally served to the client.

Let's now observe how we can technically implement each architecture.

Client-side composition

In the client-side composition case, where an application shell loads micro-frontends inside itself, the micro-frontends should have a JavaScript or HTML file as an entry point so the application shell can dynamically append the Document Object Model (DOM) nodes in the case of an HTML file or initializing the JavaScript application with a JavaScript file.

We can also use a combination of iframes to load different micro-frontends, or we could use a transclusion mechanism on the client side via a technique called client-side include. Client-side include lazy-loads components, substituting empty placeholder tags with complex components. For example, a library called *h-include* uses placeholder tags that will create an Ajax request to a URL and replace the inner HTML of the element with the response of the request.

This approach gives us many options, but using client-side includes has a different effect than using iframes. In the next chapters, we will explore this part in detail.

 According to Wikipedia (*https://oreil.ly/8p1dS*), in computer science, *transclusion* is the

> inclusion of part or all of an electronic document into one or more other documents by hypertext reference. Transclusion is usually performed when the referencing document is displayed, and it is normally automatic and transparent to the end user. The result of transclusion is a single integrated document made of parts assembled dynamically from separate sources, possibly stored on different computers in disparate places.

An example of transclusion is the placement of images in HTML. The server asks the client to load a resource at a particular location and insert it into a particular part of the DOM.

Edge-side composition

With edge-side composition, we assemble the view at the CDN level. Many CDN providers give us the option of using an XML-based markup language called Edge Side Includes (ESI). ESI (*https://oreil.ly/sdlhc*) is not a new language; it was proposed as a standard by Akamai and Oracle, among others, in 2001. ESI allows a web infrastructure to be scaled in order to exploit the large number of points of presence around the world provided by a CDN network, compared to the limited amount of data center capacity on which most software is normally hosted. One drawback to ESI is that it's not implemented in the same way by each CDN provider; therefore, a multi-CDN strategy, as well as porting our code from one provider to another, could result in a lot of refactors and potentially new logic to implement.

Server-side composition

The last possibility we have is the server-side composition, which could happen at runtime or at compile time. In this case, the origin server is composing the view by retrieving all the different micro-frontends and assembling the final page. If the page is highly cacheable, the CDN will then serve it with a long time-to-live policy. However, if the page is personalized per user, serious consideration will be required regarding the scalability of the eventual solution, when there are many requests coming from different clients. When we decide to use server-side composition, we must deeply analyze the use cases we have in our application. If we decide to have a runtime composition, we must have a clear scalability strategy for our servers in order to avoid downtime for our users.

From these possibilities, we must choose the technique most suitable for our project and team structure. As we will learn later in this journey, we also have the opportunity to deploy an architecture that exploits both client-side and edge-side composition—that's fine as long we understand how to structure our project.

Routing Micro-Frontends

The next important choice we have is how to route the application views. This decision is strictly linked to the micro-frontends composition mechanism we intend to use for the project. We can decide to route the page requests in the origin, on the edge, or at client side, as shown in Figure 3-4.

When we decide to compose micro-frontends at the origin, a server-side composition on the right side of Figure 3-4, we are forced to route the requests at origin since the entire application logic lives in the application servers. However, we need to consider that scaling an infrastructure could be nontrivial, especially when we have to manage burst traffic with many requests per second (RPS). Our servers need to be able to keep up with all the requests and scale horizontally very rapidly. Each application server then must be able to retrieve the micro-frontends for the composing page to be served.

We can mitigate this problem with the help of a CDN. The main downside is that when we have dynamic or personalized data, we won't be able to rely extensively on the CDN serving our pages because the data would be outdated or not personalized.

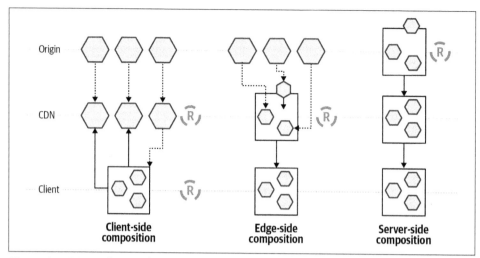

Figure 3-4. Micro-frontends routing diagram

When we decide to use edge-side composition in our architecture, the routing is based on the page URL, and the CDN serves the page requested by assembling the micro-frontends via transclusion at edge level. In this case, we won't have much room for creating smart routing—something to remember when we pick this architecture.

The final option is to use client-side routing. In this instance, we will load our micro-frontends according to the user state, such as loading the authenticated area of the application when the user is already authenticated or loading just a landing page if the user is accessing our application for the first time.

If we use an application shell that loads a micro-frontend as an SPA, the application shell is responsible for owning the routing logic, which means the application shell retrieves the routing configuration first and then decides which micro-frontend to load. This is a perfect approach when we have complex routing, such as when our micro-frontends are based on authentication, geolocalization, or any other sophisticated logic. When we are using a multipage website, micro-frontends may be loaded via client-side transclusion. There is almost no routing logic that applies to this kind of architecture because the client relies completely on the URL typed by the user in the browser or the hyperlink chosen in another page, similar to what we have when we use the ESI approach.

We won't have any scalability issue in either case. The client-side routing is highly recommended when your teams have stronger frontend skills so that it becomes natural having a client-side routing over a backend configuration.

Those routing approaches are not mutually exclusive, either. As we will see later in this book, we can combine those approaches using CDN and origin or client-side and CDN together. The important thing is determining how we want to route our application. This fundamental decision will affect how we develop our micro-frontends application.

Micro-Frontends Communication

In an ideal world, micro-frontends wouldn't need to communicate with each other because all of them would be self-sufficient. In reality, it's not always possible, because we have to notify other micro-frontends about user interaction, especially when we work with multiple micro-frontends on the same page.

When we have multiple micro-frontends on the same page, the complexity of managing a consistent, coherent user interface for our users may not be trivial. This is also true when we want communication between micro-frontends owned by different teams. Bear in mind that each micro-frontend should be unaware of the others on the same page; otherwise, we are breaking the principle of independent deployment.

In this case, we have a few options for notifying other micro-frontends that an event occurred. We can inject an eventbus, a mechanism that allows decoupled components to communicate with each other via events sent via a bus, in each micro-frontend, and notify the event to every micro-frontend. If some micro-frontends in the view are interested in the event, they can listen and react, as shown in Figure 3-5.

To inject the eventbus, we need the micro-frontends container to instantiate the eventbus and inject it inside all of the page's micro-frontends.

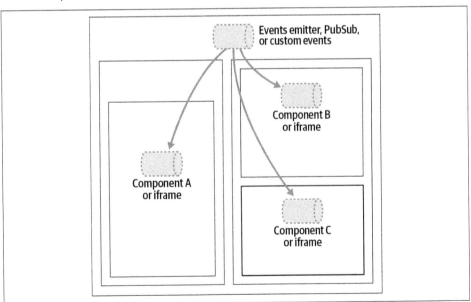

Figure 3-5. Event emitter and custom events diagram

Another solution is to use custom events (*https://oreil.ly/maiME*). These are normal events but with a custom body, which allows us to define the string that identifies the event and an optional object custom for the event. Here's an example:

```
new CustomEvent('myCustomEvent', { detail:{someObj: "customData" }})
```

The custom events should be dispatched via an object available to all the micro-frontends, such as the window object, which is the representation of a window in a browser. If you decide to implement your micro-frontends with iframes, using an eventbus would allow you to avoid challenges like which window object to use from inside the iframe, because each iframe has its own window object. No matter whether we have a horizontal or a vertical split of our micro-frontends, we need to decide how to pass data between views.

Imagine we have one micro-frontend for signing in a user and another for authenticating the user on our platform. After being successfully authenticated, the sign-in micro-frontend has to pass a token to the authenticated area of our platform. How can we pass the token from one micro-frontend to another? We have several options.

We can use a web-storage-like session, local storage, or cookies (see Figure 3-6). In this situation, we might use the local storage to store and retrieve the token independently. The micro-frontend is loaded because the web storage is always available and accessible, as long as the micro-frontends live in the same subdomain.

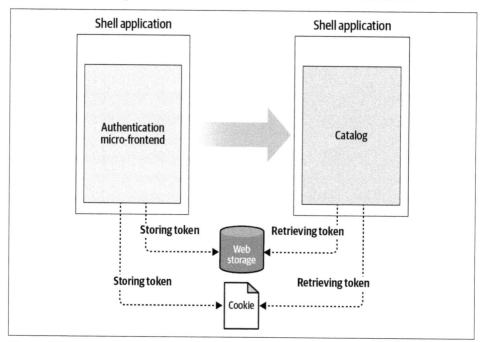

Figure 3-6. Sharing data between micro-frontends in different views

Another option could be to pass some data via query strings. For example, in the hypothetical URL *http://www.acme.com/products/details?id=123*, the text after the question mark represents the query string—in this case, the "ID 123" of a specific product selected by the user—and retrieves the full details to display via an API (see Figure 3-7). However, using query strings is not the most secure way to pass sensitive data, such as passwords and user IDs. There are better ways to retrieve that information if it's passed via the HTTPS protocol. Embrace this solution carefully.

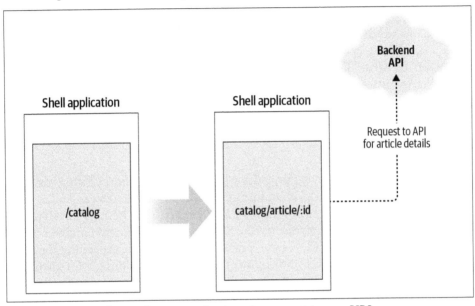

Figure 3-7. Micro-frontends communication via query strings or URL

To summarize, the micro-frontends decisions framework is composed of four key decisions: identifying, composing, routing, and communicating. In Table 3-2 you can find all the combinations available based on how you identify a micro-frontend.

Table 3-2. Micro-frontends decisions framework summary

Micro-frontends definition	Composition	Routing	Communication
Horizontal	Client side	Client side	Event emitter
	Server side	Server side	Custom events
	Edge side	Edge side	Web storage
			Query strings
Vertical	Client side	Client side	Web storage
	Server side	Server side	Query strings
		Edge side	

Micro-Frontends in Practice

Although micro-frontends are a fairly new approach in the frontend architecture ecosystem, they have been used for a few years at medium and large organizations. Many well-known companies have made micro-frontends their main system for scaling their business to the next level.

Zalando

The first one worth mentioning is Zalando, a European fashion and ecommerce company. I attended a conference presentation given by their technical leads and was impressed by what they have created and released open source. More recently, Zalando has replaced the well-known OSS project Tailor.js with Interface Framework (*https://oreil.ly/Xl26d*). Interface Framework is based on concepts similar to Tailor.js but is more focused on components and GraphQL instead of fragments.

HelloFresh

HelloFresh, a digital service that provides ready-to-cook food boxes with a variety of recipes from all over the world, is another good example. Inspired by Zalando's work, HelloFresh is now serving a multitude of SPAs orchestrated by URL. In an interesting approach to flexibility of components, the SPAs are assembled and rendered on the servers, then cached at the CDN level, providing flexibility for generating the SPAs. This approach also allows the development teams to be responsible for their own technology stacks; each SPA could have a different one, and each team is fully independent from the others.

AllegroTech

In 2016, Polish retailer and auction site AllegroTech came up with OpBox (*https://oreil.ly/T01FH*), a project that allows nontechnical people to merge UI representations (a.k.a. components) with data sources inside the same page. At first, AllegroTech tried to work with multiple components assembled at runtime with ESI lang (*https://oreil.ly/sdlhc*), but the system didn't provide the desired level of consistency. Furthermore, they had a few problems with managing specific library versions. For instance, one component could have been developed with React v13 and another one with v15, both rendered on the same page.

In the OpBox project, Allegro's teams had the opportunity to decouple the rendering part of a component (the view) from the data in order to render. As long as the contract between the component and the data source matched, they were able to assemble data and different components together, which enhanced their ability to do A/B testing and gather data from there. But it is the additional abstraction between how the page is composed and the components to display that really stands out in this implementation. In fact, a JSON file describes the page and the components needed, and the renderer then composes the page as configured inside the JSON file. Two or more components on the same page could also react to a specific user interaction or to a change in a set of data, thanks to an eventbus implementation that signals the change to all the components that are listening to it.

Spotify

In this list of case histories, I can't neglect to mention Spotify. For its desktop application, Spotify has assembled multiple components living in separate iframes that communicate via a "bridge" for the low-level implementation made with C++. If we inspect the desktop application, we can easily find the multiple parts composing it. Each *.spa* file is composed of an HTML file, multiple CSS files, a *manifest.json*, and a JavaScript bundle file minimized and optimized, as shown in Figure 3-8.

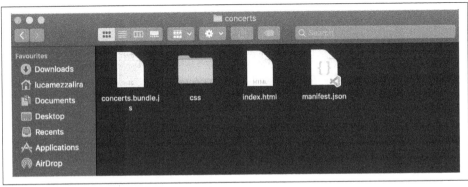

Figure 3-8. Spotify micro-frontend artifact

Those files will be loaded inside an iframe to compose the final application UI. This approach was used at the beginning for the web instance of the Spotify player (*https://oreil.ly/nyFr3*), but it was abandoned due to its poor performance, and Spotify has since moved back to an SPA architecture similar to what they have for the TV application. This doesn't mean the approach can't work, but the way it was designed caused more issues than benefits for the final users.

SAP

Another company using iframes for its applications is SAP. SAP released Luigi framework, a micro-frontends framework used for creating an enterprise application that interacts with SAP. Luigi works with Angular, React, Vue, and SAPUI—basically the most modern and well-adopted frontend frameworks, plus a well-known one, like SAPUI, for delivering applications interacting with SAP. Since enterprise applications are B2B solutions, where SEO and bandwidth are not a problem, having the ability to choose the hardware and software specifications where an application runs makes iframes adoption easy. If we think of the memory management provided by iframes out of the box, the decision to use them makes sense for that specific context.

OpenTable

Another interesting approach is OpenTable's Open Components (*https://oreil.ly/ pMI9L*) project, embraced by Skyscanner and other large organizations and released open source. Open Components are using a really interesting approach to micro-frontends: a registry similar to the Docker registry gathers all the available components encapsulating the data and UI, exposing an HTML fragment that can then be encapsulated in any HTML template.

A project using this technique receives many benefits, such as the team's independence, the rapid composition of multiple pages by reusing components built by other teams, and the option of rendering a component on the server or on the client. When I have spoken with people who work at OpenTable, they told me that this project allowed them to scale their teams around the world without creating a large communication overhead. For instance, using micro-frontends allowed them to smooth the process by repurposing parts developed in the United States for use in Australia— definitely a huge competitive advantage.

DAZN

Last but not least is DAZN, a live and video-on-demand sports platform that uses a combination of SPAs and components orchestrated by a client-side agent called Bootstrap. DAZN's approach focuses on targeting not only the web but also multiple smart TVs, set-top boxes, and consoles. Its approach is fully client side, with an orchestrator always available during the navigation of the video platform to load different SPAs at runtime when there is a change of business domain.

These are just some of the possibilities micro-frontends offer for scaling up our colocated and/or distributed teams. More and more companies are embracing this paradigm, including New Relic, Starbucks, and Microsoft.

Summary

In this chapter, we discovered the different high-level architectures for designing micro-frontends applications. We dove deep into the key decisions to make: *define, compose, orchestrate,* and *communicate.* Finally, we discovered that many organizations are already embracing this architecture in production, with successful software not merely available inside the browsers but also in other end uses, like desktop applications, consoles, and smart TVs. It's fascinating how quickly this architecture has spread across the globe. In the next chapter, I will discuss how to technically develop micro-frontends, providing real examples you can use within your own projects.

CHAPTER 4

Discovering Micro-Frontend Architectures

In the previous chapter, we learned about *decisions framework*, the foundation of any micro-frontend architecture. In this chapter, we will review the different architecture choices, applying what we have learned so far.

Micro-Frontend Decisions Framework Applied

The decisions framework helps you to choose the right approach for your micro-frontend project based on its characteristics (see Figure 4-1). Your first decision will be between a horizontal and vertical split.

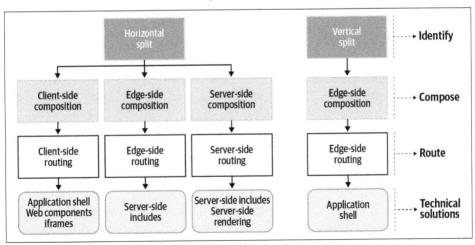

Figure 4-1. The micro-frontends decisions framework

The micro-frontends decisions framework helps you determine the best architecture for a project.

Vertical Split

A vertical split offers fewer choices, and because they are likely well known by front-end developers who are used to writing single-page applications (SPAs), only the client-side choice is shown in Figure 4-1. You'll find a vertical split helpful when your project requires a consistent user interface evolution and a fluid user experience across multiple views. That's because a vertical split provides the closest developer experience to an SPA, and therefore the tools, best practices, and patterns can be used for the development of a micro-frontend.

Although technically you can serve vertical-split micro-frontends with any composition, so far all the explored implementations have a client-side composition in which an application shell is responsible for mounting and unmounting micro-frontends, leaving us with one composition method to choose from. The relation between a micro-frontend and the application shell is always one to one, so therefore the application shell loads only one micro-frontend at a time. You'll also want to use client-side routing. The routing is usually split in two parts, with a global routing used for loading different micro-frontends being handled by the application shell (see Figure 4-2).

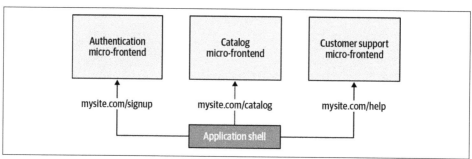

Figure 4-2. The application shell is responsible for global routing between micro-frontends

Although the local routing between views inside the same micro-frontend is managed by the micro-frontend itself, you'll have full control of the implementation and evolution of the views present inside it since the team responsible for a micro-frontend is also the subject-matter expert on that business domain of the application (Figure 4-3).

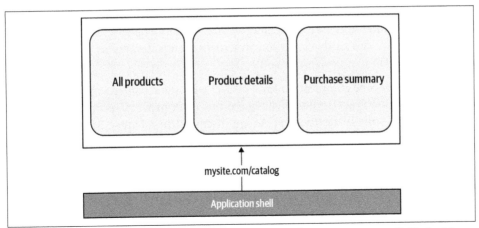

Figure 4-3. A micro-frontend is responsible for routing between views available inside the micro-frontend itself

Finally, for implementing an architecture with a vertical-split micro-frontend, the application shell loads HTML or JavaScript as the entry point. The application shell shouldn't share any business domain logic with the other micro-frontends and should be technology agnostic to allow future system evolution, so you don't want to use any specific UI framework for building an application shell. Try Vanilla JavaScript if you built your own implementation.

The application shell is always present during users' sessions because it's responsible for orchestrating the web application as well as exposing some life cycle APIs for micro-frontends in order to react when they are fully mounted or unmounted.

When vertical-split micro-frontends have to share information with other micro-frontends, such as tokens or user preferences, we can use query strings for volatile data, or web storages for tokens or user preferences, similar to how the horizontal split ones do between different views.

Horizontal Split

A horizontal split works well when a business subdomain should be presented across several views and therefore reusability of the subdomain becomes key for the project; when search engine optimization is a key requirement of your project and you want to use a server-side rendering approach; when your frontend application requires tens if not hundreds of developers working together and you have to split more granular our subdomains; or when you have a multitenant project with customer customizations in specific parts of your software.

The next decision you'll make is between client-side, edge-side, and server-side compositions. Client side is a good choice when your teams are more familiar with the frontend ecosystem or when your project is subject to high traffic with significant spikes, for instance. You'll avoid dealing with scalability challenges on the frontend layer because you can easily cache your micro-frontends, leveraging a content delivery network (CDN).

You can use edge-side composition for a project with static content and high traffic in order to delegate the scalability challenge to the CDN provider instead of having to deal with it in your infrastructure. As we discussed in Chapter 3, embracing this architecture style has some challenges, such as its complicated developer experience and the fact that not all CDNs support it. But projects like online catalog with no personalized content may be a good candidate for this approach.

Server-side composition gives us the most control of our output, which is great for highly indexed websites, such as news sites or ecommerce. It's also a good choice for websites that require great performance metrics, similar to PayPal and American Express, both of which use server-side composition.

Next is your routing strategy. While you can technically apply any routing to any composition, it's common to use the routing strategy associated with your chosen composition pattern. If you choose a client-side composition, for example, most of the time, routing will happen at the client-side level. You might use computation logic at the edge (using Lambda@Edge in case of AWS or Workers in CloudFlare) to avoid polluting the application shell's code with canary releases or to provide an optimized version of your web application to search engine crawlers leveraging the dynamic rendering capability.

On the other hand, an edge-side composition will have an HTML page associated with each view, so every time a user loads a new page, a new page will be composed in the CDN, which will retrieve multiple micro-frontends to create that final view. Finally, with server-side routing, the application server will know which HTML template is associated with a specific route; routing and composition happen on the server side.

Your composition choice will also help narrow your technical solutions for building a micro-frontends project. When you use client-side composition and routing, your best implementation choice is an application shell loading multiple micro-frontends in the same view with the webpack plug-in called Module Federation, with iframes, or with web components, for instance. For the edge-side composition, the only solution available is using edge-side includes (ESI). We are seeing hints that this may change in the future, as cloud providers extend their edge services to provide more computational and storage resources. For now, though, ESI is the only option. And when you decide to use server-side composition, you can use server-side includes (SSI) or one of the many SSR frameworks for your micro-frontend applications. Note that SSRs will give you greater flexibility and control over your implementation.

Missing from the decisions framework is the final pillar: how the micro-frontends will communicate when they are in the same or different views. This is mainly because when you select a horizontal split, you have to avoid sharing any state across micro-frontends; this approach is an antipattern. Instead, you'll use the techniques mentioned in Chapter 3, such as an event emitter, custom events, or reactive streams using an implementation of the publish/subscribe (pub/sub) pattern for decoupling the micro-frontends and maintaining their independent nature. When you have to communicate between different views, you'll use a query string parameter to share volatile data, such as product identifiers, and web storage/cookies for persistent data, such as users' tokens or local users' settings.

Observer Pattern

The observer pattern (also known as publish/subscribe pattern) is a behavioral design pattern that defines a one-to-many relationship between objects such that, when one object changes its state, all dependent objects are notified and updated automatically. An object with a one-to-many relationship with other objects that are interested in its state is called the subject or publisher. Its dependent objects are called observers or subscribers. The observers are notified whenever the state of the subject changes, and then they act accordingly. The subject can have any number of dependent observers.

Architecture Analysis

To help you better choose the right architecture for your project, we'll now analyze the technical implementations, looking at challenges and benefits. We'll review the different implementations in detail and then assess the characteristics for each architecture. The characteristics we'll analyze for every implementation:

Deployability
  Reliability and ease of deploying a micro-frontend in an environment.

Modularity
  Ease of adding or removing micro-frontends and ease of integrating with shared components hosted by micro-frontends.

Simplicity
  Ease of being able to understand or do. If a piece of software is considered simple, it has likely been found to be easy to understand and to reason about.

Testability
  Degree to which a software artifact supports testing in a given test context. If the testability of the software artifact is high, then finding faults in the system by means of testing is easier.

Performance
> Indicator of how well a micro-frontend would meet the quality of user experience described by web vitals (*https://oreil.ly/mHFq9*), essential metrics for a healthy site.

Developer experience
> The experience developers are exposed to when they use your product, be it client libraries, SDKs, frameworks, open source code, tools, API, technology, or services.

Scalability
> The ability of a process, network, software, or organization to grow and manage increased demand.

Coordination
> Unification, integration, or synchronization of group members' efforts in order to provide unity of action in the pursuit of common goals.

Characteristics are rated on a five-point scale, with one point indicating that the specific architecture characteristic isn't well supported and five points indicating that the architecture characteristic is one of the strongest features in the architectural pattern. The score indicates which architecture characteristic shines better with every approach described. It's almost impossible having all the characteristics working perfectly in an architecture due to the tension they exercise with each other. Our role would be to find the trade-off suitable for the application we have to build, hence the decision to create a score mechanism to evaluate all of these architectural approaches.

Architecture and Trade-offs

As I pointed out elsewhere in this book, I firmly believe that the perfect architecture doesn't exist; it's always a trade-off. The trade-offs are not only technical but also based on business requirements and organizational structure. Modern architecture considers other forces that contribute to the final outcome as well as technical aspects. We must recognize the sociotechnical aspects and optimize for the context we operate in instead of searching for the "perfect architecture" (which doesn't exist) or borrowing the architecture from another context without researching whether it would be appropriate for our context.

In *Fundamentals of Software Architecture*, Neal Ford and Mark Richards highlight very well these new architecture practices and invite the readers to optimize for the "least worst" architecture. As they state, "Never shoot for the best architecture, but rather the least worst architecture."

Before settling on a final architecture, take the time to understand the context you operate in, your teams' structures, and the communication flows between teams. When we ignore these aspects, we risk creating a great technical proposition that's completely unsuitable for our company. It's the same when we read case studies from other companies embracing specific architectures. We need to understand how the company works and how that compares to how our company works. Often the case studies focus on how a company solved a specific problem, which may or may not overlap with your challenges and goals. It's up to you to find out if the case study's challenges match your own.

Read widely and talk with different people in the community to understand the forces behind certain decisions. Taking the time to research will help you avoid making wrong assumptions and become more aware of the environment you are working in.

Every architecture is optimized for solving specific technical and organizational challenges, which is why we see so many approaches to micro-frontends. Remember: there isn't right or wrong in architecture, just the best trade-off for your own context.

Vertical-Split Architectures

For a vertical-split architecture, a client-side composition, client-side routing, and an application shell, as described above, are fantastic for teams with a solid background of building SPAs for their first foray into micro-frontends, because the development experience will be mostly familiar. This is probably also the easiest way to enter the micro-frontend world for developers with a frontend background.

Application Shell

A persistent part of a micro-frontend application, the application shell is the first thing downloaded when an application is requested. It will shepherd a user session from the beginning to the end, loading and unloading micro-frontends based on the endpoint the user requests. The main reasons to load micro-frontends inside an application shell include:

Handling the initial user state (if any)
> If a user tries to access an authenticated route via a deep link but the user token is invalid, the application shell redirects the user to the sign-in view or a landing page. This process is needed only for the first load, however. After that, every micro-frontend in an authenticated area of a web application should manage the logic for keeping the user authenticated or redirecting them to an unauthenticated page.

Retrieving global configurations
> When needed, the application shell should first fetch a configuration that contains any information used across the entire user sessions, such as the user's country if the application provides different experiences based on country.

Fetching the available routes and associated micro-frontends to load

To avoid needlessly deploying the application shell, the route configurations should be loaded at runtime with the associated micro-frontends. This will guarantee control of the routing system without deploying the application shell multiple times.

Setting logging, observability, or marketing libraries

Because these libraries are usually applied to the entire application, it's best to instantiate them at the application shell level.

Handling errors if a micro-frontend cannot be loaded

Sometimes micro-frontends are unreachable due to a network issue or bug in the system. It's wise to add an error message (a 404 page, for instance) to the application shell or load a highly available micro-frontend to display errors and suggest possible solutions to the user, like suggesting similar products or asking them to come back later.

You could achieve similar results by using libraries in every micro-frontend rather than using an orchestrator like the application shell. However, ideally you want just one place to manage these things from. Having multiple libraries means ensuring they are always in sync between micro-frontends, which requires more coordination and adds complexity to the entire process. Having multiple libraries also creates risk in the deployment phase, where there are breaking changes, compared to centralizing libraries inside the application shell.

Never use the application shell as a layer to interact constantly with micro-frontends during a user session. The application shell should only be used for edge cases or initialization. Using it as a shared layer for micro-frontends risks having a logical coupling between micro-frontends and the application shell, forcing testing and/or redeployment of all micro-frontends available in an application. This situation is also called a distributed monolith and is a developer's worst nightmare.

In this pattern, the application shell loads only one micro-frontend at a time. That means you don't need to create a mechanism for encapsulating conflicting dependencies between micro-frontends because there won't be any clash between libraries or CSS styles (see Figure 4-4), as long as both are removed from the window object when a micro-frontend is unloaded.

The application shell is nothing more than a simple HTML page with logic wrapped in a JavaScript file. Some CSS styles may or may not be included in the application shell for the initial loading experience, such as for showing a loading animation like a spinner. Every micro-frontend entry point is represented by a single HTML page containing the logic and style of a single view or a small SPA containing several routes that include all the logic needed to allow a user to consume an entire subdomain of the application without a new micro-frontend needing to load. A JavaScript file could be loaded instead as a micro-frontend entry point, but in this case we are limited by the initial customer experience, because we have to wait until the JavaScript file is interpreted before it can add new elements into the domain object model (DOM).

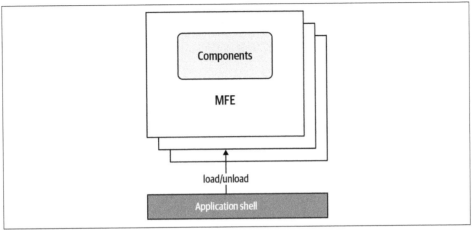

Figure 4-4. Vertical-split architecture with client-side composition and routing using the application shell

The vertical split works well when we want to create a consistent user experience while providing full control to a single team. A clear sign that this may be the right approach for your application is when you don't have many repetitions of business subdomains across multiple views but every part of the application may be represented by an application itself.

Identifying micro-frontends becomes easy when we have a clear understanding of how users interact with the application. If you use an analytics tool like Google Analytics, you'll have access to this information. If you don't have this information, you'll need to get it before you can determine how to structure the architecture, business domains, and your organization. With this architecture, there isn't a high reusability of micro-frontends, so it's unlikely that a vertical-split micro-frontend will be reused in the same application multiple times.

However, inside every micro-frontend we can reuse components (think about a design system), generating a modularity that helps avoid too much duplication. It's more likely, though, that micro-frontends will be reused in different applications maintained by the same company. Imagine that in a multitenant environment, you have to develop multiple platforms and you want to have a similar user interface with some customizations for part of every platform. You will be able to reuse vertical-split micro-frontends, reducing code fragmentation and evolving the system independently based on the business requirements.

Challenges

Of course, there will be some challenges during the implementation phase, as with any architecture pattern. Apart from domain-specific ones, we'll have common challenges, some of which have an immediate answer, while others will depend more on context. Let's look at four major challenges: a sharing state, the micro-frontends composition, a multiframework approach, and the evolution of your architecture.

Sharing state

The first challenge we face when we work with micro-frontends in general is how to share states between micro-frontends. While we don't need to share information as much with a vertical-split architecture, the need still exists.

Some of the information that we may need to share across multiple micro-frontends are fine when stored via web storage, such as the audio volume level for media the user played or the fonts recently used to edit a document.

When information is more sensitive, such as personal user data or an authentication token, we need a way to retrieve this information from a public API and then share across all the micro-frontends interested in this information. In this case, the first micro-frontend loaded at the beginning of the user's session would retrieve this data, stored in a web storage with a retrieval time stamp. Then every micro-frontend that requires this data can retrieve it directly from the web storage, and if the time stamp is older than a preset amount of time, the micro-frontend can request the data again. And because the application loads only one micro-frontend at a time and every micro-frontend will have access to the selected web storage, there is no strong requirement to pass through the application shell for storing data in the web storage.

However, let's say that your application relies heavily on the web storage, and you decide to implement security checks to validate the space available or type of message stored. In this scenario, you may want to instead create an abstraction via the application shell that will expose an API for storing and retrieving data. This will centralize where the data validation happens, providing meaningful errors to every micro-frontend in case a validation fails.

Composing micro-frontends

You have several options for composing vertical-split micro-frontends inside an application shell. Remember, however, that vertical-split micro-frontends are composed and routed on the client side only, so we are limited to what the browser's standards offer us. There are four techniques for composing micro-frontends on the client side:

ES modules

JavaScript modules can be used to split our applications into smaller files to be loaded at compile time or at runtime, fully implemented in modern browsers. This can be a solid mechanism for composing micro-frontends at runtime using standards. To implement an ES module, we simply define the module attribute in our script tag and the browser will interpret it as a module:

```
<script type="module" src="catalogMFE.js"></script>
```

This module will be always deferred and can implement cross-origin resource sharing (CORS) authentication. ES modules can also be defined for the entire application inside an import map, allowing us to use the syntax to import a module inside the application. As of publication time, the main problem with import maps is that they are not supported by all the browsers. You'll be limited to Google Chrome, Microsoft Edge (with Chromium engine), and recent versions of Opera, limiting this solution's viability.

SystemJS

This module loader supports import maps specifications, which are not natively available inside the browser. This allows them to be used inside the SystemJS implementation, where the module loader library makes the implementation compatible with all the browsers. This is a handy solution when we want our micro-frontends to load at runtime, because it uses a syntax similar to import maps and allows SystemJS to take care of the browser's API fragmentation.

Module Federation

This is a plug-in introduced in webpack 5 used for loading external modules, libraries, or even entire applications inside another one. The plug-in takes care of the undifferentiated heavy lifting needed for composing micro-frontends, wrapping the micro-frontends' scope and sharing dependencies between different micro-frontends or handling different versions of the same library without runtime errors. The developer experience and the implementation are so slick that it would seem like writing a normal SPA. Every micro-frontend is imported as a module and then implemented in the same way as a component of a UI framework. The abstraction made by this plug-in makes the entire composition challenge almost completely painless.

HTML parsing

When a micro-frontend has an entry point represented by an HTML page, we can use JavaScript for parsing the DOM elements and append the nodes needed inside the application shell's DOM. At its simplest, an HTML document is really just an XML document with its own defined schema. Given that, we can treat the micro-frontend as an XML document and append the relevant nodes inside the shell's DOM using the DOMParser object (*https://oreil.ly/q9X8P*). After parsing the micro-frontend DOM, we then append the DOM nodes using adoptNode (*https://oreil.ly/oopaw*) or cloneNode (*https://oreil.ly/RVMKg*) methods. However, using cloneNode or adoptNode doesn't work with the script element, because the browser doesn't evaluate the script element, so in this case we create a new one, passing the source file found in the micro-frontend's HTML page. Creating a new script element will trigger the browser to fully evaluate the JavaScript file associated with this element. In this way, you can even simplify the micro-frontend developer experience because your team will provide the final results knowing how the initial DOM will look. This technique is used by some frameworks, such as qiankun, which allows HTML documents to be micro-frontend entry points.

All the major frameworks composed on the client side implement these techniques, and sometimes you even have options to pick from. For example, with single SPA you can use ES modules, SystemJS with import maps, or Module Federation.

All these techniques allow you to implement static or dynamic routes. In the case of static routes, you just need to hardcode the path in your code. With dynamic path, you can retrieve all the routes from a static JSON file to load at the beginning of the application or create something more dynamic by developing an endpoint that can be consumed by the application shell and where you apply logic based on the user's country or language for returning the final routing list.

Multiframework approach

Using micro-frontends for a multiframework approach is a controversial decision, because many people think that this forces them to use multiple UI frameworks, like React, Angular, Vue, or Svelte. But what is true for frontend applications written in a monolithic way is also true for micro-frontends.

Although technically you can implement multiple UI frameworks in an SPA, it creates performance issues and potential dependency clashes. This applies to micro-frontends as well, so using a multiframework implementation for this architecture style isn't recommended.

Instead, follow best practices like reducing external dependencies as much as you can, importing only what you use rather than entire packages that may increase the final JavaScript bundle. Many JavaScript tools implement a tree-shaking mechanism to help achieve smaller bundle sizes.

There are some use cases in which the benefits of having a multiframework approach with micro-frontends outweigh the challenges, such as when we can create a healthy flywheel for developers, reducing the time to market of their business logic without affecting production traffic.

Imagine you start porting a frontend application from an SPA to micro-frontends. Working on a micro-frontend and deploying the SPA codebase alongside it would help you to provide value for your business and users.

First, we would have a team finding best practices for approaching the porting (such as identifying libraries to reuse across micro-frontends), setting up the automation pipeline, sharing code between micro-frontends, and so on. Second, after creating the minimum viable product (MVP), the micro-frontend can be shipped to the final user, retrieving metrics and comparing with the older version. In a situation like this, asking a user to download multiple UI frameworks is less problematic than developing the new architecture for several months without understanding if the direction is leading to a better result. Validating your assumptions is crucial for generating the best practices shared by different teams inside your organization. Improving the feedback loop and deploying code to production as fast as possible demonstrates the best approach for overcoming future challenges with microarchitectures in general.

You can apply the same reasoning to other libraries in the same application but with different versions, such as when you have a project with an old version of Angular and you want to upgrade to the latest version.

Remember, the goal is creating the muscles for moving at speed with confidence and reducing the potential mistakes automating what is possible and fostering the right mindset across the teams. Finally, these considerations are applicable to all the micro-frontend architecture shared in this book.

Architecture evolution and code encapsulation

Perfectly defining the subdomains on the first try isn't always feasible. In particular, using a vertical-split approach may result in coarse-grained micro-frontends that become complicated after several months of work because of broadening project scope as the team's capabilities grow. Also, we can have new insights into assumptions we made at the beginning of the process. Fear not! This architecture's modular nature helps you face these challenges and provides a clear path for evolving it alongside the business. When your team's cognitive load starts to become unsustainable, it may be time to split your micro-frontend. One of the many best practices for splitting a micro-frontend is code encapsulation, which is based on a specific user flow. Let's explore it!

The concept of encapsulation comes from object-oriented programming (OOP) and is associated with classes and how to handle data. Encapsulation binds together the attributes (data) and the methods (functions and procedures) that manipulate the data in order to protect the data. The general rule, enforced by many languages, is that attributes should only be accessed (that is, retrieved or modified) using methods that are contained (encapsulated) within the class definition.

Imagine your micro-frontend is composed of several views, such as a payment form, sign-up form, sign-in form, and email and password retrieval form, as shown in Figure 4-5.

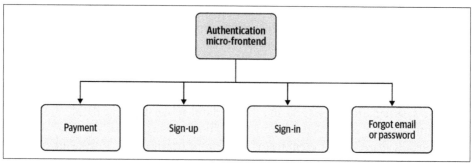

Figure 4-5. Authentication micro-frontend composed of several views that may create a high cognitive load for the team responsible for this micro-frontend

An existing user accessing this micro-frontend is more likely to sign in to the authenticated area or want to retrieve their account email or password, while a new user is likely to sign up or make a payment. A natural split for this micro-frontend, then, could be one micro-frontend for authentication and another for subscription. In this way, you'll separate the two according to business logic without having to ask the users to download more code than the flow would require (see Figure 4-6).

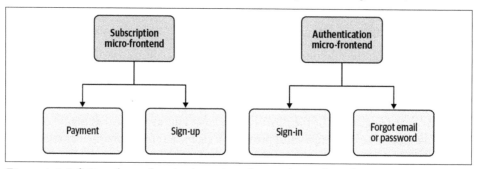

Figure 4-6. Splitting the authentication micro-frontend to reduce the cognitive load, following customer experience more than technical constraints

This isn't the only way to split this micro-frontend, but however you split it, be sure you're prioritizing a business outcome rather than a technical one. Prioritizing the customer experience is the best way to provide a final output that your users will enjoy.

Encapsulation helps with these situations. For instance, avoid having a unique state representing the entire micro-frontend. Instead, prefer state management libraries that allow composition of state, like MobX-State-Tree (*https://oreil.ly/ayXTf*) does. The data will be expressed in tree structure, which you can compose at will. Spend the time evaluating how to implement the application state, and you may save time later while also reducing your cognitive load. It is always easier to think when the code is well identified inside some boundaries than when it's spread across multiple parts of the application.

When libraries or even logic are used in multiple domains, such as in a form validation library, you have a few options:

Duplicate the code

Code duplication isn't always a bad practice; it depends on what you are optimizing for and overall impact of the duplicated code. Let's say that you have a component that has different states based on user status and the view where it's hosted, and that this component is subject to new requirements more often in one domain than in others. You may want to centralize it. Keep in mind, though, that every time you have a centralized library or component, you have to build a solid governance for making sure that when this shared code is updated, it also gets updated in every micro-frontend that uses this shared code as well. When this happens, you also have to make sure the new version doesn't break anything inside each micro-frontend and you need to coordinate the activity across multiple teams. In this case, the component isn't difficult to implement and it will become easier to build for every team that uses it, because there are fewer states to take care of. That allows every implementation to evolve independently at its own speed. Here, we're optimizing for speed of delivery and reducing the external dependencies for every team. This approach works best when you have a limited amount of duplication. When you have dozens of similar components, this reasoning doesn't scale anymore; you'll want to abstract into a library instead.

Abstract your code into a shared library

In some situations, you really want to centralize the business logic to ensure that every micro-frontend is using the same implementation, as with integrating payment methods. Imagine implementing in your checkout form multiple payment methods with their validation logic, handling errors, and so on. Duplicating such a complex and delicate part of the system isn't wise. Creating a shared library instead will help maintain consistency and simplify the integration across the entire platform. Within the automation pipelines, you'll want to add a version check on every micro-frontend to review the latest library version. Unfortunately, while dealing with distributed systems helps you scale the organization and deliver with speed, sometimes you need to enforce certain practices for the greater good.

Delegate to a backend API

The third option is to delegate the common part to be served to all your vertical-split micro-frontends by the backend, thus providing some configuration and implementation of the business logic to each micro-frontend. Imagine you have multiple micro-frontends that are implementing an input field with specific validation that is simple enough to represent with a regular expression. You might be tempted to centralize the logic in a common library, but this would mean enforcing the update of this dependency every time something changes. Considering the logic is easy enough to represent and the common part would be using the same regular expression, you can provide this information as a configuration field when the application loads and make it available to all the micro-frontends via the web storage. That way, if you want to change the regular expression, you won't need to redeploy every micro-frontend implementing it. You'll just change the regular expression in the configuration, and all the micro-frontends will automatically use the latest implementation.

Code Duplication over Wrong Abstractions

Many well-known people in the industry have started to realize that abstracting code is not always a benefit, especially in the long run. In certain cases, code duplication brings more benefits to a premature or a hasty abstraction. Moreover, duplicated code can be easily abstracted if and when needed; it's more challenging to try to move away from abstractions once they're present in the code. If you are interested in this topic, read "The Wrong Abstraction" (*https://oreil.ly/s4xcD*), a 2016 blog post by Sandi Metz. Kent Dodds's AHA programming (*https://oreil.ly/VGJwa*) or "Avoid Hasty Abstractions" concept is strongly inspired by the work Metz describes in his blog and talk. Also, the well-known DRY principle (don't repeat yourself) appears to be misapplied by many developers, who just looked in the code for duplicated lines of code and abstracted them. In the second edition of *Pragmatic Programmer* (Addison-Wesley), where the DRY principle was first introduced, the authors provide a great explanation of this point:

> In the first edition of this book we did a poor job of explaining just what we meant by Don't Repeat Yourself. Many people took it to refer to code only: they thought that DRY means "don't copy-and-paste lines of source."

> That is part of DRY, but it's a tiny and fairly trivial part. *DRY is about the duplication of knowledge, of intent*. It's about expressing the same thing in two different places, possibly in two totally different ways. [emphasis added]

It's important to understand that no solution fits everything. Consider the context your implementation should represent and choose the best trade-off in the guardrails you are operating with. Could you have designed the micro-frontends in this way from the beginning? Potentially, you could have, but the whole point of this architecture is to avoid premature abstractions, optimize for fast delivery, and evolve the architecture when it is required due to complexity or just a change of direction.

Implementing a Design System

In a distributed architecture like micro-frontends, design systems may seem a difficult feature to achieve, but in reality the technical implementation doesn't differ too much from that of a design system in an SPA. When thinking about a design system applied to micro-frontends, imagine a layered system composed of design tokens, basic components, user interface library, and the micro-frontends that host all these parts together, as shown in Figure 4-7.

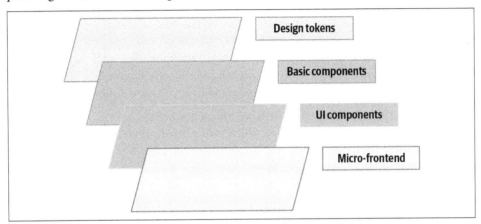

Figure 4-7. How a design system fits inside a micro-frontends architecture

The first layer, design tokens, allows you to capture low-level values to then create the styles for your product, such as font families, text colors, text size, and many other characteristics used inside our final user interface. Generally, design tokens are listed in JSON or YAML files, expressing every detail of our design system.

We don't usually distribute design tokens across different micro-frontends because each team will implement them in their own way, risking the introduction of bugs in some areas of the application and not in others, increasing the code duplication across the system, and, in general, slowing down the maintenance of a design system. However, there are situations when design tokens can be an initial step for creating a level of consistency for iterating later on, with basic components shared across all the micro-frontends. Often, teams do not have enough space for implementing the final design system components inside every micro-frontend. Therefore, make sure if you go down this path that you have the time and space for iterating on the design system.

The next layer is basic components. Usually, these components don't hold the application business logic and are completely unaware of where they will be used. As a result, they should be as generic as can be, such as a label or button, which will provide the consistency we are looking for and the flexibility to be used in any part of the application.

This is the perfect stage for centralizing the code that will be used across multiple micro-frontends. In this way, we create the consistency needed in the UI to allow every team to use components at the level they need.

The third layer is a UI components library, usually a composition of basic components that contain some business logic that is reusable inside a given domain. We may be tempted to share these components as well, but be cautious in doing so. The governance to maintain and the organization structure may cause many external dependencies across teams, creating more frustration than efficiencies. One exception is when there are complex UI components that require a lot of iterations and there is a centralized team responsible for them. Imagine, for instance, building a complex component such as a video player with several functionalities, such as closed captions, a volume bar, and trick play. Duplicating these components is a waste of time and effort; centralizing and abstracting your code is by far more efficient.

Note, though, that shared components are often not reused as much as we expect, resulting in a wasted effort. Therefore, think twice before centralizing a component. When in doubt, start duplicating the component and, after a few iterations, review whether these components need to be abstracted. The wrong abstraction is way more expensive than duplicated code.

The final layer is the micro-frontend that is hosting the UI components library. Keep in mind the importance of a micro-frontend's independence. The moment we get more than three or four external dependencies, we are heading toward a distributed monolith. That's the worst place to be because we are treating a distributed architecture like a monolith that we wanted to move away from, no longer creating independent teams across the organization.

To ensure we are finding the right trade-offs between development speed and independent teams and UI consistency, consider validating the dependencies monthly or every two months throughout the project life cycle. In the past, I've worked at companies where this exercise was done every two weeks at the end of every sprint, and it helped many teams postpone tasks that may not have been achievable during a sprint due to blocks from external dependencies. In this way, you'll reduce your teams' frustration and increase their performance.

On the technical side, the best investment you can make for creating a design system is in web components. Since you can use web components with any UI framework, should you decide to change the UI framework later, the design system will remain the same, saving you time and effort. There are some situations in which using web components is not viable, such as projects that have to target old browsers. Chances are, though, you won't have such strong requirements and you can target modern browsers, allowing you to leverage web components with your micro-frontend architecture.

While getting the design system ready to be implemented is half the work, to accomplish the delivery inside your micro-frontends architecture, you'll need a solid governance to maintain that initial investment. Remember, dealing with a distributed architecture is not as straightforward as you can imagine. Usually, the first implementation happens quite smoothly because there is time allocated to that. The problems come with subsequent updates. Especially when you deal with distributed teams, the best approach is to automate the system design version validation in the continuous integration (CI) phase. Every time a micro-frontend is built, the *package.json* file should check that the design system library is up to date with the latest version.

Implementing this check in CI allows you to be as strict as needed. You may decide to provide a warning in the logs, asking to update the version as soon as possible, or prevent artifact creation if the micro-frontend is one or more major versions behind.

Some companies have custom dashboards for dealing with this problem, not only for design systems but also for other libraries, such as logging or authentication. In this way, every team can check in real time whether their micro-frontend implements the latest versions.

Finally, let's consider the team's structure. Traditionally, in enterprise companies, the design team is centralized, taking care of all the aspects of the design system, from ideation to delivery, and the developers just implement the library the design team provides. However, some companies implement a distributed model wherein the design team is a central authority that provides the core components and direction for the entire design system, but other teams populate the design system with new components or new functionalities of existing ones. In this second approach, we reduce potential bottlenecks by allowing the development teams to contribute to the global design system. Meanwhile, we keep guardrails in place to ensure every component respects the overall plan, such as regular meetings between design and development, office hours during which the design team can guide development teams, or even collaborative sessions where the design team sets the direction but the developers actually implement the code inside the design system.

Developer Experience

For vertical-split micro-frontends, the developer's experience is very similar to SPAs. However, there are a couple of suggestions that you may find useful to think about up front. First of all, create a command line tool for scaffolding micro-frontends with a basic implementation and common libraries you would like to share in all the micro-frontends such as a logging library. While not an essential tool to have from day one, it's definitely helpful in the long term, especially for new team members. Also, create a dashboard that summarizes the micro-frontend version you have in different environments. In general, all the tools you are using for developing an SPA are still relevant for a vertical-split micro-frontend architecture. We will discuss this topic more in depth in Chapter 7, where we review how to create automation pipelines for micro-frontend applications.

Search Engine Optimization

Some projects require a strong SEO strategy, including micro-frontend projects. Let's look at two major options for a good SEO strategy with vertical-split micro-frontends. The first one involves optimizing the application code in a way that is easily indexable by crawlers. In this case, the developer's job is implementing as many best practices as possible for rendering the entire DOM in a timely manner (usually under five seconds). Time matters with crawlers, because they have to index all the data in a view and also structure the UI in a way that exposes all the meaningful information without hiding behind user interactions. Another option is to create an HTML markup that is meaningful for crawlers to extract the content and categorize it properly. While this isn't impossible, in the long run, this option may require a bit of effort to maintain for every new feature and project enhancement.

Another option would be using dynamic rendering to provide an optimized version of your web application for all the crawlers trying to index your content. Google introduced dynamic rendering to allow you to redirect crawler requests to an optimized version of your website, usually prerendered, without penalizing the positioning of your website in the search engine results (see Figure 4-8).

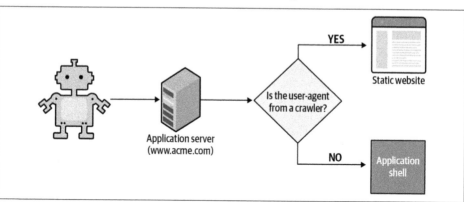

Figure 4-8. When a crawler requests a specific page, the application server should retrieve the user-agent and serve the crawler's requests to a prerendered version of the website, otherwise serving the micro-frontend implementation

There are a couple of solutions for serving a prerendered version of your application to a crawler. First, for the prerendering phase, you can create a customized version of your website that fetches the same data of the website your users will consume. For instance, you can create a server-side rendering output stored in an objects storage that translates a template into static HTML pages at compile time, maintaining the same user-facing URL structure. Amazon S3 is a good choice for this. You can also decide to server-side render at runtime, eliminating the need to store the static pages and serving the crawlers a just-in-time version created ad hoc for them. Although this solution requires some effort to implement, it allows you the best customization and optimization for improving the final output to the crawler.

A second option would be using an open source solution like Puppeteer or Rendertron to scrape the code from the website created for the users and then deploy a web server that generates static pages regularly.

After generating the static version of your website, you need to know when the request is coming from a browser and when from a crawler. A basic implementation would be using a regular expression that identifies the crawler's user-agents. A good Node.js library for that is *crawler-user-agents* (*https://oreil.ly/sB59e*). In this case, after identifying the user-agent header, the application server can respond with the correct implementation. This solution can be applied at the edge using technologies like AWS Lambda@Edge or Cloudflare Workers. In this case, CDNs of some cloud providers allow a computation layer after receiving a request. Because there are some constraints on the maximum execution time of these containers, the user-agent identification represents a good reason for using these edge technologies. Moreover, they can be used for additional logic, introducing canary releases or blue-green deployment, as we will see in Chapter 6.

Performance and Micro-Frontends

Is good performance achievable in a micro-frontend architecture? Definitely! Performance of a micro-frontend architecture, like in any other frontend architecture, is key for the success of a web application. And a vertical-split architecture can achieve good performance thanks to the split of domains and, therefore, the code to be shared with a client.

Think for a moment about an SPA. Typically, the user has to download all the code specifically related to the application, the business logic, and the libraries used in the entire application. For simplicity, let's imagine that an entire application code is 500 KB. The unauthenticated area, composed of sign-in, sign-up, the landing page, customer support, and few other views, requires 100 KB of business logic, while the authenticated area requires 150 KB of business logic. Both use the same bundled dependencies that are each 250 KB (see Figure 4-9).

A new user has to download all 500 KB, despite the action having to fulfill inside the SPA. Maybe one user just wants to understand the business proposition and visits just the landing page, another user wants to see the payment methods available, or an authenticated user is interested mainly in the authenticated area where the service or products are available. No matter what users are trying to achieve, they are forced to download the entire application.

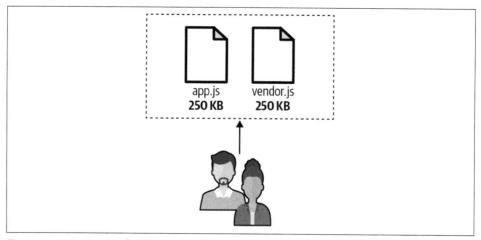

Figure 4-9. Any user of an SPA has to download the entire application regardless of the action they intend to perform in the application

In a vertical-split architecture, however, our unauthenticated user who wants to see the business proposition on the landing page will be able to download the code just for that micro-frontend, while the authenticated user will download only the codebase for the authenticated area. We often don't realize that our users' behaviors are different from the way we interpret the application, because we often optimize the application's performance as a whole rather than by how users interact with the site. Optimizing our site according to user experiences results in a better outcome.

Applying the previous example to a vertical-split architecture, a user interested only in the unauthenticated area will download less than 100 KB of business logic plus the shared dependencies, while an authenticated user will download only the 250 KB plus the shared dependencies.

Clearly a new user who moves beyond the landing page will download almost 500 KB, but this approach will still save some kilobytes if we have properly identified the application boundaries because it's unlikely a new user will go through every single application view. In the worst-case scenario, the user will download 500 KB as they would for the SPA, but this time not everything up front. Certainly, there is additional logic to download due to the application shell, but usually the size is only in the double digits, making it meaningless for this example. Figure 4-10 shows the advantages of a vertical-split micro-frontend in terms of performance.

A good practice for managing performance on a vertical-split architecture is introducing a performance budget. A performance budget is a limit for micro-frontends that a team is not allowed to exceed. The performance budget includes the final bundle size, multimedia content to load, and even CSS files. Setting a performance budget is an important part of making sure every team optimizes its own micro-frontend properly and can even be enforced during the CI process. You won't set a performance budget until later in the project, but it should be updated every time there is a meaningful refactoring or additional features introduced in the micro-frontend codebase.

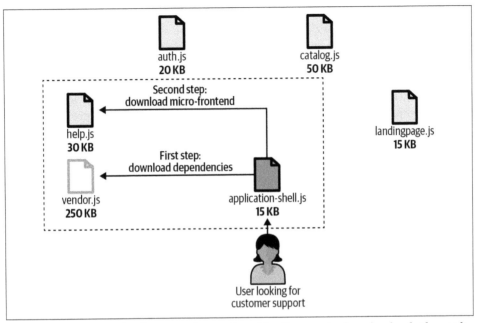

Figure 4-10. A vertical-split micro-frontend enables the user to download only the application code needed to accomplish the action the user is looking for

Time to display the final result to the user is a key performance indicator, and metrics to track include time-to-interactive or first contentful paint, the size of the final artifact, font size, and JavaScript bundle size, as well as metrics like accessibility and SEO. A tool like Lighthouse (*https://oreil.ly/ip4Ap*) is useful for analyzing these metrics and is available in a command-line version (*https://oreil.ly/3aPf5*) to be used in the continuous integration process. Although these metrics have been discussed extensively for SPA optimization, bundle size may be trickier when it comes to micro-frontends.

With vertical-split architectures, you can decide either to bundle all the shared libraries together or to bundle the libraries for each micro-frontend. The former can provide greater performance because the user downloads the bundle only once, but you'll need to coordinate the libraries to update for every change across all the micro-frontends. While this may sound like an easy task, it can be more complicated than you think when it happens regularly. Imagine you have a breaking change on a specific shared UI framework; you can't update the new version until all the micro-frontends have done extensive tests on the new framework version. So while we gain in performance in this scenario, we must first overcome some organizational challenges. The latter solution—maintaining every micro-frontend independently—reduces the communication overhead for coordinating the shared dependencies but might increase the content the user must download. As seen before, however, a user may decide to stay within the same micro-frontend for the entire session, resulting in the exact same kilobytes downloaded.

Once again, there isn't right or wrong in any of these strategies. Make a decision on the requirements to fulfill and the context you operate in. Don't be afraid to make a call and monitor how users interact with your application. You may discover that, overall, the solution you picked, despite some pitfalls, is the right one for the project. Remember, you can easily reverse this decision, so spend the right amount of time thinking which path your project requires, but be aware that you can change direction if a new requirement arises or the decision causes more harm than benefits.

Available Frameworks

There are some frameworks available for embracing this architecture. However, building an application shell on your own won't require too much effort, as long as you keep the application shell decoupled from any micro-frontend business logic. Polluting the application shell codebase with domain logic is not only a bad practice but also may invalidate all effort and investment of using micro-frontends in the long run due to code and logic coupling.

Two frameworks that are fully embracing this architecture are single-spa (*https://single-spa.js.org*) and qiankun (*https://qiankun.umijs.org*). The concept behind single-spa is very simple: it's a lightweight library that provides undifferentiated heavy lifting for the following:

Registration of micro-frontends
> The library provides a root configuration to associate a micro-frontend to a specific path of your system.

Life cycle methods
> Every micro-frontend is exposed to many stages when mounted. Single-spa allows a micro-frontend to perform the right task for the life cycle method. For instance, when a micro-frontend is mounted, we can apply logic for fetching an API. When unmounted, we should remove all the listeners and clean up all DOM elements.

Single-spa is a mature library, with years of refinement and many integrations in production. It's open source and actively maintained and has a great community behind it. In the latest version of the library, you can develop horizontal-split micro-frontends, too, including server-side rendering ones. Qiankun is built on top of single-spa, adding some functionality from the latest releases of single-spa.

Module Federation (*https://oreil.ly/E5nO2*) may also be a good alternative for implementing a vertical-split architecture, considering that the mounting and unmounting mechanism, dependencies management, orchestration between micro-frontends, and many other features are already available to use. Module Federation is typically used for composing multiple micro-frontends in the same view (horizontal split). However, nothing is preventing us from using it for handling vertical-split micro-frontends. Moreover, it's a webpack plug-in. If your projects are already using webpack, it may help you avoid learning new frameworks for composing and orchestrating your project's micro-frontends. In the next chapter, we will explore the Module Federation for implementing vertical and horizontal split architectures.

Use Cases

The vertical-split architecture is a good solution when your frontend developers have experience with SPA development. It will also scale up to a certain extent, but if you have hundreds of frontend developers working on the same frontend application, a horizontal split may suit your project better, because you can modularize your application even further.

Vertical-split architecture is also great when you want UI and UX consistency. In this situation, every team is responsible for a specific business domain, and a vertical split will allow them to develop an end-to-end experience without the need to coordinate with other teams.

Another reason to choose this architecture pattern is the level of reusability you want to have across multiple micro-frontends. For instance, if you reuse mainly components of your design system and some libraries, like logging or payments, a vertical split may be a great architecture fit. However, if part of your micro-frontend is replicated in multiple views, a horizontal split may be a better solution. Again, let the context drive the decision for your project.

Finally, this architecture is my first recommendation when you start embracing micro-frontends because it doesn't introduce too much complexity. It has a smooth learning curve for frontend developers, it distributes the business domains to dozens of frontend developers without any problem, and it doesn't require huge upfront investment in tools but more in general in the entire developer experience.

Architecture Characteristics

Deployability (5/5)
  Because every micro-frontend is a single HTML page or an SPA, we can easily deploy our artifacts on a cloud storage or an application server and stick a CDN in front of it. It's a well-known approach, used for several years by many frontend developers for delivering their web applications. Even better, when we apply a

multi-CDN strategy, our content will always be served to our user no matter which fault a CDN provider may have.

Modularity (2/5)

This architecture is not the most modular. While we have a certain degree of modularization and reusability, it's more at the code level, sharing components or libraries but less on the features side. For instance, it's unlikely a team responsible for the development of the SPA catalog micro-frontend shares it with another micro-frontend. Moreover, when we have to split a vertical-split micro-frontend in two or more parts because of new features, a bigger effort will be required for decoupling all the shared dependencies implemented, since it was designed as a unique logical unit.

Simplicity (4/5)

Taking into account that the primary aim of this approach is reducing the team's cognitive load and creating domain experts using well-known practices for frontend developers, the simplicity is intrinsic. There aren't too many mindset shifts or new techniques to learn to embrace this architecture. The overhead for starting with single-spa or Module Federation should be minimal for a frontend developer.

Testability (4/5)

Compared to SPAs, this approach shows some weakness in the application shell's end-to-end testing. Apart from that edge case, however, testing vertical-split micro-frontends doesn't represent a challenge with existing knowledge of unit, integration, or end-to-end testing.

Performance (4/5)

You can share the common libraries for a vertical-split architecture, though it requires a minimum of coordination across teams. Since it's very unlikely that you'll have hundreds of micro-frontends with this approach, you can easily create a deployment strategy that decouples the common libraries from the micro-frontend business logic and maintains the commonalities in sync across multiple micro-frontends. Compared to other approaches, such as server-side rendering, there is a delay on downloading the code of a micro-frontend because the application shell should initialize the application with some logic. This may impact the load of a micro-frontend when it's too complex or makes many roundtrips to the server.

Developer experience (4/5)

A team familiar with SPA tools won't need to shift their mindset to embrace the vertical split. There may be some challenges during end-to-end testing, but all the other engineering practices, as well as tools, remain the same. Not all the tools available for SPA projects are suitable for this architecture, so your developers may need to build some internal tools to fill the gaps. However, the out-of-the-box tools available should be enough to start development, allowing your team to defer the decisions to build new tools.

Scalability (5/5)

The scalability aspect of this architecture is so great that we can even forget about it when we serve our static content via a CDN. We can also configure the time-to-live according to the assets we are serving, setting a higher time for assets that don't change often, like fonts or vendor libraries, and a lower time for assets that change often, like the business logic of our micro-frontends. This architecture can scale almost indefinitely based on CDN capacity, which is usually great enough to serve billions of users simultaneously. In certain cases, when you absolutely must avoid a single point of failure, you can even create a multiple-CDN strategy, where your micro-frontends are served by multiple CDN providers. Despite being more complicated, it solves the problem elegantly without investing too much time creating custom solutions.

Coordination (4/5)

This architecture, compared to others, enables a strong decentralization of decision making, as well as autonomy of each team. Usually, the touching points between micro-frontends are minimal when the domain boundaries are well defined. Therefore, there isn't too much coordination needed, apart from an initial investment for defining the application shell APIs and keeping them as domain unaware as possible.

Table 4-1 gathers the architecture characteristics and its associated score for this micro-frontend architecture.

Table 4-1. Architecture characteristics summary for developing a micro-frontends architecture using vertical split and application shell as composition and orchestrator

Architecture characteristics	Score (1 = lowest, 5 = highest)
Deployability	5/5
Modularity	2/5
Simplicity	4/5
Testability	4/5
Performance	4/5
Developer experience	4/5
Scalability	5/5
Coordination	4/5

Horizontal-Split Architectures

Horizontal-split architectures provide a variety of options for almost every need a micro-frontend application has. These architectures have a very granular level of modularization thanks to the possibility to split the work of any view among multiple teams. In this way, you can compose views reusing different micro-frontends built by multiple teams inside your organization. Horizontal-split architectures are suggested not only to companies that already have a sizable engineering department but also to projects that have a high level of code reusability, such as a multitenant business-to-business (B2B) project in which one customer requests a customization or ecommerce with multiple categories with small differences in behaviors and user interface. Your team can easily build a personalized micro-frontend just for that customer and for that domain only. In this way, we reduce the risk of introducing bugs in different parts of the applications, thanks to the isolation and independence that every micro-frontend should maintain.

At the same time, due to this high modularization, horizontal-split architecture is one of the most challenging implementations because it requires solid governance and regular reviews for getting the micro-frontends boundaries rights. Moreover, these architectures challenge the organization's structure unless they are well thought out up front. It's very important with these architectures that we review the communication flows and the team's structure to enable the developers to do their job and avoid too many external dependencies across teams. Also, we need to share best practices and define guidelines to follow to maintain a good level of freedom while providing a unique, consolidated experience for the user.

One of the recommended practices when we use horizontal-split architectures is to reduce the number of micro-frontends in the same view, especially when multiple teams have to merge their work together. This may sound obvious, but there is a real risk of over-engineering the solution to have several tiny micro-frontends living together in the same view, which creates an antipattern. This is because you are blurring the line between a micro-frontend and a component, where the former is a business representation of a subdomain and the latter is a technical solution used for reusability purposes.

Components Versus Micro-Frontends

A good rule of thumb to understand if we are building a component or a micro-frontend is that, with a component, we tend to extend for different use cases, exposing multiple properties for covering all the use cases for different scenarios. Instead, with a micro-frontend, we encapsulate the logic, allowing communication via events.

Moreover, managing the output of multiple teams in the same view requires additional coordination in several stages of the software development life cycle. Another sign of over-engineering a page is having multiple micro-frontends fetching from the same API. In that case, there is a good chance that you have pushed the division of a view too far and need to refactor. Remember that embracing these architectures provides great power, and therefore we have great responsibility for making the right choices for the project. In the next sections we will review the different implementations of horizontal-split architectures: client side, edge side, and server side.

Client Side

A client-side implementation of the horizontal-split architecture is similar to the vertical-split one in that there is an application shell used for composing the final view. The key difference is that, here, a view is composed of multiple micro-frontends, which can be developed by the same or different teams. Due to the horizontal split's modular nature, it's important not to fall into the trap of thinking too much about components. Instead, stick to the business perspective.

Imagine, for example, you are building a video-streaming website and you decide to use a horizontal-split architecture using a client-side composition. There are several teams involved in this project; however, for simplicity, we will only consider two views: the landing page and the catalog. The bulk of work for these two experiences involve the following teams:

Foundation team
> This team is responsible for the application shell and the design system, working alongside the UX team but from a more technical perspective.

Landing page team
> The landing page team is responsible for supporting the marketing team to promote the streaming service and creating all the different landing pages needed.

Catalog team
> This team is responsible for the authenticated area where a user can consume a video on demand. It works in collaboration with other teams for providing a compelling experience to the service subscribers.

Playback experience team
> Considering the complexity for building a great video player available in multiple platforms, the company decides to have a team dedicated to the playback experience. The team is responsible for the video player, video analytics, implementation of the digital rights management (DRM), and additional security concerns related to the video consumption from unauthorized users.

When it comes to implementing one of the many landing pages, three teams are responsible for the final view presented to every user. The foundation team provides the application shell, footer, and header and composes the other micro-frontends present in the landing page. The landing page team provides the streaming service offering, with additional details about the video platform. The playback experience team provides the video player for delivering the advertising needed to attract new users to the service. Figure 4-11 shows the relationship between these elements.

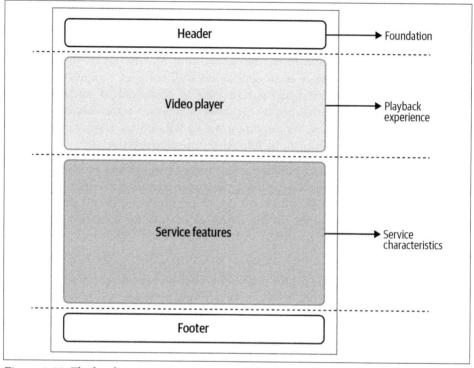

Figure 4-11. The landing page view is composed by the application shell, which loads two micro-frontends: the service characteristics and the playback experience

This view doesn't require particular communication between micro-frontends, so once the application shell is loaded, it retrieves the other two micro-frontends and provides the composed view to the user. When a subscriber wants to watch any video content, after being authenticated, they will be presented with the catalog that includes the video player (see Figure 4-12).

In this case, every time a user interacts with a tile to watch the content, the catalog micro-frontend has to communicate with the playback micro-frontend to provide the ID of the video selected by the user. When an error has to be displayed, the catalog team is responsible for triggering a modal with the error message for the user. And when the playback has to trigger an error, the error will need to be communicated to the catalog micro-frontend, which will display it in the view. This means we need a strategy that keeps the two micro-frontends independent but allows communication between them when there is a user interaction or an error occurs.

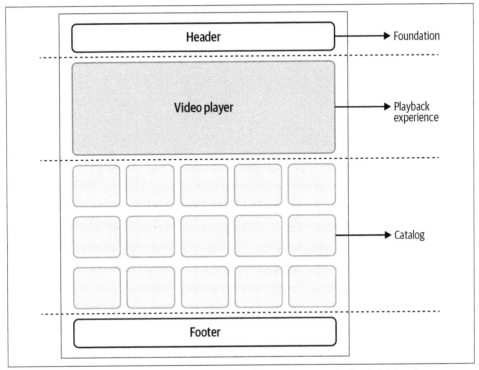

Figure 4-12. The catalog view is composed by the application shell, which loads two micro-frontends: the playback experience and the catalog itself

There are many strategies available to solve this problem, like using custom events or an event emitter, but we will discuss the different approaches later on in this chapter. Why wasn't there a specific composition strategy for this example? Mainly because every client-side architecture has its own way of composing a view. Also, in this case we will see, architecture by architecture, the best practice for doing so.

Do you want to discover where the horizontal-split architecture really shines? Let's fast-forward a few months after the release of the video-streaming platform. The product team asks for a nonauthenticated version of the catalog to improve the discoverability of the platform assets, as well as providing a preview of their best shows to potential customers. This boils down to providing a similar experience of the catalog without the playback experience. The product team would also like to present additional information on the landing page so users can make an informed decision about subscribing to the service. In this case, the foundation team, catalog team, and landing page team will be needed to fulfill this request (see Figure 4-13).

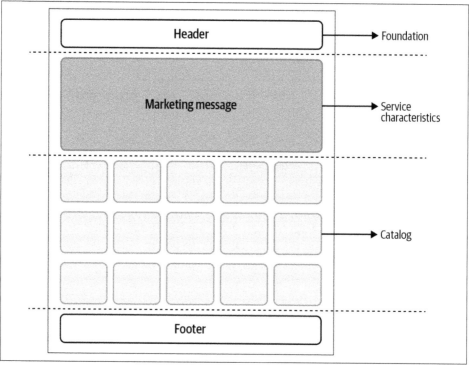

Figure 4-13. This new view is composed by the catalog (owned by the catalog team) and the marketing message (owned by the landing page team)

Evolving a web application is never easy, for both technical and collaboration reasons. Having a way to compose micro-frontends simultaneously and then stitching them together in the same view, with multiple teams collaborating without stepping on each other's toes, makes life easier for everyone and enables the business to evolve at speed and in any direction.

Challenges

As with every architecture, horizontal splits have benefits and challenges that are important to recognize to ensure they're a good fit for your organization and projects. Evaluating the trade-offs before embarking on a development puts you one step closer to delivering a successful project.

Micro-frontend communication

Embracing a horizontal-split architecture requires understanding how micro-frontends developed by different teams share information, or states, during the user session. Inevitably, micro-frontends will need to communicate with each other. For some projects, this may be minimal, while in others, it will be more frequent. Either way, you need a clear strategy up front to meet this specific challenge. Many developers may be tempted to share states between micro-frontends, but this results in a socio-technical antipattern. On the technical side, working with a distributed system that has shared code with other micro-frontends owned by different teams means that the shared state requires it to be designed, developed, and maintained by multiple teams (see Figure 4-14).

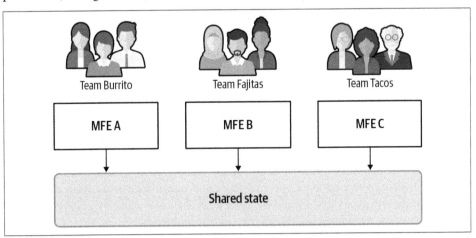

Figure 4-14. Shared state between multiple micro-frontends represents an antipattern

Every time a team makes a change to the shared state, all the others must validate the change and ensure it won't impact their micro-frontends. Such a structure breaks the encapsulation micro-frontends provide, creating an underlying coupling between teams that has frequent, if not constant, external dependencies to take care of.

Moreover, we risk jeopardizing the agility and the evolution of our system because a key part of one micro-frontend is now shared among other micro-frontends. Even worse is when a micro-frontend is reused across multiple views and a team is responsible for maintaining multiple shared states with other micro-frontends. On the organization side, this approach risks coupling teams, resulting in the need for a lot of coordination that can be avoided while maintaining intact the boundaries of every micro-frontend.

The coordination between teams doesn't stop on the design phase, either. It will be even more exasperating during testing and release phases because now all the micro-frontends in the same view depend on the same state that cannot be released independently. Having constant coordination to handle instead of maintaining a micro-frontend's independent nature can be a team's worst nightmare. In the microservices world, this is called a distributed monolith: an application deployed like a microservice but built like a monolith.

One of micro-frontends' main benefits is the strong boundaries that allow every team to move at the speed they need, loosely coupling the organization, reducing the time of coordination, and allowing developers to take destiny in their hands. In the micro-services world, to achieve a loose coupling between microservices and therefore between teams, we use the choreography pattern, which uses an asynchronous communication, or event broker, to notify all the consumers interested in a specific event. With this approach we have:

- Independent microservices that can react to (or not react to) external events triggered by one or more producers
- Solid, bounded context that doesn't leak into multiple services
- Reduced communication overhead for coordinating across teams
- Agility for every team so they can evolve their microservice based on their customers' needs

With micro-frontends, we should think in the same way to gain the same benefits. Instead of using a shared state, we maintain our micro-frontends' boundaries and communicate any event that should be shared on the view using asynchronous messages, something we're used to dealing with on the frontend.

Other possibilities are implementing either an event emitter or a reactive stream (if you are in favor of the reactive paradigm) and sharing it across all the micro-frontends in a view (see Figure 4-15).

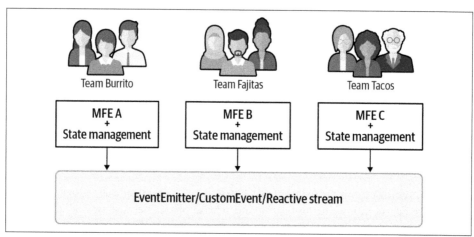

Figure 4-15. Every micro-frontend in the same view should own its own state and should communicate changes via asynchronous communication using an event emitter or CustomEvent or reactive streams

In Figure 4-15, Team Fajitas is working on a micro-frontend (MFE B) that needs to react when a user interacts with an element in another micro-frontend (MFE A), run by Team Burrito. Using an event emitter, Team Fajitas and Team Burrito can define how the event name and the associated payload will look and then implement them, working in parallel (see Figure 4-16).

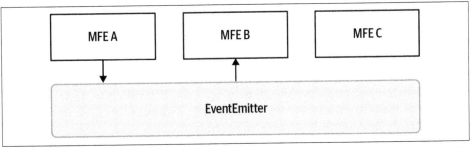

Figure 4-16. MFE A emits an event using the EventEmitter as a communication bus; all the micro-frontends interested in that event will listen and react accordingly

When the payload changes for additional features implemented in the platform, Team Fajitas will need to make a small change to its logic and can then start integrating these features without waiting for other teams to make any change and maintaining its independence.

The third micro-frontend in our example (MFE C, run by Team Tacos) doesn't care about any event shared in that view because its content is static and doesn't need to react to any user interactions. Team Tacos can continue to do its job knowing its part won't be affected by any state change associated with a view.

A few months later a new team, Team Nachos, is created to build an additional feature in the application. Team Nachos' micro-frontend (MFE D) lives alongside MFE A and MFE B (see Figure 4-17).

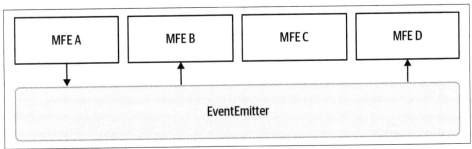

Figure 4-17. A new micro-frontend was added in the same view and has to integrate with the rest of the application reacting to the event emitted by MFE A. Because of the loose coupling nature of this approach, MFE D just listens to the events emitted by MFE A. In this way, all micro-frontends and teams maintain their independence.

Because every micro-frontend is well encapsulated and the only communication protocol is a pub/sub system like the event emitter, the new team can easily listen to all the events it needs to for plugging in the new feature alongside the existing micro-frontends. This approach not only enhances the technical architecture but also provides a loose coupling between teams while allowing them to continue working independently.

Once again, we notice how important our technology choices are when it comes to maintaining independent teams and reducing external dependencies that would cause more frustration than anything else. As well, having the team document all the events in input and output for every horizontal-split micro-frontend will help facilitate the asynchronous communication between teams. Providing an up-to-date, self-explanatory list of contracts for communicating in and out of a micro-frontend will result in clear communication and better governance of the entire system. What these processes help achieve is speed of delivery, independent teams, agility, and a high degree of evolution for every micro-frontend without affecting others.

Clashes with CSS classes and how to avoid them

One potential issue in horizontal-split architecture during implementation is CSS classes clash. When multiple teams work on the same application, there is a strong possibility of having duplicate class names, which would break the final application layout. To avoid this risk, we can prefix each class name for every micro-frontend, creating a strong rule that prevents duplicate names and, therefore, undesired outcomes for our users. Block Element Modifier, or BEM (*http://getbem.com*), is a well-known naming convention for creating unique names for CSS classes. As the name suggests, we use three elements to assign to a component in a micro-frontend:

Block
An element in a view. For example, an avatar component is composed of an image, the avatar name, and so on.

Element
A specific element of a block. In the previous example, the avatar image is an element.

Modifier
A state to display. For instance, the avatar image can be active or inactive.

Based on the example described, we can derive the following class names:

```
.avatar {}
.avatar__image {}
.avatar__image--active {}
.avatar__image--inactive {}
```

While following BEM can be extremely beneficial for architecting your CSS strategy, it may not be enough for projects with multiple micro-frontends. So we build on the BEM structure by prefixing the micro-frontend name to the class.

For our avatar example, when it's used in the "My account" micro-frontend, the names become:

```
.myaccount_avatar {}
.myaccount_avatar__image {}
.myaccount_avatar__image--active {}
.myaccount_avatar__image--inactive {}
```

Although this makes names long, it guarantees the isolation needed and makes clear what every class refers to. Any other naming convention for CSS class names you want to create is also acceptable, but just remember to add prefixes when used with micro-frontends.

 For a good guide to starting with BEM, check out Inna Belaya's article "BEM for Beginners: Why You Need BEM" (*https://oreil.ly/ NGTiB*) at *Smashing* magazine. You can read additional content on the topic (*https://oreil.ly/KzYGh*) at *Smashing* as well.

Multiframework approach

Using multiple frameworks isn't great for vertical-split architectures due to performance issues. On horizontal-split architectures, it's even more dangerous. When this problem is not addressed in the design phase, it can cause runtime errors in the final view.

Imagine having multiple versions of React in the same view. It does not lead to a great experience for the user. When the browser downloads two versions for a rendering view, performance issues can crop up. Consider, too, the potential variables clashing when we load the libraries or append new components in the view.

There are many ways to address this problem. For instance, iframes create a sandbox so that what loads inside one iframe doesn't clash with another iframe. Module Federation allows you to share libraries and provides a mechanism for avoiding clashing dependencies. Import maps allow us to define scopes for every dependency (*https:// oreil.ly/bG4Or*) so we can define different versions of the same libraries to different scopes. And web components can "hide" behind the shadow DOM the frameworks need for a micro-frontend.

Still, using a multiframework approach is strongly discouraged due to performance issues. Having more kilobytes to download in order to render a page is not a great customer experience, and our job as developers and architects should be to provide the best user experience possible. Multiframework isn't acceptable in other frontend architectures, like SPAs, and micro-frontends should not be an exception.

The only acceptable time to use a multiframework strategy is when we have to migrate a legacy application to a new one, resulting in the micro-frontends being iteratively released rather than releasing all at once. In this case, the multiframework strategy allows you to provide customer value and lowers risks in deploying your artifacts.

Authentication

Horizontal-split architectures present an interesting challenge when it comes to system authentication, because, more often than not, multiple teams are working on the same view, and they need to maintain a unique experience for the customer. When a user enters into an authenticated area of a web application, all the micro-frontends composing the page have to communicate with the respective APIs providing tokens.

Let's say we have three different teams creating a micro-frontend, each composing a view for the customer. These micro-frontends have to fetch data from the backend, which is a distributed system composed of multiple microservices (see Figure 4-18).

How can different micro-frontends retrieve and store a token safely without multiple round trips to the backend? The best option we have is storing the token in the localStorage, the sessionStorage, or a cookie. In this case, all the micro-frontends will retrieve the same token in the defined web storage solution by convention.

Different security restrictions will be applied based on the web storage selected for hosting the token. For instance, if we use localStorage or sessionStorage, all the micro-frontends have to be hosted in the same subdomain; otherwise the localStorage or sessionStorage where the token is stored won't be accessible. In the case of cookies, we can use multiple subdomains but must use the same domain.

We also have to consider when we have multiple micro-frontends consuming the same API with the same request body that it's very likely that these micro-frontends can be merged into a unique micro-frontend.

Don't be afraid to review the domain boundaries of micro-frontends, because they will evolve alongside the business. Additionally, because there isn't a scientific way to define boundaries, taking a step back and reassessing the direction taken can sometimes be more beneficial than ignoring the problem. The longer we ignore the problem, the more disruption the teams will experience. It's far better to invest time at the beginning of the project for refactoring a bunch of micro-frontends.

Finally, this approach is applicable also to the vertical-split architecture, and we don't even have to be worried about multiple teams looking for a token considering we load just one micro-frontend per time.

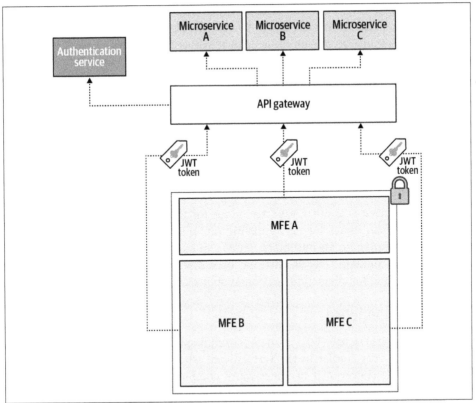

Figure 4-18. Every micro-frontend in a horizontal-split architecture has to fetch data from an API passing a JWT token to the backend to validate that the user is entitled to retrieve the data requested

Micro-frontends refactoring

Another benefit of the horizontal-split architecture is the ability to refactor specific micro-frontends when the code becomes too complicated to be manageable by a single team or a new team starts owning a micro-frontend they didn't develop. While you can do this with a vertical split as well, the horizontal-split micro-frontends have far less logic to maintain, making them a great benefit, especially for enterprise organizations that have to work on the same platform for many years.

Because every micro-frontend is independent, refactoring the code to make it more understandable for the team is a benefit because this activity won't impact anyone else in the company. While you need to keep tech leadership's guidelines in mind, refactoring a well-designed micro-frontend requires far less time than refactoring a large monolithic codebase. This characteristic makes micro-frontends more maintainable in the long run. Additionally, when a complete rewrite is needed, having the domain experts—the team—in charge of rewriting something they know inside out requires significantly less work than rewriting an unfamiliar application from scratch. And because of the micro-frontends' nature, you can decide to rewrite them iteratively and ship them in production to gain immediate benefits of your work, instead of working for several months before releasing everything all at once.

I'm not encouraging refactoring or rewriting just because they're easier. But sometimes the team gains additional business knowledge, or they have to implement a tactical solution due to a hard delivery date; making a refactor or a rewrite from scratch can make life easier in the long run, speeding up new-feature development or reducing the possibility of bugs in the production environment.

Search Engine Optimization

Dynamic rendering is another valid technique for this architecture, especially when we decide to use iframes for encapsulating our micro-frontends. In that situation, redirecting a crawler to an optimized version of static HTML pages helps with the search engine's ranking. Overall, what has been discussed so far about dynamic rendering is also valid for client-side horizontal-split architectures.

Developer Experience

The developer experience (DX) of the horizontal-split architecture with a client-side composition is very similar to the vertical split when a team is developing its own micro-frontend. However, it becomes more complex when the team needs to test micro-frontends inside a view with other micro-frontends. The main challenge is keeping up with the versions and having a quick turnaround for assembling a view on the developer's laptop.

As we will describe in Chapter 7, we can use webpack DevServer Proxy for testing locally, with micro-frontends available in testing, staging, or production environments. Often, companies that embrace this architecture create tools for improving their teams' feedback loop, often in the form of command line tools that can enhance the standard tools available for the frontend developers' community, like Rollup, webpack, or Snowpack. It's important to note that it's very likely this architecture will require some internal investments to create a solid DX. Currently, frameworks and tools (webpack Module Federation, for instance) are trying an opinionated approach; while this isn't necessarily a bad thing, in large companies, additional effort will most likely be required to maintain the guidelines and standards the tech leadership designed based on the industry the company operates in.

Maintaining control with effective communication

Although horizontal-split architectures are the most versatile, they also present intrinsic implementation challenges from an organizational point of view, with coordinating a final output for the use being the main one. When we have multiple micro-frontends owned by different teams composed in the same view, we have to create a social mechanism for avoiding runtime issues in production due to dependency clashes or CSS classes overriding each other. As well, observability tools must be added to quickly identify which micro-frontends are failing in production and provide the team with clear information so they can diagnose the issue in their micro-frontend.

The best way to avoid issues is to keep the communication channels open and maintain a fast feedback loop that keeps all teams in sync, such as a weekly or biweekly meeting with a member from every micro-frontend team responsible for a view. Synching the work between teams has to happen either in a live meeting or via asynchronous communication, such as emails or instant messaging clients.

We must also reduce the number of teams working on the same page and make one team responsible for the final output presented to the users. This doesn't mean that the team responsible for the final look and feel of a view should do all the work. However, shared responsibilities often lead to misunderstandings, so having one team lead the effort creates a better experience for your users.

As we saw in our client-side video player example, we have three teams involved in delivering the catalog page. It's very likely that the catalog team would perform any additional checks on the playback experience because after a user clicks on a movie or a show, it should play in the video player. In this case, then, the catalog team should be responsible for the final outcome and should coordinate the effort with the playback experience team for providing the best output for their users.

When possible, reducing external dependencies should be a periodic job for an engineer manager or a team lead. Don't blindly accept the status quo. Instead, embrace a continuous improvement mindset and challenge the work done so far to find better ways to serve your customers.

Strongly encourage your teams to document their micro-frontend inputs and outputs, the events a micro-frontend expects to receive, and those that will trigger to keep the teams in sync and to allow the discussion of potential breaking changes. Especially for the latter case, keeping track of breaking changes using requests for comments (RFCs) or similar documents is strongly recommended for several reasons. First, it creates asynchronous communication between teams, which is especially when teams are distributed across time zones. It also maintains a record of decisions with the context the company was operating in when the decision was made. Finally, not everyone performs well during meetings; sometimes one person will monopolize the discussion, preventing others from sharing their opinion. Moving from verbal to written communications helps everyone have their voice be heard.

Use Cases

One reason to embrace the horizontal-split architecture is the micro-frontends' reusability across the application or multiple applications. Imagine a team responsible for the payment micro-frontend of an ecommerce website, and the micro-frontend contains different states based on the type of view and payments available. The payment micro-frontend is present in every view in which the user wants to perform a payment action, including a landing page, a product detail view, or even a subscription page for another product. This situation is applicable at a larger scale on a B2B application, where similar UX constructs are replicated in several system views.

Another use case for this architecture is for enterprise applications, for which we often deal with dashboards containing a variety of data that we want to collect into different views for different purposes, such as financial and monitoring. New Relic uses this approach to provide monitoring tools for cloud services, as well as a frontend one that implements micro-frontends (*https://oreil.ly/j29Du*) for scaling the organization, allowing multiple teams to contribute different data representations, all collected into a unique dashboard.

In Figure 4-19, you can see how New Relic divided its application so that a small number of teams work in the same view, reducing the amount of communication needed for composing the final view but allowing the team to be well encapsulated inside its business domain.

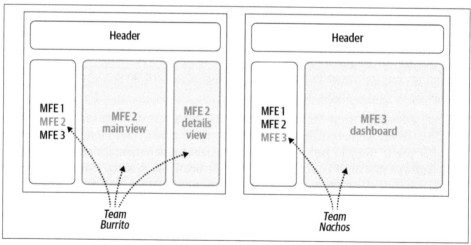

Figure 4-19. New Relic micro-frontend implementation. Every team is responsible for their own domain, and when a user selects a dashboard, the related micro-frontend is lazy-loaded inside the application shell.

This approach allows New Relic teams to work on their own micro-frontends, and by following some contracts for deploying micro-frontends in production, they can see the final results in their web application.

The final use case for this architecture is when we are developing a multitenant application for which the vast majority of the interface is the same but allowing customers to build specific features to make the software suitable for their specific organization. For example, let's say we are developing a digital till system for restaurants, and we want to configure the tables on the floor on a customer-by-customer basis. The application will have the same functionality for every single customer, but a restaurant chain can request specific features in the digital till system. The micro-frontend team responsible for the application can implement these features without forking the code for every customer; instead, they will create a new micro-frontend for handling the specific customer's needs and deploy it in their tenant.

Module Federation

Micro-frontend architectures received a great gift with the release of webpack 5: a new native plug-in called Module Federation. Module Federation allows chunks of JavaScript code to load synchronously or asynchronously, meaning multiple developers or even teams can work in isolation and take care of the application composition, lazy-loading different JavaScript chunks behind the scenes at runtime, as shown in Figure 4-20.

A Module Federation application is composed of two parts:

The host
    Represents the container of one or more micro-frontends or libraries loaded.

The remote
    Represents the micro-frontend or library that will be loaded inside a host at runtime. A remote exposes one or more objects that can be used by the host when the remote is lazy-loaded into an application.

The part of Module Federation that really shines is the simplicity of exposing different micro-frontends, or even shared libraries such as a design system, allowing a simple asynchronous integration. The developer experience is incredibly smooth. As when you're working with a monolithic codebase, you can import remote micro-frontends and compose a view in the way you need.

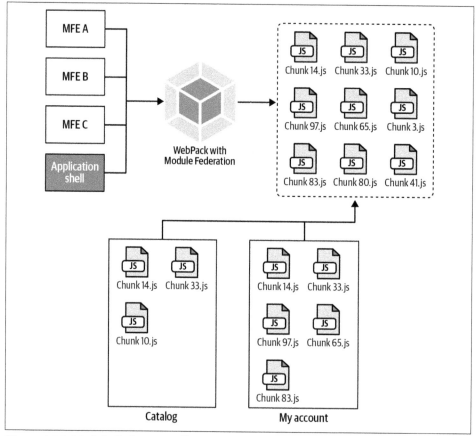

Figure 4-20. Module Federation allows multiple micro-frontends to be loaded asynchronously, providing the user with a seamless experience

Testing locally or pointing to a specific endpoint online doesn't make a difference because we can work in a similar way to handle multiple environments, with webpack having a common configuration augmented by a specific one for every environment (test, stage, or production).

Another important feature of webpack with Module Federation is the ability to share external libraries across multiple micro-frontends without the fear of potential clashes happening at runtime. In fact, we can specify which libraries are shared across multiple micro-frontends, and Module Federation will load just one version for all the micro-frontends using the library.

Imagine that all your micro-frontends are using Vue.js 3.0.0. With Module Federation, you will just need to specify that Vue version 3 is a shared library; at compile time, webpack will export just one Vue version for all the micro-frontends using it. And if you wanted to intentionally work with different versions of Vue in the same project? Module Federation will wrap the two libraries in different scopes to avoid the clashes that could happen at runtime, or you can even specify the scope for a different version of the same library using Module Federation APIs.

Module Federation is available not only when we want to run an application fully client side but also when we want to use it with server-side rendering. In fact, we can asynchronously load different components without needing to deploy the application server that composes the page again and serve the final result to a client request.

Unfortunately, the great simplicity of code sharing across projects is also the weakest point of this plug-in. When you work in a team that's not disciplined enough, sharing libraries, code snippets, and micro-frontends across multiple views can result in a very complicated architecture to maintain, thanks to the frictionless integration. So it's critical to create guidelines that follow the micro-frontend decisions framework in order not to regret the freedom Module Federation provides.

Performance

With webpack, you can use a long list of official plug-ins to optimize your code when it is bundled, as well as even more plug-ins from independent developers and companies on GitHub.

Module Federation benefits from this ecosystem because many of these plug-ins can manipulate a micro-frontend's output and work in conjunction with the plug-in. One of the main challenges we face when working with micro-frontends is how to share dependencies across this distributed architecture, and Module Federation can help there too. Let's say you have multiple teams working in the same application. Each team owns a single micro-frontend, and the teams have agreed to use the same UI library for the entire application. You can share these libraries automatically with Module Federation from the plug-in configuration, and they'll be loaded only once at the beginning of the project.

You can also load micro-frontends dynamically inside JavaScript logic instead of defining all of them in the webpack configuration file.

Optimizing the micro-frontends code from webpack is definitely a great option, mainly because, while the tool was created for bundling JavaScript, now it can optimize other static assets, such as CSS or HTML files.

With so many organizations and independent developers using webpack, the ecosystem is more alive than ever, and the community-created enhancements are great for supporting any type of workload.

Composition

Using Module Federation for a micro-frontend architecture is as simple as importing an external JavaScript chunk lazy-loaded inside a project. Composition takes place at runtime either on the client side, when we use an application shell for loading different micro-frontends, or on the server side, when we use server-side rendering. When we load a micro-frontend on an application shell at runtime, we can fetch the micro-frontend directly from a CDN or from an application server. And the same is true when we are working with a server-side rendering architecture. In this case, composition takes place at the origin, and we can load micro-frontends at runtime before serving them to a client request.

In the next chapter, we will dive deeply into Module Federation composition, providing more insights into how to achieve horizontal- and vertical-split composition with code examples.

Shared code

Module Federation makes sharing code very simple, providing a frictionless developer experience. However, we have to carefully consider why we are embracing micro-frontends in the first place. This plug-in allows you to have bidirectional sharing across micro-frontends, therefore flattening the hierarchical nature of an application where a host micro-frontend can share code with a remote micro-frontend and vice versa. I tend to discourage this practice because a unidirectional implementation brings several advantages, such as the following:

- Code is easier to debug, as we know what code is coming from where.
- It's less prone to errors, as we have more control over our code.
- It's more efficient, as the micro-frontend knows the boundaries of each part of the system.

In the past, we have seen a similar approach with frontend architecture moving from a bidirectional data flow to a unidirectional one with the release of Facebook's Flux (*https://oreil.ly/4FflK*), which made developers' lives easier and the applications more stable. The same reasoning was applied to React and how we deal with props objects injected from the parent component to one or more child components. Additionally, reactive architectures have fully embraced this pattern with interesting implementations, like Model-View-Intent (MVI) applied on Elm (*https://elm-lang.org*) or Cycle.js (*https://oreil.ly/iU68m*).

Developer experience

Webpack with Module Federation makes developers' lives easier, especially when they're familiar with the main tool. The people behind the plug-in did an incredible job abstracting all the complexity needed to create a smooth DX, and now developers can load asynchronously or synchronously shared code in the form of libraries or micro-frontends. Even better, Module Federation fits perfectly inside the webpack ecosystem and can be used with other plug-ins or configurations available in the webpack configuration file.

By default, this plug-in produces small JavaScript chunks for every micro-frontend, enabling dependencies to be shared across micro-frontends when specified in the plug-in's configuration. However, when we use the optimization capability webpack offers out of the box, we can instruct the output to use fewer but larger chunks, maybe dividing our output in vendor and business logic files. These two files can then be cached in different ways, which is valuable since the business logic will be iterated more frequently than a project's external dependencies will be changed or upgraded.

Use cases

Because this plug-in provides such extensive flexibility, we can apply to it any horizontal- or vertical-split micro-frontend use case. We can compose an application on the client or server side and then easily route using any available routing libraries for our favorite UI framework. Finally, we can use an event emitter library or custom events for communications across micro-frontends. Webpack with Module Federation covers almost all micro-frontends use cases, providing a great DX for every team or developer used to working with webpack.

Architecture characteristics

Deployability (4/5)

Webpack divides a micro-frontend into JavaScript chunks, making them easy to deploy in any cloud service from any automation pipeline. And because they are all static files, they are highly cacheable. While we have to handle the scalability of the application servers responding to any client requests in an SSR approach, the ease of integration and rapid feedback are definitely big pluses for this approach.

Modularity (4/5)

This plug-in's level of modularity is very high, but so is its risk. If we're not careful, we can create many external dependencies across teams; therefore, we have to use Module Federation wisely to avoid creating organizational friction.

Simplicity (5/5)

Webpack's new system solves many problems behind the scenes, but the abstraction created by Module Federation makes the integration of micro-frontends very similar to other, more familiar frontend architectures like SPA or SSR.

Testability (4/5)

Although Module Federation offers an initial version of a federated test using Jest for integration testing, we can still apply unit and end-to-end testing similar to how we're used to working with other frontend architectures.

Performance (4/5)

With Module Federation, we gain a set of capabilities, such as sharing common libraries or UI frameworks, that won't compromise the final artifact's performance. Bear in mind that the mapping between a micro-frontend and its output files could be one to many, so a micro-frontend may be represented by several small JavaScript files, which may increase the initial chattiness between a client and a CDN performing multiple roundtrips for loading all the files needed for rendering a micro-frontend.

Developer experience (5/5)

This is probably one of the best developer experiences currently available for working with micro-frontends. Module Federation integrates very nicely in the webpack ecosystem, hiding the complexity of composing micro-frontends and enabling the implementation of more traditional features, taking care of tedious topics like code sharing and asynchronous import of our static artifacts or libraries.

Scalability (5/5)

Module Federation's approach makes scaling easy, especially when the application is fully client side. The static JavaScript chunks easily served via a CDN make this approach extremely scalable for a vertical-split architecture.

Coordination (3/5)

When we follow the decisions framework shared in the first chapters of this book in conjunction with Module Federation, we can really facilitate the life of our enterprise organization. However, the accessible approach provided by this plug-in can lead to abuse of the modularity, resulting in increased coordination and potential refactors in the long term.

Table 4-2 gathers the architecture characteristics and their associated score for this micro-frontend architecture.

Table 4-2. Architecture characteristics summary for developing a micro-frontend architecture using webpack with Module Federation

Architecture characteristics	Score (1 = lowest, 5 = highest)
Deployability	4/5
Modularity	4/5
Simplicity	5/5
Testability	4/5
Performance	4/5
Developer experience	5/5
Scalability	5/5
Coordination	3/5

Iframes

Iframes are probably not the first thing that comes to mind in relation to micro-frontends, but they provide an isolation between micro-frontends that none of the other solutions can offer.

An iframe is an inline frame used inside a webpage to load another HTML document inside it. When we want to represent a micro-frontend as an independent artifact completely isolated from the rest of the application, iframes are one of the strongest isolations we can have inside a browser. An iframe gives us granular control over what can run inside it. The less-privileged implementation using the sandbox attribute (*https://oreil.ly/Q6tIb*) prevents any JavaScript logic from executing or any forms from being submitted:

```
<iframe sandbox src="https://mfe.mywebsite.com/catalog/">
```

An iframe gives us access to specific functionalities, combining `sandbox` with other sandbox attribute values, such as `allow-forms` or `allow-scripts`, to ease the sandbox attribute restrictions, allowing form submission or JavaScript file execution, respectively:

```
<iframe sandbox="allow-scripts allow-forms" ↵
src="https://mfe.mywebsite.com/catalog"/>
```

Additionally, the iframe can communicate with the host page when we use the post Message method (*https://oreil.ly/9EJnL*). In this way, the micro-frontend can notify the broader application when there is a user interaction inside its context, and the application can trigger other activities, such as sharing the event with other iframes or changing part of the UI interface present in the host application.

Iframes aren't new, but they are still in use for specific reasons and have found a place within the micro-frontend ecosystem. So far, the main use cases for implementing micro-frontends with iframes are coming from desktop applications and B2B applications, when we control the environment where the application is consumed. Note, though, that this approach is strongly discouraged for consumer websites because iframes are really bad for performance. They are CPU-intensive, especially when multiple iframes are used in the same view.

A proposal for adding a *ShadowRealm* (*https://oreil.ly/h29kZ*), a sandbox like iframes that is lighter and closer to modern web APIs, is in draft to the TC39 (*https://tc39.es*), the committee responsible for evolving the ECMAScript programming language and authoring the specification. A ShadowRealm object would abstract the notion of a distinct global environment with its own global object, copy of the standard library, and intrinsics. This is the dynamic equivalent of a same-origin iframe without DOM. Basically, this is a lighter implementation of an iframes sandbox with the same isolation capabilities but without the performance issues that multiple iframes can have when rendered inside the same view.

We can find a list of use cases where ShadowRealms can be used in the proposal repository (*https://oreil.ly/UGmNC*). Sandboxing is just one of them, and there are some interesting scenarios possible. The proposal may never go beyond the draft stage, but it looks very interesting and could be a great fit for the micro-frontend ecosystem.

Best practices and drawbacks

There are some best practices to follow when we want to compose micro-frontends in a horizontal split with iframes. First, we must define a list of templates where the iframes will be placed; having a few layouts can help simplify managing an application with iframes (see Figure 4-21).

Using templates allows your teams to understand how to implement their micro-frontends' UI and minimizes edge cases thanks to some guardrails to follow.

Try to avoid too many interactions across micro-frontends; too many interactions can increase the complexity of the code to be maintained. If you need to share a lot of information across micro-frontends, iframes may not be the right approach for the project. This architecture allows teams to build their micro-frontends in isolation without any potential clash between libraries. However, to create a UI consistency, you will need to share the design system at build-time.

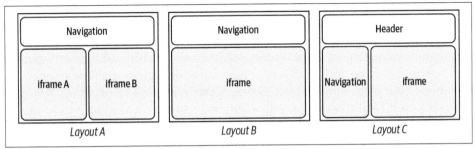

Figure 4-21. Different layouts for composing micro-frontends with iframes. Minimizing the number of iframes in a page would result in better performance despite there being an intrinsic performance overhead when we integrate one or more iframes into a view.

Using iframes for responsive websites can be challenging, as dealing with a fluid layout with iframes and their content can be fairly complicated. Try to stick with fixed dimensions as much as you can. If fixed dimensions aren't possible, one of the other architectures in this chapter may work better for you.

When you have to store data in webstorage or a cookie, use the webstorage or cookie in the application shell to avoid issues with retrieving data across multiple iframes. In this situation, communication between the host page and every micro-frontend living inside an iframe has to be well implemented and thoroughly tested.

When using a pub/sub pattern between iframes and the host page, you have to share an event emitter instance between the main actors of a page. To do this, create an event emitter and append it to the iframe `contentWindow` object so that you can communicate via the emit or dispatch method across all the micro-frontends listening to it. Alternatively, you can rely on an open source library such as Poster (*https://oreil.ly/ UwZS1*), which abstracts the communication API between the host and every micro-frontend in an iframe:

index.js

```
var iframe = document.getElementById("myIframe");
var poster = new Poster(iframe.contentWindow);

poster.post("msg", "hello, world!");
```

catalog-mfe.js

```
var poster = new Poster(window.parent);

poster.on("msg", function (msg) {
  console.log("msg = " + msg); // "msg = hello, world"
});
```

Frameworks such as Luigi from SAP provide solutions for the pitfalls listed so far, which we'll discuss in more depth in the "Available framework" section that follows.

Developer experience

Dealing with iframes makes developers' lives easier, considering the sandboxed environment they use. One of the main challenges of using this approach is with end-to-end testing, when retrieving objects programmatically across multiple iframes can result in a huge effort due to object nesting. Overall, a micro-frontend will be represented by an HTML entry point, with additional resources loaded such as JavaScript or CSS files—very similar to what we are used to in other frontend architectures, like SPAs.

Available framework

There aren't many options available for simplifying the developer experience of micro-frontends inside iframes; usually we can create an in-house strategy, or you can use Luigi framework. Luigi from SAP (*https://oreil.ly/oZFTr*) is a micro-frontends framework used for building intranet applications, which simplifies integration with SAP, but it also can be used outside an SAP context and provides a set of libraries for managing common challenges like routing or localization.

The Luigi framework uses iframes for encapsulating micro-frontends and having a true sandbox around the code. Luigi is the main framework for applications that need to extract data from SAP and aggregate it in a more user-friendly interface. These applications are also mainly running in intranet environments, where it's possible to control which browser version a micro-frontend application runs in without needing to index the content on the main search engines. Given these things, iframes are probably a good fit for using some web standards without the need to create proprietary solutions to handle micro-frontend challenges. In fact, out of the box, Luigi provides a typical implementation for an enterprise application, composed in two main parts:

Main view
> An application shell that provides an abstraction for handling authentication integration with an authentication provider, navigation between views, localization, and general application settings

Luigi client
> A micro-frontend that can interact with the main view via a postMessage mechanism abstracted by the Luigi APIs and several other APIs to allow capabilities like web storage integration or life cycle hooks

After implementing these two parts, a developer then can implement a micro-frontend without the risk of interfering with other parts of the application because the implementation uses iframes to create the requested isolation between key elements of the architecture (see Figure 4-22).

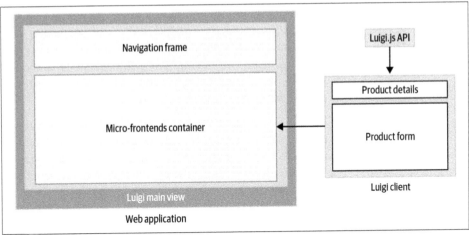

Figure 4-22. A micro-frontend architecture (at left) with the Luigi framework is composed of two parts: the main view and a Luigi client. The Luigi.js API provides an abstraction for common operations, such as communication between a micro-frontend and the host.

Use cases

Iframes are definitely not the solution for every project, yet iframes can be handy in certain situations. Iframes shine when there isn't much communication between micro-frontends and we must enforce the encapsulation of our system using a sandbox for every micro-frontend. The sandboxes release the memory, and there won't be dependency clashes between micro-frontends, removing some complexities of other implementations.

Drawbacks include accessibility, performance, and lack of indexability by crawlers, so best use cases for iframes are in desktop, B2B, or intranet applications. For example, Spotify used to use iframes to encapsulate its micro-frontends in desktop applications, preventing teams from leaking anything outside an iframe while allowing communication between them via events. That helps a desktop application to not download all the dependencies for rendering a micro-frontend; they are all available with the executable download. If you have a desktop application to develop, then, and multiple teams will contribute to specific domains, iframes might be a possible solution. (Note that Spotify recently decided to add its web modular architecture (*https://oreil.ly/qg6GJ*) to the desktop application to unify the codebase and allow reusability across multiple targets.)

Many large organizations also use iframes in intranet applications as strong security boundaries between teams. For instance, when a company has dozens of teams working on the same project and it wants to enforce the teams' independence, iframes could be a valid solution to avoid code or dependency clashes without creating too many tools to work with.

Imagine you have to build a dashboard where multiple teams will contribute their micro-frontends, composing a final view with a snapshot of different metrics and data points to consult. Iframes can help isolate the different domains without the risk of potential clashes between codebases from different teams. They can even prevent specific features inside an iframe using the sandbox attribute.

The final use case is when we have to maintain a legacy application that isn't actively developed but is just in support mode and it has to live alongside the development of a new application, which will both have to be presented to users. In this case, the legacy application can be easily isolated in an iframe living alongside a micro-frontends architecture without the risk of polluting it.

Architecture characteristics

Deployability (5/5)
> The deployability of this architecture is nearly identical to the vertical-split one, with the main difference being we will have more micro-frontends in the horizontal split because we will be dealing with multiple micro-frontends per view.

Modularity (3/5)
> Iframes provide a good level of modularity, thanks to the ability to organize a view in multiple micro-frontends. At the same time, we will need to find the right balance to avoid abusing this characteristic.

Simplicity (3/5)
> For a team working on a micro-frontend, iframes are not difficult. The challenge is in communicating across iframes, orchestrating iframe sizes when the page is resized without breaking the layout. In general, dealing with the big picture in absence of frameworks may require a bit of work.

Testability (3/5)
> Testing in iframes doesn't have any particular challenges apart from the one described for horizontal-split architectures. However, end-to-end testing may become verbose and challenging due to the DOM tree structure of iframes inside a view.

Performance (2/5)
> Performance is probably the worst characteristic of this architecture. If not managed correctly, performance with iframes may be far from great. Although iframes solve a huge memory challenge and prevent dependency clashing, these features don't come free. In fact, iframes aren't a solution for accessible websites because they aren't screen-reader-friendly. Moreover, iframes don't allow search

engines to index the content. If either of these is a key requirement for your project, it's better to use another approach.

Developer experience (3/5)

The iframes DX experience is similar to the SPA one. Automation pipelines are set up in a similar manner, and final outputs are static files, like an SPA. The main challenge is creating a solid client-side composition that allows every team working with micro-frontends to test their artifacts in conjunction with other micro-frontends. Some custom tools for speeding up our teams' DX may be needed. The most challenging part, though, is creating end-to-end testing due to the DOM replication across multiple iframes and the verbosity for selecting an object inside it.

Scalability (5/5)

The content served inside an iframe is highly cacheable at the CDN level, so we won't suffer from scalability challenges at all. At the end, we are serving static content, like CSS, HTML, and JavaScript files.

Coordination (3/5)

As with all horizontal-split architectures, it's important to avoid too many teams collaborating in the same view. Thanks to the sandbox nature of iframes, code clashes aren't a concern, but we can't have interactions spanning across the screen when we have multiple iframes, because coordinating these kinds of experiences is definitely not suitable for this architecture.

Table 4-3 gathers the architecture characteristics and their associated score for this micro-frontend architecture.

Table 4-3. Architecture characteristics summary for developing a micro-frontend architecture using horizontal split and iframes

Architecture characteristics	Score (1 = lowest, 5 = highest)
Deployability	5/5
Modularity	3/5
Simplicity	3/5
Testability	3/5
Performance	2/5
Developer experience	3/5
Scalability	5/5
Coordination	3/5

Web Components

Web components are a set of web platform APIs that allow you to create custom, reusable, and encapsulated HTML tags for use in web pages and web apps. You may argue that web components are not the first thing that comes to mind when thinking about micro-frontends. However, they have interesting characteristics that make web components a suitable solution for building micro-frontend architecture. For instance, we can encapsulate our styles inside web components without fear of leaking in the main application. As well, all the major UI frameworks, like React, Angular, and Vue, are capable of generating web components, and the number of open source libraries to simplify creating this web standard is increasing, particularly with projects like Svelte, which can compile to web components, and LitElement from Google. Web components are also great tools for creating shared libraries for micro-frontend projects used with the same or different UI framework. In fact, in several 2019 surveys about the state of frontend development, web components were one of the most used solutions for building micro-frontends. They play a pivotal role in micro-frontend architecture, either for sharing components across micro-frontends or for encapsulating micro-frontends.

Web components technologies

Web components consist of three main technologies, which can be used together to create custom elements with encapsulated functionality that can be reused wherever you like without fear of code collisions.

Custom elements
> They are an extension of HTML components. We can use them as containers of our micro-frontends, allowing us to interact with the external world via callbacks or events, for instance. Moreover, we can configure exposed properties to configure our micro-frontends accordingly when needed.

Shadow DOM
> A set of JavaScript APIs for attaching an encapsulated "shadow" DOM tree to an element, rendered separately from the main DOM. In this way, you can keep an element's features private, so they can be scripted and styled without the fear of collision with other parts of the document.

HTML templates
> The template and slot elements enable you to write markup templates that are not displayed in the rendered page. These can then be reused multiple times as the basis of a custom element's structure.

Among these three technologies, custom elements and shadow DOM are those that make web components useful for micro-frontend architectures. Both elements allow encapsulation of the code needed in a subdomain without affecting the application shell. Custom elements are used as wrappers of a micro-frontend, while the shadow DOM allows us to encapsulate the micro-frontend's styles without causing them to override another style of micro-frontend.

An important aspect to consider when we are working with web components as wrappers of our micro-frontends is avoiding domain logic leaks. The moment we are allowing the container of our micro-frontends, wrapped inside web components, to customize their behaviors, we are exposing the domain logic to the external world, causing the container of a micro-frontend to know how to interact with a specific API contract via attributes.

It's essential to make sure the communication between a micro-frontend wrapped by a web component and the rest of the view happens in a decoupled and unified way. We may risk blurring the line between components and micro-frontends, where the former should be open to extension, while the latter should be close to extension but open to communication.

Compatibility challenges

Before choosing web components for our next micro-frontend project, we need to take into consideration if the requirements are suitable for them. When we have to target many versions of web browsers, including the old ones and Internet Explorer, the only option provided by web components are polyfills (*https://oreil.ly/ypFGt*). There are two ways for integrating polyfills for web components. The first is including them all. The package size would be quite large, but you are bulletproof, extending the retrocompatibility of your code for older browsers. The second option is loading at runtime only the polyfills needed. In this case, the package size is by far smaller, but it could require a bit of time before loading the right polyfills, considering we have to identify which ones are needed on the browser in which we are running the application.

Another compatibility challenge to be aware of is that there are some bugs on WebKit (*https://oreil.ly/vIM7J*) engine that affect web components' customized built-in elements. Also, older versions of Safari (7 and 8, for instance) don't support importNode or cloneNode methods for appending HTML templates to the DOM. For more information about the web components' fragmentation across all the major browsers divided by vendor and version, I recommend checking out the Can I Use website (*https://oreil.ly/ESH4s*).

SEO and web components

When our micro-frontend project requires search engine optimization, dealing with web components may be nontrivial. In fact, the best way to allow a crawler indexing the content rendered inside a web component is exposing its content in the light DOM:

```
<my-account-mfe>
 <h2>Welcome to My Account</h2>
</my-account-mfe>
```

In this way, the vast majority of the crawlers available worldwide would be capable of indexing the content of your application. The usage of content inside the shadow DOM is discouraged when you deploy an application that should not be indexed only by major search engines like Google. Therefore, when a SEO is a key requirement for your micro-frontend project, dynamic rendering can be an option if you have to use web components.

Use cases

Embracing web components for your micro-frontend architecture is a great choice when you need to support multitenant environments. Given their broad compatibility with all the major frameworks, web components are the perfect candidate for use in multiple projects with the same or different frontend stack, as with multitenant projects. In multitenant projects, our micro-frontends should be integrated in multiple versions of the same application or even in multiple applications, which makes web components a simple, effective solution.

Let's say your organization is selling a customer-support solution in which the chat micro-frontend should be live alongside any frontend technology your customers use. Web components can also play an important role in shared libraries. In a design system, for instance, using a web standard allows you to evolve your applications without having to start from scratch every time, because part of the work is reusable no matter what direction your tech teams or business will take. This is a great investment to make.

Architecture characteristics

Deployability (4/5)
> Loading web components at runtime is easily doable. We just need a CDN for serving them, and they can then be integrated everywhere. They are also easy to integrate with compile time integration; we add them as we import libraries in JavaScript. Although technically you can render them server side, the DX is not as sleek as other solutions proposed by UI frameworks like React.

Modularity (3/5)
> Web components' high degree of modularity allows you to decompose an application into well-encapsulated subdomains. Moreover, because they are a web standard, we can use them in several situations without too many problems when we operate inside browsers that support them. The risk of using them as a micro-frontend wrapper is that it can confuse new developers who are joining a project, blurring the line between components and micro-frontends. This often results in

a proliferation of "micro-frontends"' in a view, but probably we should call them nano-frontends.

Simplicity (4/5)

Using web components should be a simple task for anyone who is familiar with frontend technologies. The main challenge is not splitting our micro-frontends too granularly. Because web components can also be used for building component libraries, the line between micro-frontends and components can be blurred. However, focusing on the business side of our application should lead us to correctly identify micro-frontends from components in our applications.

Testability (4/5)

Leveraging different testing strategies using web components doesn't present too many challenges, but we have to be familiar with their APIs. Web components' APIs differ from UI frameworks, making it challenging to do what we are used to doing with our favorite framework.

Performance (4/5)

One of the main benefits of web components is that we are extending HTML components, meaning we aren't making them extremely dense with external code from libraries. As a result, they should be one of the best solutions for rendering your micro-frontends client side.

Developer experience (4/5)

The DX of your projects shouldn't be too different from your favorite framework. You have to learn another framework to simplify your life, though there aren't too many differences in the development life cycle, especially in the syntax, but that's why there are web component frameworks for simplifying the developer's life.

Scalability (5/5)

Whether we implement our web components at compile or runtime, we will be delivering static files. A simple infrastructure can easily serve millions of customers without the bother of maintaining complex infrastructure solutions to handle traffic.

Coordination (3/5)

The main challenge is making sure we have the micro-frontends' granularity right, because this will impact application delivery speed and avoid external dependencies that may lead to developer frustrations. We need to have a strong sense of discipline when identifying what is represented by a component or by a micro-frontend.

Table 4-4 gathers the architecture characteristics and their associated score for this micro-frontend architecture.

Table 4-4. Architecture characteristics summary for developing a micro-frontends architecture using web components

Architecture characteristics	Score (1 = lowest, 5 = highest)
Deployability	4/5
Modularity	3/5
Simplicity	4/5
Testability	4/5
Performance	4/5
Developer experience	4/5
Scalability	5/5
Coordination	3/5

Server Side

Horizontal-split architectures with a server-side composition are the most flexible and powerful solutions available in the micro-frontend ecosystem, thanks to cloud, which is the perfect environment for developers wanting to focus on the value stream more than infrastructure operationalization. In the cloud, we have the agility to spin up the infrastructure as requests increase and reduce it again when traffic goes back to normal. We can also set up our baseline without too many headaches, focusing on what really matters: the value created for our users.

Server-side composition is usually chosen when our applications have a strong requirement for SEO because this technique speeds up the page load time and the page is fully rendered without the need of any JavaScript logic. Server-side rendering also helps with the position of your application on search engine results pages, considering every search engine takes into account the page load speed.

In a server-side composition, the final view is created on the server side, where we can control the speed of the final output using techniques like caching in different layers (e.g., in a service, in-memory, or CDN), reducing the hops between services to retrieve all the micro-frontends, as well as the type of compute used for running the logic to compose our micro-frontends. Nowadays we have all the tools and resources needed to impact how fast a view is composed and served to our users.

Many of the challenges described in the horizontal split with client-side composition are challenges on the server side too, so rather than repeating them here, let's focus on a few additional challenges this approach creates.

Scalability and response time

Despite the infrastructure flexibility cloud provides, we have to set up the infrastructure correctly in the first place based on our application's traffic patterns. While a cloud provider's auto-scaling functionalities can help you to achieve this goal, the type of compute layer you choose will affect how fast you can ramp up your application. Containers are faster to run than virtual machines, and managed containers like serverless ones delegate the operationalization of our infrastructure to the cloud provider, so we just need to focus on comparing different services' implementations and plug-and-play options to achieve our goals.

Of course, not all web applications behave in the same way, so there's a risk that our chosen auto-scaling solution will not be fast enough to copy with our specific traffic surges. A classic example would be the beginning of Black Friday sales or a global live event available only on our platform. In these cases, we would need to ensure that we meet the predictive load by manually increasing our solution's baseline infrastructure before the users join our platform.

Another challenge we face with this architecture is understanding how we can speed up the response time of services and maybe microservices, and whether we need to consume them every time or if we can cache the response for specific micro-frontends instead of embracing eventual consistency. An in-memory cache solution like Redis can be a great ally in this situation, allowing us to store the microservice response for a short time, thereby increasing our micro-frontend composition's throughput. We can also store the entire micro-frontend DOM inside an in-memory cache and fetch it from there instead of composing it every time.

Alternatively, we can use a CDN, which can increase a web page's delivery speed, reducing the latency between the client and the content requested.

Latency, response time, cache eviction, and similar metrics become our measure of success in these situations, but creating the right infrastructure is not a trivial process, especially when there is a lack of knowledge or experience.

Infrastructure ownership

Composition layer ownership is another challenge with this architecture. In the best implementations, a cross-functional team of frontend and backend developers work together to manage the micro-frontend composition layer end to end. In this way, they can collaborate on the best outputs at the composition layer level, improving how data flows through it.

Some companies may decide to split the composition layer from micro-frontend development. The risk here is that a frontend developer will be working in a silo, requiring additional mechanisms to keep the teams in sync to consolidate the integration of the two layers. Frontend developers must clearly understand what's going on in the composition layer and be able to help enhance it on code, infrastructure, monitoring, and logging levels. In this way, they can optimize the micro-frontend code written based on the implementation made in the composition layer.

Composing micro-frontends

Composing micro-frontends in a server-side architecture may deviate from what we have seen till now, but deviations are in the details, not the substance. As we can see from Figure 4-23, the typical architecture is composed of three layers.

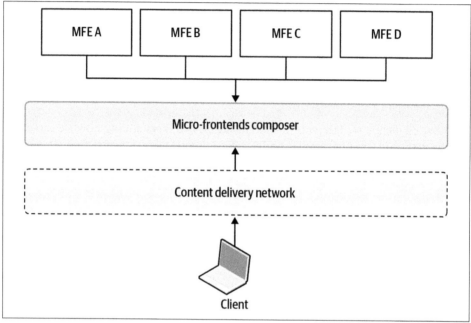

Figure 4-23. A typical high-level architecture for a server-side micro-frontend architecture, where a composer is responsible for stitching together the different micro-frontends at runtime. A CDN can be used for offloading traffic to the origin.

The three layers are as follows:

Micro-frontends
> These can be deployed as static assets, maybe prepared at compile time during the automation pipeline, or as dynamic assets in which an application server prepares a template and its associated data for every user's requests.

Composer
> This layer is used to assemble all the micro-frontends before returning the final view to a user. In this case, we can have an NGINX or HTTPd instance for leveraging SSI's directives or a more complex scenario leveraging Kubernetes and custom application logic for stitching everything together.

CDN

Whenever possible, you should add a CDN layer in front of your application server in order to cache as many requests as possible. And if you can cache a page for a few minutes, you can offload a lot of traffic from the composer and increase your web application's performance, thanks to the shorter roundtrip for the response.

Many frameworks out there will do the undifferentiated heavy lifting of implementing this type of architecture. To choose the best one for your project, you'll have to understand the project's business goals to evaluate the frameworks against the business requirements and architecture characteristics you aim for.

In the next section, I'll cover some of these frameworks so that you can see how they align with the pattern described above. However, every framework emphasizes different aspects than others, and not all the DXs are first class, so you may end up investing more time streamlining the DX before realizing the expected outcome from your chosen framework.

Micro-frontend communication

When you choose the server-side approach, you likely won't have many communications inside the view but instead have communication between the view and the APIs. This is because at the end, the page will reload after every significant user action on it. Still, there are situations in which one micro-frontend has to notify another that something happened in the session, such as a user adding a product to the cart. The micro-frontend that owns the domain will need to show the new product on a dropdown to show the user that the change was made in the cart. To accomplish this, we will add some logic on the frontend, and, using an event emitter or custom event, we will keep the micro-frontends loosely coupled while allowing them to communicate when something happens inside the application. In Figure 4-24, we can see how this mechanism works in practice:

1. A user adds a product to the cart. This event is communicated to the backend, which acknowledges the added product within the user's session.

2. The product micro-frontend notifies the checkout experience micro-frontend that a new product was added to the cart.

3. The checkout experience micro-frontend fetches the new list of products in the cart and displays the new information in the UI.

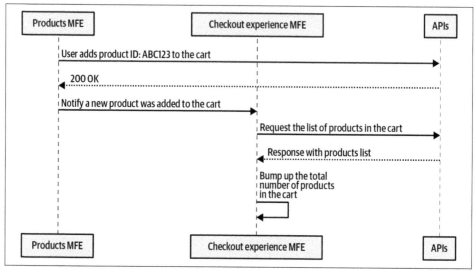

Figure 4-24. An example of how the product's micro-frontend notifies the checkout experience micro-frontend to refresh the cart interface when a user adds a product to the cart

There aren't many of these types of interactions per view in most web applications, so the code won't negatively impact performance or the maintainability of the final solution.

Available frameworks

Some of the available frameworks for this category include Podium (*https://podium-lib.io*), Mosaic (*https://www.mosaic9.org*), Puzzle.js (*https://oreil.ly/eXf6w*), and Ara Framework (*https://oreil.ly/AtnzZ*), with Mosaic probably being one of the most famous because it was one of the first open source frameworks to embrace this architecture style. Mosaic is really a collection of frameworks and tools made famous by Zalando, a fashion ecommerce site, one of the first to leverage the concept of micro-frontends. There are many forks of Tailor.js, the tool used to stitch together different HTML fragments in the Mosaic suite, which testifies how good the solution was. As of publication time, however, Zalando had decided to create a new version of Mosaic with a more opinionated approach based on React and GraphQL.

To implement a micro-frontend architecture with a server-side composition, we explore the high-level architectures of a couple other frameworks that are currently in use by American Express (Amex), OpenTable, and Skyscanner, well-known brands that decided to scale their organizations and frontend development using micro-frontends. Then we'll spend some time revisiting a well-known approach, SSI, since it falls in this category and there are still organizations leveraging this approach for their micro-frontend applications.

Amex released the open source project OneApp, a Node.js server used for serving server-side rendered micro-frontends on a single HTML page by using Holocron modules, another open source project from Amex. Every module represents a micro-frontend implementation with a set of utilities for simplifying the development experience, as well as for augmenting existing libraries such as Redux for store management. The view is a combination of Holocron modules called the Holocron roots.

As we can see in Figure 4-25, when a user requests a page, OneApp retrieves the associated root module, triggering the retrieval of the associated micro-frontends in order to render the final view. Next, the view is server-side rendered and served to the user. For performance reasons, the OneApp server periodically pulls the modules map JSON from the CDN, storing it in memory as a fast way to retrieve the module associated with a view without introducing too much latency in every request.

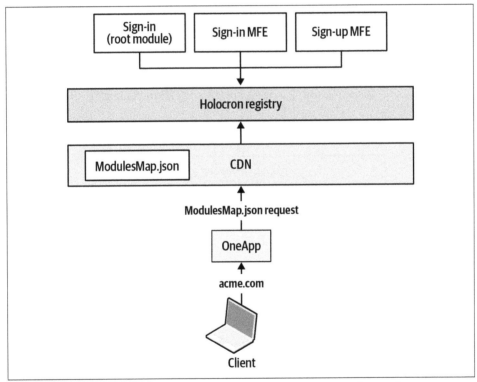

Figure 4-25. Holocron is a server-side rendering system for micro-frontends

The pain point of this architecture is the use of Redux as global state management for sharing the application state between micro-frontends. As discussed, every micro-frontend should be completely independent, but in Holocron this isn't the case. Instead, custom events are used for communication between micro-frontends.

Although this isn't the most common communication technique for React applications, it's definitely a step closer to fully embracing micro-frontend principles. And because Holocron modules can be stored anywhere and don't necessarily need to be retrieved from a CDN, a virtual machine, an object storage, or a container may also be a suitable solution.

OpenComponents (*https://oreil.ly/0ETxx*) is another micro-frontend framework for server-side horizontal-split architectures. This opinionated framework provides several features out of the box, including prewarming of a CDN via runtime agents, a micro-frontend registry, and tools for simplifying the DX. Every micro-frontend is encapsulated inside a computational layer completely isolated from the others. This approach enables each team to focus on the implementation of their own domain without taking into account the entire application. Moreover, every micro-frontend has a set of utilities, such as observability, monitoring, or dashboards. For managing burst traffic at specific times of the day, such as from a constant flow of people reserving tables at restaurants, the traffic prewarming the CDN in use is offloaded every time a new micro-frontend is created or when a change to an existing one is made (see Figure 4-26).

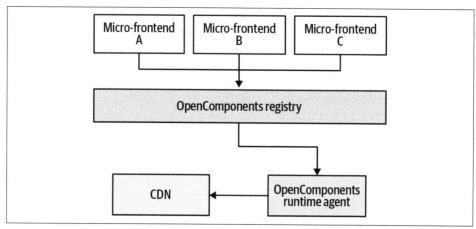

Figure 4-26. The OpenComponents architecture shows how a server-side rendered micro-frontend is flowing from development to an environment

Interestingly, OpenComponents allows not only server-side rendering but also client-side rendering, so you can choose the right technique for every use case. When SEO is a key goal of a project, for example, you can choose SSR, while when you need a more SPA-like experience, you can use client-side rendering. Once again, you can see how all these frameworks had to make an investment in the developer experience to accelerate their adoption. As you compare frameworks, keep in mind that the vast majority of the time, these frameworks were built by midsize to large organizations, for which the final benefits definitely overcame the initial investment of resources and time.

SSI are used for dividing a final view into multiple parts, usually called fragments, that are composed by a server before returning a static page to the client request. Back in the 1990s, SSI were used to decouple an HTML page's static content from other parts that may or not have been dynamic. SSI have directives—placeholders that the server interprets in order to perform a specific action on a page. That action might be including a micro-frontend or running logic, like including different fragments based on specific parameters, such as providing different UIs based on the user status.

SSI directives look like this:

```
<!--# include virtual="acme.com/mfe/catalog" -->
```

In particular, the include directive is very important for micro-frontends because when the server interprets this directive, it will add the fragment into the final DOM. Figure 4-27 summarizes how the logic applied by a server, like NGINX or HTTPd, composes micro-frontends using SSI.

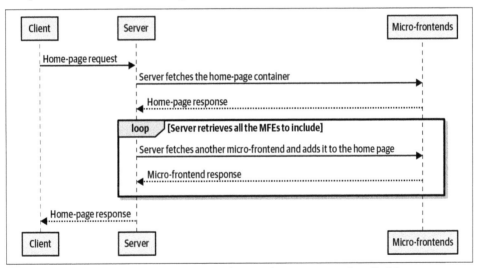

Figure 4-27. The sequence diagram shows how a client request is handled by a server when SSI are used

When a client requests a page, the server retrieves the page containing the different directives. The server interprets all the directives and fetches the different fragments in parallel. When the directives are fully loaded, the server returns the final response to the client.

Clearly, when a fragment takes time to return, the page's time to the first byte is affected. Luckily for us, we can set up timeouts as well as stub content to replace a fragment that times out or returns an empty body. Another challenge of this approach is avoiding overlaps in our CSS classes. As discussed before, creating prefixes for every class can help avoid undesired outcomes for your customers. Finally, it's important to highlight that SSI won't enrich your user's website experience, so you will need to add some JavaScript logic to the page to run on the client side if you want the benefits of both s and page interactivity.

The main benefit of SSI is the server-side composition of the final page, which makes it easier for a search engine crawler to index the page. This is a plus for all server-side composition frameworks, but considering SSI were created several years ago, we can say they were the first technique to integrate this feature out of the box.

Use cases

The typical use cases for this architecture are business-to-consumer (B2C) websites, for which the content has to be highly discoverable by search engines, or B2B solutions with modular layouts, such as dashboards where the user interface doesn't require too many drifts in the layout, as with a customer-facing solution. A tangible example of these types of implementations is OpenTable, an online restaurant-reservation service company based in San Francisco, with offices all over the world. The platform contains a host of tools that streamline the DX, making it easy to build micro-frontends thanks to OpenComponents.

This architecture is recommended for B2B applications, with many modules that are reused across different views. It's important, however, that full stack or backend developers with the appropriate skills facilitate the introduction of this implementation. This architecture generally isn't a good choice for very interactive, fluid layouts, mainly due to the coordination needed across teams to create a cohesive final result or when there are bugs in production that may require more effort in discovering their root cause.

Architecture characteristics

Deployability (4/5)
These architectures may be challenging when you have to handle burst traffic or with high-volume traffic. When we decide to deploy a new micro-frontend, we'll also likely have to deploy some API to fetch the data, creating more infrastructure and configuration to handle. To limit the extra work and avoid production issues, automate repetitive tasks as much as possible.

Modularity (5/5)
This architecture key characteristic is the control we have over not only how we compose micro-frontends but also how we manage different levels of caching

and final output optimization. Because we can control every aspect of the front-end with this approach, it's important to modularize the application to fully embrace this approach.

Simplicity (3/5)

This architecture isn't the easiest to implement. There are many moving parts, and observability tools on both the frontend and backend need to be configured so that you'll understand what's happening when the application doesn't behave as expected. Taking into account the architectures seen so far, this is the most powerful and the most challenging, especially on large projects with burst traffic.

Testability (4/5)

This is probably the easiest architecture to test, considering it doesn't differ too much from server-side rendering applications. There may be some challenges when we expect every micro-frontend to hydrate the code on the client side because we'll have some additional logic to test, but since we're talking about micro-frontends, it won't be too much additional effort.

Performance (5/5)

With this implementation, we have full control of the final result being served to a client, allowing us to optimize every single aspect of our application, down to the byte. That doesn't mean optimization is easier with this approach, but it definitely provides all the possibilities needed to make a micro-frontend application highly performant.

Developer experience (3/5)

There are frameworks that provide an opinionated way to create a smooth developer experience, but it's very likely you will need to invest time creating custom tools to improve project management and introducing dashboards, additional command line tools, and so on. Also, a frontend developer may need to boost their backend knowledge, learning how to run servers locally, scale them in production, work in the cloud or on premises efficiently, manage the observability of the composition layer, and more. Full stack developers are more likely to embrace this approach but not always.

Scalability (3/5)

Scalability may be a nontrivial task for high-volume projects because you'll need to scale the backend that composes the final view to the user. A CDN can work, but you will have to deal with different levels of caching. CDNs are helpful with static content, but less so with personalized ones. Moreover, when you need to maintain a low response latency and you aren't in control of the API you are consuming, you will have another challenge to solve on top of the scalability of the micro-frontend composition layer.

Coordination (3/5)

Considering all the moving parts included in this architecture, the coordination has to be well designed. The structure has to enable different teams to work independently, reducing the risks of too many external dependencies that can jeopardize a sprint and cause frustration for developers. Furthermore, developers have to keep both the big picture and the implementation details in mind, making the organization structure a bit more complicated, especially with large organizations and distributed teams.

Table 4-5 gathers the architecture characteristics and their associated score for this micro-frontend architecture.

Table 4-5. Architecture characteristics summary for developing a micro-frontend architecture using horizontal split and server-side composition

Architecture characteristics	Score (1 = lowest, 5 = highest)
Deployability	4/5
Modularity	5/5
Simplicity	3/5
Testability	4/5
Performance	5/5
Developer experience	3/5
Scalability	3/5
Coordination	3/5

Edge Side

Edge Side Includes, or ESI, was created in 2001 by companies like Akamai and Oracle. It's a markup language used for assembling different HTML fragments into an HTML page and serving the final result to a client. Usually, ESI is performed at the CDN level, where it offers great scalability options because of the CDN's architecture. Different points of presence across the globe serve every user requesting static content. Every request is redirected to the closest point of presence, reducing the latency between the user and where the content is stored. Additionally, because CDNs are great for caching static assets, this combination of capillarity across the globe and cacheability makes ESI a potential solution for developing micro-frontends that don't require dynamic content, such as catalog applications.

Another alternative for using ESI is using proxies like NGINX or Varnish, both of which offer ESI implementations. Unfortunately, ESI specifications are not fully supported everywhere. We often find only a subset of the features available in CDN provider or a proxy solution, which may compromise the flexibility needed for a business, reducing the possibility of the frontend architecture evolution. Moreover, the frontend community hasn't embraced this standard as it has with others, such as

React, Vue, or Angular. The fragmentation between vendors, the lack of tools, and the friction on the developer experience have all played a pivotal role in the adoption of this technology.

Implementation details

As we said, every micro-frontend is composed with an HTML page as entry point with either a reverse proxy or a CDN provider. ESI language and composition are very similar to SSI, except that the markup is interpreted before the page is served to a client. ESI is composed by a template containing multiple fragments that represent, in this case at least, our micro-frontends. Here are the main functionalities:

Inclusion
> ESI can compose pages by assembling included content, which is fetched from the network. The template uses transclusion to replace the placeholder tag within it with the micro-frontend it has retrieved.

Variable support
> ESI supports the use of variables based on HTTP request attributes. These variables can be used by ESI statements or written directly into the processed markup.

Conditional processing
> ESI allows conditional logic with Boolean comparisons to influence how a template is processed.

Exception and error handling
> ESI allows you to handle errors or exceptions with alternative content to create a smoother user experience.

This is how ESI looks before being served to a browser:

```
<html>
 <body>
 Welcome to MFE with ESI
<esi:include src="https://www.myorigin.com/MFE_A.html"/>
<esi:include src="https://www.myorigin.com/MFE_B.html"/>
 </body>
</html>
```

When the markup language is interpreted, the final result will be a static HTML page completely renderable by a browser.

Transclusion

ESI uses a technique called transclusion for including existing content inside a new document without the need to duplicate it. In early 2000, this mechanism was used to reduce the cut-and-paste process that every developer was using to create web pages.

Now we can use it to reuse content and generate new views based on simple constructs like conditional processing or variable support. This provides a useful mechanism to reduce the time it takes to build websites despite the poor developer experience.

Client-side includes (CSI) also leverage transclusion, such as the h-include (*https://oreil.ly/cWgCr*). Applying transclusion inside the browser uses the same logic for interpreting an ESI tag. In fact, each `<h-include>` element will create a request to the URL and replace the innerHTML of the element with the response of the request. Using CSI with ESI will help supplement ESI's limitation, adding the possibility of serving dynamic content inside a predefined template. In this way, we can use ESI to leverage a CDN's scalability. When we further combine this with JavaScript's ability to load HTML fragments directly on the client side, we can make our websites far more interactive.

Challenges

While ESI may seem like a viable option, there are some challenges to be aware of. First, ESI specifications are not implemented in all CDN providers or proxy servers the way Varnish and NGINX are. This lack of adoption increases the chance that you will have to evolve your infrastructure in the future. Your web application requires a certain resilience, and if you are considering a multi-CDN strategy, ESI probably won't be the right solution for you.

Another problem that ESI won't solve is the integration of dynamic contents. Let's say you want to integrate personalized content in your micro-frontends. A caching strategy won't help because you may end up with a list of personalized content per user, and segmenting your content for a group of users may result in segments too large to be meaningfully cached by a CDN. In these cases, ESI should be integrated in conjunction with JavaScript running inside the browser and consuming some APIs. Depending on the business requirements, you might also use the CSI transclusion mechanism. CSI leverages the same mechanism as ESI but on the client side, so that once the application is loaded inside a browser, a JavaScript code will scan the DOM to find and replace tags and then mount new DOM elements instead of the placeholders. However, you may want to just load some DOM elements or even some external JavaScript files that would run the logic to render personalized content inside an ESI application. Obviously, all these roundtrips may impact micro-frontend application performance, so you'll want to find the right balance to implement micro-frontends with a combination of ESI and CSI, and you'll need to spend the time finding the best way to stitch everything together.

Last but not least, ESI doesn't shine for a frictionless developer experience, with the poor adoption contributing to the lack of investment in this markup language.

Developer experience

The DX is one of ESI's main challenges. It's very important to create a smooth, functional environment for developers so that they can concentrate on developing new features, hardening algorithms, and, in general, striving in their daily job. However, ESI requires developers to use different tools to ensure the final result is the one expected by the user.

Imagine we decide to embrace ESI and use Akamai for handling the transclusion at the CDN level. Akamai implements the full specifications for using ESI, but how would you test that locally? Akamai offers an ESI test server (*https://oreil.ly/tBS78*) provided as a Docker container for local development and for integration with your automation pipelines. The testing server mimics the Akamai servers' behaviors when receiving a request, fetching the page to serve, interpreting the ESI tags, and serving the final HTML page to a browser. Other CDN providers don't implement the entire specification, so you risk using a technique that could end up with false positives and invalidate the quick feedback loop for your developers.

Finally, this architecture is not widely embraced by the frontend community, resulting in a lack of documentation, tools, and support compared to more modern solutions described in this chapter.

Use cases

One of the main use cases for edge-side composition is for managing large static websites where multiple teams are contributing to the same final application. The IKEA catalog was implemented in some countries using a combination of ESI and CSI in this way.

Another potential application would be using ESI for the static part of a website and serving the rest with micro-frontends rendered at client side. This technique is also known as micro-caching, but it is complicated to put in place as well as to debug. Because of the poor developer experience, not many companies have implemented this technology, and despite its age, it has never seen the mainstream.

Architecture characteristics

Deployability (3/5)
> Similar to the client-side composition, this approach guarantees an easy deployment and artifacts consumptions via CDN. Because we are talking about a horizontal split, we need to increase the effort of managing potential network errors that would prevent a micro-frontend from being composed on the CDN level. Finally, not all the CDN supports ESI, which could be a problem in the long run for your project, especially when you have to change CDN providers. However, managing multiple environments and deploying micro-frontends in local environment is not a smooth experience.

Modularity (4/5)

Transclusion facilitates modular design, so we can reuse micro-frontends in multiple pages. ESI becomes even more interesting when mixed with CSI, covering the static parts with ESI and the more dynamic ones with CSI.

Simplicity (2/5)

If horizontal-split architectures can become quite complex in the long run, the edge-side ones can be even more complex because of the poor developer experience and the need of a CDN or Varnish to test your code.

Testability (3/5)

ESI doesn't shine in testing either. Unit testing may be similar to what we're used to implementing for other architectures, but to implement an integration and end-to-end testing strategy, we need to rely on a more complex infrastructure, which could slow down the feedback loop for a team.

Performance (3/5)

Since ESI is a composition on the CDN level most of the time, the application can have great performance out of the box thanks to the cache for static content. However, we need to consider that when a micro-frontend hangs due to network issues, none of the pages will be served until the request timed out—not exactly the best customer experience.

Developer experience (2/5)

The DX of any solution is a key factor in adoption; the more complicated a solution is, the less developers will embrace it. ESI is definitely a complicated solution. To locally test your implementation, you will need a Varnish, NGINX, or Akamai testing server inside a virtual machine or a docker container. And if you are using a CDN, be ready for a long feedback loop on whether your code is behaving correctly. There are other tools available, but it's still a clunky experience compared to the other architectures.

Scalability (4/5)

If your project is static content, ESI is probably one of the best solutions you can have, thanks to the composition at the CDN level. And with a mix of static and dynamic content, using ESI in conjunction with CSI, the scalability of your solution will be bulletproof.

Coordination (3/5)

Edge-side composition allows you to leverage micro-frontend principles, allowing you to have independent teams and artifacts. However, due to the poor DX, you may need more coordination across teams, especially when there are changes in the production environment that affect all the teams. Similar to the recommendation for server-side composition, plan your team structure accordingly and be sure to iterate to validate decisions.

Table 4-6 gathers the architecture characteristics and their associated score for this micro-frontend architecture.

Table 4-6. Architecture characteristics summary for developing a micro-frontends architecture using horizontal split and edge-side composition

Architecture characteristics	Score (1 = lowest, 5 = highest)
Deployability	3/5
Modularity	4/5
Simplicity	2/5
Testability	3/5
Performance	3/5
Developer experience	2/5
Scalability	4/5
Coordination	3/5

Summary

In this chapter, we have applied the micro-frontend decisions framework to multiple architectures. Defining the four pillars (defining, composing, routing, and communicating) offered by the micro-frontends decisions framework helps us to filter our choices and select the right architecture for a project. We have analyzed different micro-frontend architectures, highlighting their challenges and scoring the architecture characteristics so that we can easily select the right architecture based on what we have to optimize for. Finally, because we understand that the perfect architecture doesn't exist, we realized that we have to find the *less worse architecture* based on the context we operate in. In the next chapter, we will analyze a technical implementation and focus our attention on the main challenges we may encounter in a micro-frontend implementation.

CHAPTER 5

Micro-Frontend Technical Implementation

In this chapter, we will use the micro-frontend decisions framework to build a basic ecommerce website using one of the technical approaches discussed in Chapter 4. As we've discussed, there isn't a one-size-fits-all solution when it comes to architecture. The project's goals, the organization's structure and communications, and the technical skills available with the company are some of the factors we have to consider when we need to choose an approach.

After identifying the context we'll operate in, we can use the micro-frontend decisions framework to help define the key pillars for our architecture's technical direction. Instead of creating the same example in multiple frameworks, I'll focus on helping you build the right mental model, which will allow you to master any micro-frontend framework rather than memorizing only one or two of the options available.

We will definitely explore some code, but I will stress the importance of understanding *why* a decision is made. This way, despite the approach and framework you use in your next project, you will be able to decide what the right direction is, independent of how familiar you are with a specific micro-frontend framework.

Remember the old saying "Give a man a fish, and you feed him for a day. Teach a man to fish, and you feed him for a lifetime"? Let's learn to fish.

The Project

Our project is an internal swag ecommerce website for an enterprise organization. The site is composed of several subdomains, including:

- Login
- Payment

- Swag catalog
- Account management
- Employee support
- FAQ

For our example in this chapter, we'll use only three of them: authentication, catalog, and account management. The ecommerce site must have a consistent user interface so that users will have a cohesive experience while they shop for their favorite swag. We will have several teams responsible for delivering this project. To hit the project deadline, the tech department decides to reuse an internal engine developed for its B2C ecommerce solutions. It's a monolithic backend architecture that's been battle-tested after several years of development and hardening in production environments. However, the tech department wants to move away from siloing the frontend and backend expertise, so it decides to use micro-frontends and to set up independent teams responsible for a subdomain of the new ecommerce site. It will also use back-end developers to rearchitect the backend using microservices and incorporate agility at the business and technical levels.

The next step is to assign the teams responsible for the different subdomains:

- *Team Sashimi* will be responsible for the authentication subdomain. Because this is an internal ecommerce site, the team will implement the sign-in form using the centralized authentication system available, which employees use to access every system inside the organization. It will also be responsible for the user authentica-tion and personal details for the account details micro-frontend. One team mem-ber will be a full stack developer, and the rest will focus on the backend integration with Microsoft Active Directory (AD) (*https://oreil.ly/KgqEp*).
- *Team Maki* will own the core domain—the swag catalog. It's the largest team and will be responsible for the main user experience. The team will be split between frontend and backend developers.
- *Team Nigiri* will cover the payments subdomain. It will integrate different pay-ment methods, such as credit cards and PayPal.

The flow we'll implement is composed of three sections. Figure 5-1 shows that the authentication and catalog micro-frontends will be vertical-split micro-frontends, while the account management will be composed of two horizontal-split micro-frontends. We can have just one developer working on the authentication frontend because the heavier part of the implementation is on the backend. For the catalog, however, we want a richer user experience, so we will have a team with deep knowl-edge of frontend practices. Finally, because account management is an intersection of different subdomains, the two teams responsible for those subdomains will help develop this view.

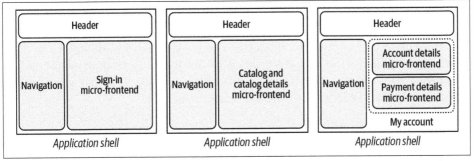

Figure 5-1. The swag ecommerce sections: sign-in, catalog with product details, and account management

Following the micro-frontend decisions framework and testing their assumptions with proof of concepts, the teams have decided to use:

A hybrid approach for identifying micro-frontends

> Instead of using either a horizontal or vertical split for the whole project, the teams decided to use the right approach for each subdomain. A vertical split is more suitable for achieving the business requirements for authentication and the catalog, while a horizontal split for the account management subdomain fulfills the business need to have multiple subdomains.

A client-side composition

> A client-side composition supports the requirements of the internal ecommerce site and is within the team's skill sets. This composition also allows future evolutions to other platforms, like a desktop application and even a progressive web application.

Client-side routing

> Once we decide to use client-side composition, the decisions framework helps us easily decide that the routing should happen on the client side as well. We also have to consider that there will be two types of routing: a global routing handled by the micro-frontend container (also called the application shell), which will be responsible for routing between micro-frontends, and a local routing inside the catalog subdomains, where the Maki team will develop micro-frontends with multiple views.

Communication between micro-frontends embracing decisions framework suggestions

> Again following the decisions framework suggestions, the team will use web storage for sharing the JSON web token (JWT) needed for consuming authenticated APIs. Because the account management view will have two micro-frontends and could have more in the future, we want to maintain the teams and the artifacts independently from each other. As a result, we'll use an event emitter

to communicate between micro-frontends present in the same view, defining up front the events triggered by every micro-frontend and the related payload.

The technology chosen for the ecommerce site is webpack with Module Federation. After several proofs of concept, the teams felt that Module Federation would provide everything they needed to successfully release this project. The main reasons for embracing Module Federation over other solutions are:

Existing webpack knowledge
Webpack is widely used inside the organization. Many developers have used this JavaScript bundler for other projects, so they don't have to learn a new framework. Module Federation fits nicely in their technology stack, considering it's just a plug-in of a well-known tool for the company.

Client-side composition
With the micro-frontend composition based on the client side, Module Federation will provide a simple way to asynchronously load JavaScript bundles. It was developed initially for this specific use case and then extended to server-side rendering, so if in the future the requirements change, the teams will be able to change the micro-frontend implementation while maintaining Module Federation as stable assets for the evolution of their platform.

A seamless developer experience
The teams have significant expertise with webpack. As well, the implementation in the automation pipeline and the local development tools remain the same, so it's a great way for the teams to be immediately productive.

Module Federation was chosen for specific reasons for this project. For other projects, Module Federation may or may not be the right choice. When we are designing an architecture, we have to think about the trade-offs before blindly selecting a technology. Analyze your team structures, developers' skills, the tech stack used in other projects by the company, and the project's business goals before deciding which micro-frontend architecture is suitable for your use case. After analyzing the context you're working in, use the micro-frontend decisions framework to create a solid foundation for future decisions for your project.

Module Federation 101

Before jumping into the technical implementation, we need to understand a few basic concepts to appreciate the reasoning behind some technical decisions. Module Federation allows a JavaScript application to dynamically run code from another bundle or build on both the client and server. It's a plug-in available for webpack 5 and to some extent for webpack 4 and Rollup, with limited functionalities. Module Federation provides two key concepts that we have to understand before working with it:

Host

> The container that loads shared libraries, micro-frontends, or components at runtime

Remote

> The JavaScript bundle we want to load inside a host

As we can see in Figure 5-2, a host can load multiple remotes. In our case, the host represents the application shell, while a remote represents a micro-frontend.

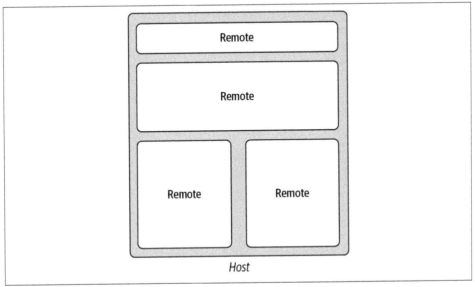

Figure 5-2. Module Federation is composed of two key elements: the host, which is responsible for loading some JavaScript bundles at runtime, and the remote, which is responsible for any type of JavaScript bundles, such as shared libraries, micro-frontends, or even components

With Module Federation, sharing can be bidirectional, allowing a remote to share parts or the whole bundle with a host and vice versa. However, bidirectional sharing can complicate your architecture very quickly. The best approach is sharing unidirectionally, so that a host never shares anything with remotes. This makes debugging easier and will reduce the potential for domain leaks to the host, which could cause design coupling between hosts and remotes.

Behind the scenes, Module Federation orchestrates two webpack plug-ins: *Container-Plugin* and *ContainerReferencePlugin*. The first is responsible for creating a container to asynchronously load and synchronously evaluate a module, while the second is responsible for overriding the container created as placeholder with the remote module and making the code acting as present in the initial bundle.

Leveraging this architecture allows us to not only specify remotes in the webpack configuration but also load them using JavaScript in our code. For instance, we can fetch the routes from an API and generate a dynamic view of remotes based on the user's country or role.

Because Module Federation is a webpack plug-in, we can use other webpack capabilities to optimize our code in the best way for our project. For instance, Module Federation creates many JavaScript chunk files by default, but we may prefer a less chatty implementation for our remote, loading just two or three files. In this case, we could use the *MinChunkSizePlugin* (*https://oreil.ly/XHstO*) that forces webpack to slice the chunks with a minimum of kilobytes per file. We could also use the *DefinePlugin* (*https://oreil.ly/LvYkc*) to replace variables in your code with other values or expressions at compile time. Using this plug-in, we can easily create some logic to provide the right base path when we are testing code locally or when it's running on our development environments. Combined with other plug-ins available in the webpack ecosystem, Module Federation can be a powerful, suitable way to tweak your outputs for your context.

Meanwhile, the frontend community has started to embrace Module Federation for their projects, and new dedicated tools are being released to improve the developer experience, including dashboards for understanding the relations between shared dependencies across remotes like Atriom (*https://oreil.ly/pEnOx*) and a live reloading plug-in (*https://oreil.ly/wnRKo*) to use in conjunction with Module Federation.

We should have enough Module Federation knowledge to dive deeply into the implementation details. The project we're exploring here shares many of the configurations available for Module Federation in a micro-frontend project. For more details, check out the official documentation (*https://oreil.ly/E5nO2*).

Technical Implementation

Now that we've reviewed the context where the application will be developed and applied the decisions framework and selected the technical strategy, it's time to look at the implementation details. The swag ecommerce repository is available on GitHub (*https://oreil.ly/dMnO2*), so you can review the entire project or clone and play with it. I intentionally developed the example without any server interaction so that you can run it locally without any external dependencies.

Just to recap, the application is composed of an application shell that is available during the entire user's session, loading different micro-frontends, such as the authentication, the catalog, and the account management micro-frontends. For the technology stack, the teams chose React with webpack and Module Federation, enabling every team to create independent micro-frontends. Using Module Federation, they can share common dependencies and load them only once during a user's session. This creates a seamless experience for users without compromising developer experience. Let's dive deeply into the key aspects of the main parts of this application.

Project Structure

Before going ahead with the case study, I want to say a few words on the structure I created for the swag ecommerce project. When you clone the repository, you will see multiple folders, as shown in Figure 5-3.

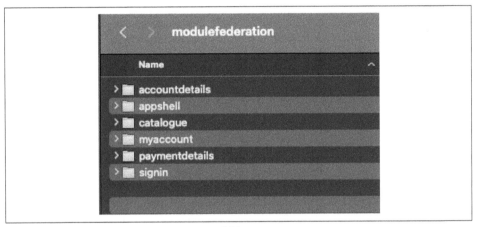

Figure 5-3. The swag ecommerce project folder structure

Every folder represents an independent project. Because they are present in the same repository, this is a monorepo approach, but they could easily be extracted in a poly-repo approach. More information about the differences between these two versions of control strategies is covered in Chapter 6.

All the folders have the same structure, as you can see in Figure 5-4.

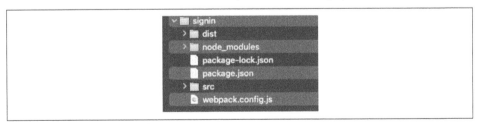

Figure 5-4. Micro-frontend structure

Every micro-frontend folder contains the following:

dist folder
After building a micro-frontend, we can find all the optimized files to be deployed in an environment.

node_modules folder
This folder contains all the micro-frontend dependencies.

package.json
This file gathers all the metadata about the project and defines functional attributes of the project that npm uses to install dependencies, run scripts, and identify the entry point to our package.

src folder
This folder contains all the micro-frontend business logic.

webpack.config.js
This file is the webpack configuration used to configure the Module Federation plug-in for serving our micro-frontends.

This is really a typical JavaScript project folder structure; Module Federation doesn't require you to change the way you usually work. It orchestrates all the dependencies and the logic for loading and removing dependencies behind the scenes without you having to change your favorite folder structure.

Application Shell

As described before, the application shell is present for the entire user's session. Considering it's necessary for orchestrating micro-frontends and doesn't fit in with any business subdomain, the teams decided to assign implementation of the shell to a new team formed by principal engineers, called Sasazushi. Because building this part of the system won't require a lot of effort and maintenance should be minimal, thanks to the fact that the application shell doesn't own any business domain, the principal engineers were chosen to be on this team as well as their main teams.

Sasazushi is responsible for:

- Avoiding domains leak in the application shell
- Implementing the global routing between micro-frontends
- Making sure the micro-frontends are mounted and unmounted correctly
- Generating the cross-domain dependencies in one or multiple JavaScript chunks

Additionally, because the team is composed of principal engineers, the team will be responsible for the overall performance of the system, creating such mechanisms as recurring meetings with the teams to share optimization best practices or review specific bottlenecks they identify during the performance assessment.

Let's start analyzing the webpack configuration. Since Module Federation is a webpack plug-in, we just need to import it as we would any other JavaScript library:

```
const { ModuleFederationPlugin } = require("webpack").container;
```

The most basic webpack configuration is composed by an entry file, an output folder, and the mode we want our code transpiled to, such as development or production:

```
module.exports = {
  entry: "./src/index",
  mode: "development",
  output: {
   publicPath: "auto",
  },
// additional configuration
}
```

Then usually we add rules to support specific language features. For instance, before ES6 was available in browsers, we would have had to transpile specific features, like generators (*https://oreil.ly/xPYtn*), in code that browsers would interpret. In our case, we are using Babel with the React preset to add JSX support:

```
// ...

module: {
   rules: [
    {
     test: /\.jsx?$/,
     loader: "babel-loader",
     exclude: /node_modules/,
     options: {
      presets: ["@babel/preset-react"],
     },
    },
   ],
  }

// ...
```

However, the most important part for our micro-frontend architecture is configuring Module Federation to load remote micro-frontends. Since the application shell is the container for our micro-frontends, it's the host, to use Module Federation vocabulary. That means we'll have to configure all the remote micro-frontends we want to lazy-load inside our application shell. In our example, the plug-in was configured like that in the following code snippet:

```
plugins: [
    new ModuleFederationPlugin({
     name: "AppShell",
```

```
    remotes: {
     MyAccount: "MyAccount@http://localhost:3004/remoteEntry.js",
     Catalog: "Catalog@http://localhost:3002/remoteEntry.js",
     SignIn: "SignIn@http://localhost:3003/remoteEntry.js"
     // you can also specify a remote entry from a web server URL
     //SignIn:"SignIn@http://www.mysite.com/signin/remoteEntry.js"
    },
    shared: {
      react: {
       singleton: true,
      },
      "react-dom": {
       singleton: true,
      },
      "react-router-dom": {
       singleton: true
      },
      "@material-ui/core": {
       singleton: true
      },
      "@material-ui/icons": {
       singleton: true
      }
    }
   })
  ],
 }
```

After defining the name—in this case *AppShell*—in a host, we list all the remotes we want to load in our application inside the *remote* object. Every remote is composed of an ID and the URL where a JavaScript file that contains a map of all the JavaScript chunks generated for that micro-frontend will be fetched from; these two values are separated by an @ symbol. Looking at our configuration, we see that the catalog micro-frontend has an ID called *Catalog* and a local URL like *http://localhost:3002/remoteEntry.js*. This means that when the application shell loads the catalog micro-frontend, Module Federation will fetch the *remoteEntry.js* file to understand which JavaScript chunks have to be loaded and which dependencies are shared, right after it loads our code from a remote server. In this case, the server is running in our development environment, but it can easily be a remote URL, like what we see in the commented code for the sign-in micro-frontends.

The next part of the plug-in's configuration specifies which libraries we want to share across the micro-frontends. When we work with other micro-frontend frameworks, we have to consider how to share dependencies across micro-frontends.

Oftentimes developers will create an independent repository to commit the shared libraries and dependencies to. They then create a new automation pipeline for building and deploying the shared code and create a governance on updates responsibility, package dimensions, rollback and deployment strategy, and so on. With Module

Federation, though, we just have to specify the dependencies we want to share in every remote and host. In our case, that's all the micro-frontends and the application shell. Then webpack and Module Federation will create multiple JavaScript files, downloading them only once for every user's session across all micro-frontends.

It may seem obvious but, trust me, it's not always the case. The simplicity Module Federation provides when we attempt to optimize our micro-frontends is really phenomenal.

Defining shared libraries in the Module Federation configuration is as simple as presented in the following code snippet:

```
//...

shared: {
    react: {
      singleton: true,
    },
    "react-dom": {
      singleton: true,
    },
    "react-router-dom": {
      singleton: true
    },
    "@material-ui/core": {
      singleton: true
    },
    "@material-ui/icons": {
      singleton: true
    }
}

//...
```

In the *shared* object, we list all the libraries we want to share. We can also use the Module Federation advanced APIs for the following:

- Loading the library just once, using the `singleton` property, as in our example
- Loading all the shared libraries before the application code is fetched, using `eager` property
- Configuring the version of the libraries to be loaded, using the `requiredVersion` property
- Configuring the variable name and the scope in which a shared library should be instantiated, using `shareKey` and `shareScope` properties, respectively

These are just some of the configurations we can apply to the shared modules. Considering the extensibility of the API provided, I wouldn't be surprised if more capabilities will be added to the shared code feature in the future.

Module Federation allows us to load our dependencies either synchronously, using the eager property in the plug-in configuration, or asynchronously. It's recommended to load them asynchronously, so that the user won't need to load all the dependencies in a larger bundle up front and metrics like time to first byte (TTFB) and time to interactive (TTI) won't be degraded. To asynchronously load our dependencies, we have to split the initialization of our application into multiple files. We'll split the application shell into three main files: *index.js*, *bootstrap.js*, and *app.js*. The file *index.js* will be the entry point of our application, requiring just one line of code:

```
import("./bootstrap");
```

Bootstrap.js will be responsible for instantiating the application shell and appending the React application in a div element present in the HTML template called "root":

```
import React from "react";
import ReactDOM from "react-dom";
import App from "./App";
ReactDOM.render(<App />, document.getElementById("root"));
```

Finally, *app.js* will contain two important elements. The first, the Main component, will implement the application's basic user interface with a header and a side menu. The second, React Router, one of the popular routing solutions for React applications, will handle the application's global routing:

```
import React from "react";
import {BrowserRouter as Router} from "react-router-dom";
import Main from "./Main";

const App = () => {
  return(
    <Router>
      <Main></Main>
    </Router>
  )
}

export default App;
```

Bear in mind that for the global routing strategy, you can use other libraries with React or even create your own router library—although reinventing the wheel may not be very productive. The important thing to remember is that we don't have to use specific routing libraries for building micro-frontend architecture.

There are a few key concepts to explore inside the `Main` component code. Let's start with the global routing. With an application shell, the routing happens on the client side, making the application shell responsible for routing the user between micro-frontends. Usually, we have different level in a URL, for instance: *https://www.mysite.com*. The root is always level 0 of URL depth. When the user clicks a link to another page, we move to level 1: *https://www.mysite.com/catalog*. Every additional link clicked in the catalog will add one or more levels in the URL.

The application shell only has to maintain the logic for the root and the first level. Usually, the moment a user selects a link from the home page, we move into a new website area, which represents a new business subdomain, resulting in a micro-frontend being loaded. This is exactly how the swag ecommerce site we are exploring is structured:

```
<main className={clsx(classes.content, {
        [classes.contentShift]: open,
    })}>
    <div className={classes.drawerHeader} />
    <Switch>
        <Route path="/myaccount" render={_ => renderMFE(MyAccount)}/>
        <Route path="/shop" render={_ => renderMFE(Catalog)}/>
        <Route path="" render={_ => renderMFE(SignIn)}/>
    </Switch>
</main>
```

As we can see, the `Route` object is composed by the path (first level) and the corresponding micro-frontend to load. Since version 16, React has used an experimental API called Suspense (*https://oreil.ly/kpvjw*) to signal to the framework that some code has to be loaded and in the meanwhile provides a component to be rendered as placeholder:

```
<Suspense fallback={<Spinner />}>
 <CatalogMFE />
</Suspense>
```

With the Suspense component and with the possibility to lazy-load a component, we can use the following syntax to load remote micro-frontends, and Module Federation will fetch the module and make it available to the application shell. In fact, the `renderMFE` function used in the `Route` object leverages this technique:

```
const Catalog = React.lazy(() => import("Catalog/Catalog"));
const SignIn = React.lazy(() => import("SignIn/SignIn"));
const MyAccount = React.lazy(() => import("MyAccount/MyAccount"));
 const renderMFE = (MFE) => {
```

```
    return(
      <React.Suspense fallback="Loading...">
        <MFE />
      </React.Suspense>
    )
  }
```

When the user selects the new area of ecommerce from the home page, the router will load the new micro-frontend similarly to how we would lazy-load a normal React component in a single-page application (SPA). The import contains the identifier specified in the Module Federation configuration we wrote in *webpack.config.js* file, which specifies which micro-frontend to load. Module Federation will take care of importing the remote module for you.

The last part in the application shell worth highlighting is the implementation of the design system. Material-UI (*https://material-ui.com*), a popular design system framework, is used in all our micro-frontends. We don't have to understand the Material-UI APIs in depth, but we do need to make sure our styles won't clash once we load micro-frontends inside the application shell. To achieve this, we will use prefixes, as described in Chapter 4. With Material-UI, the trick is adding a prefix for every micro-frontend, including the application shell, using the **seed** property:

```
const generateClassName = createGenerateClassName({
  seed:'appshell'
});
```

Configuring the **seed** property will prefix every CSS class name with the value present in the seed. In our example, all our styles in the application shell will have the prefix *appshell*. For example, a heading 6 element customized with Material-UI will have a class name similar to the following:

```
appshell-MuiTypography-h6
```

In this way, we can make sure that every team works with its own micro-frontend implementation without the risk of clashing with other micro-frontends living in the same or other views. There are other design system libraries that you could apply the same approach to, but this system provides you the safety of working in parallel without stepping on the other teams' toes.

Authentication Micro-Frontend

Because the authentication micro-frontend doesn't require too much work on the frontend side, Team Sashimi is largely skilled in backend integration. In fact, authentication has to be integrated with the single sign-on (SSO) system used inside the company to authorize employees' access to internal applications. A centralized SSO is a typical approach within enterprise organizations, but it's also strongly recommended for smaller entities because it provides greater control over access to a company's vital systems.

The authentication micro-frontend is the first Module Federation remote we describe, so we'll start with its configuration. A remote configuration doesn't differ too much from the host, but it has some additional fields, such as those we can see in the following code snippet:

```
// additional code before

{
    name: "SignIn",
    filename: "remoteEntry.js",
    exposes:{
     "./SignIn": "./src/SignIn"
    },
    shared: {
    // all the dependencies we want to share in this micro-frontend
    },
}

// additional code after
```

The filename field is for specifying a remote's entry point. Within the file specified in this field, we have a map of all the chunks generated by webpack and loaded by Module Federation when a micro-frontend should be rendered in the application shell. The exposes field is used to list all the modules we want to expose to a host for integration inside an application. For micro-frontends, it is very likely that this field will have just one entry because every micro-frontend is represented by an independent artifact. However, when we expose a federated library, such as a design system, we can list all the available entry points so that every host consuming the library will be able to select only what it needs and nothing more. The shared field has exactly the same logic described for the application shell configuration.

We won't review the remote configuration for every micro-frontend. They're similar to the authentication one, with the main changes being the values of fields based on the subdomain a micro-frontend represents. If you want to take a deeper look, feel free to review the GitHub repository (*https://oreil.ly/ECQqm*) for a full demo.

The part to highlight in the authentication micro-frontend is how the JWT token is shared with other micro-frontends. For micro-frontends that consume a private API, we need a mechanism to retrieve the token quickly and use it to fetch the data needed to populate the user interface.

Sharing a token on web storage or cookie is a common pattern that's also described in the decisions framework, and that's exactly what we are going to do in the authentication micro-frontend. In fact, after calling the sign-in API, we receive a JWT token that is stored in the session storage:

```
// additional code before

const SignIn = () => {
  let history = useHistory();

  const onSignIn = () => {
    window.sessionStorage.setItem("token", token);
    history.push("/shop");
  }

// additional code after

}
```

By convention, all the micro-frontends retrieve the token from the session storage and use it to consume the private API for their domain. It should go without saying that every micro-frontend that should be displayed after a user is authenticated should implement some logic to validate the token and ensure the user is entitled to access the content. In a horizontal-split architecture, where we have multiple micro-frontends on the same page, the micro-frontend container should validate the user and then either load the page's micro-frontends for authorized users or show an error message to unauthorized users. In a vertical-split architecture, before rendering any component, each micro-frontend should evaluate whether the token is valid and whether the user's role, if any, is entitled to access that content.

Catalog Micro-Frontend

The catalog domain is probably the most complex and largest of all the micro-frontends. It's the reason users are going to the website, so it has to not only be simple to use but also provide all the information the user is looking for. Team Maki is responsible for this micro-frontend, and its goal is to implement multiple views so users can discover what's available in the catalog and get the details of each product. In the future, the team may have to add new functionalities, such as sharing product images taken by a buyer or adding a review score with comments.

The team will implement all these features and prepare the codebase in a modular fashion, such that, in the future, it will be easy to hand over part of the domain to another team if needed. Strong encapsulation and a solid modularity will allow Team Maki to easily decouple part of the domain and collaborate with other teams to provide a great user experience.

This vertical-split micro-frontend's peculiarity is that we have to handle multiple views inside the same micro-frontend, a sort of SPA specific to the catalog domain. This shouldn't preclude the possibility of adding shared or domain-specific components, such as a personalized products component, implemented by other teams inside this domain. Although the application shell is responsible for the global routing, for this micro-frontend we have to implement a local routing (that is, a routing implemented at a micro-frontend level) that works in conjunction with the global one. In our example, the local routing doesn't differ much from the global routing, as shown in the following code snippet:

```
// additional code before

const Catalog = () => {
  let { path } = useRouteMatch();

  return(
    <div>
      <h1>
        Shop
      </h1>
      <Switch>
        <Route exact path={`${path}`} component={Home}/>
        <Route exact path={`${path}/product/:productId`} component={Details}/>
      </Switch>
    </div>
  )
}

// additional code after
```

Using the React Router library, we initially retrieve the first level of URL depth. We then incrementally append the product ID to the depth level when a user selects a specific product. From the second level onward, the structure and management are usually fully handled inside the micro-frontend, so the domain can evolve autonomously, eliminating the need to coordinate its enhancements with other teams. This also prevents domains creating overlapping first-level URLs because only one team is responsible for the global routing. When we implement the details page, we can use the product ID to request from an API the data to display:

```
// additional code before

const Details = () => {
  // we retrieve the product ID from the URL
  const {productId} = useParams()
  // we can add some logic for fetching the product details from an API
  return(
    <div>
        // we display the product ID
      {`Details page, product id: ${productId}`}
      <Link to="/shop">All products</Link>
    </div>
  )
}

// additional code after
```

In this way, we prepare our codebase for potential future splits without too much effort. Query strings are a good way to hand over ephemeral information to another view or even to another micro-frontend. Since this type of data is consumed in the flush by another part of the system and doesn't need to be stored for long, using query strings for passing them across the system is strongly recommended.

Account Management Micro-Frontend

Team Nigiri, responsible for the payment subdomain, and Team Sashimi, responsible for authentication, authorization, and the user's account, have to collaborate for the account management view, with part of the payment information and part of the user's details converging in the same view. Because these domains are assigned to different teams, we need a different approach from the other micro-frontends. Instead of a vertical-split micro-frontend architecture, we'll use a horizontal split to compose the final view and allow the two domains to communicate with each other for specific user interactions. To achieve this, we'll need to create a new host and two remotes. We know every remote is associated with a team, but what about the new host? Together, Teams Nigiri and Sashimi define the strategy for evaluating this common container of their subdomains. The new host has a clear implementation path that consists of:

- Loading two micro-frontends: a user's details and payment details
- Verifying whether a user is authenticated or not, presenting an error message or redirecting the user to the sign-in page

Because of that, Team Nigiri decides to take ownership of the new host and collaborate with Team Sashimi to define mechanisms to ensure the developer experience is as smooth as possible and the releases of the host don't cause any issues with Team Sashimi's work.

You may be asking yourself where the new host will technically be presented to the user. Module Federation allows us to nest multiple hosts, and there isn't a strong hierarchical structure. In fact, there is a very thin line between remote and host because a remote can expose some libraries used by the host and vice versa. As mentioned in Chapter 4, we need to pay attention to this thin line: when it's crossed and we start to share dependencies bidirectionally, we risk creating unmaintainable code that offers more problems than benefits in the long run. My recommendation is to force a hierarchical relation between host and remote where the sharing is always unidirectional so that the host will never expose any module with its remotes. This simple but effective practice simplifies a micro-frontends architecture implementation, reducing the risk of potential bugs. Moreover, it improves application debugging, which reduces the coupling between modules and avoids creating a big ball of mud in which multiple modules depend on each other. When we reduce the coupling and external dependencies in this way, each team will have the power to make the right decisions for the project, taking into account that we sometimes have to compromise to achieve the organization's business goals.

On the technical side, we have to account for some small changes to handle the horizontal approach. First, we need a container for the two micro-frontends. We'll create a host called MyAccount, which will have a different Module Federation configuration from the others. This container has to be a host, because it concerns the user's details and payment micro-frontends, but it also must be a remote for the application shell. To do this, we add the `remotes` and `exposes` objects, as seen in the following code snippet:

```
// additional code before

name: "MyAccount",
filename: "remoteEntry.js",
exposes:{
    "./MyAccount": "./src/MyAccount"
},
remotes: {
    AccountDetails: "AccountDetails@http://localhost:3005/remoteEntry.js",
    PaymentDetails: "PaymentDetails@http://localhost:3006/remoteEntry.js"
},

// additional code after
```

With just this change, we can have a host that is also a remote. We should avoid abusing this practice, however, because you can quickly end up with many small applications that represent components rather than the entire business domain. It's critical to design the boundaries correctly. When we aren't sure whether to add a new micro-frontend or incorporate a new feature inside an existing one, we need to go back to the whiteboard and ensure our decision respects the principles behind micro-frontends (review Chapter 2 if needed). A good rule of thumb described in Chapter 4 is understanding how extensible a micro-frontend is: when the business domain leaks into its container, you have to review whether you are implementing a micro-frontend or a component.

Important to note in this implementation is the communication between micro-frontends. As the micro-frontend decisions framework states, we need to share information between micro-frontends without code shared across different domains, as with a global state. An ideal solution is leveraging the publish/subscribe pattern for maintaining the domains decoupled. The teams decide to implement an event emitter that decouples the two micro-frontends present in the account management view but allows them to communicate using each other's emitting events, as shown in Figure 5-5.

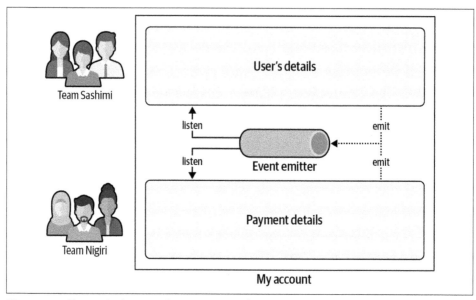

Figure 5-5. Teams Sashimi and Nigiri are implementing an event emitter shared between micro-frontends for communicating the domain's boundaries

In the host, we instantiate the event emitter and then inject the instance to the two micro-frontends, leveraging the properties mechanism:

```
// more code before

const AuthenticatedView = (props) => {
  return(
    <React.Suspense fallback="Loading...">
      <AccountDetails emitter={props.emitter}/>
      <PaymentDetails emitter={props.emitter}/>
    </React.Suspense>
  )
}

//...
let view;
// simply checking the token but it has to be a more robust ↵
authorization strategy to implement
if(token){
  const emitter = createNanoEvents();
  view = <AuthenticatedView emitter={emitter}/>
} else {
  // share a different view if the user is not authenticated
}

// more code after
```

AuthenticatedView uses the same pattern implemented for the application shell, in which we lazy-load our micro-frontends and use React Suspense until the micro-frontends are ready. The micro-frontends are loaded only when the token is available in sessionStorage. To simplify this example, I didn't present a specific authorization implementation, but you should add any authorization strategy implemented for the rest of the application. Finally, the event emitter is assigned in a property called emitter, which is available in both micro-frontends.

All micro-frontends use the event emitter to notify us that something has happened inside its business domain. In this way, a micro-frontend can evolve while maintaining the compatibility needed in the system. With this approach, it's critical that we document correctly the events every micro-frontend is listening to and emitting. When we do, the work required to add a new micro-frontend inside a view becomes trivial, because the documentation should cover the event name as well as the payload passed through the event. We should take a similar approach when we use reactive streams or custom events. The technical implementation becomes very simple because in the payment micro-frontend we can emit an event when a user changes the payment method:

```
const onPaymentChanged = () => {
    props.emitter.emit("paymentChanged", "May 2021");
}
```

The account details micro-frontend, meanwhile, has listened for the paymentChanged event in order to apply the change in its code:

```
const [lastPaymentDate, setPaymentChanged] = useState("Jan 2021")

props.emitter.on("paymentChanged", date => setPaymentChanged(date))

return (
    <div>
        <h3>Account Details</h3>
        <ul>
            <li><i>name:</i> Luca</li>
            <li><i>surname:</i> Mezzalira</li>
            <li><i>email:</i> guesswho@acme.com</li>
            <li><i>member since:</i> Jan 2021</li>
            <li><i>payment changed: </i>{lastPaymentDate}</li>
            <li><a href="#">Change account details</a></li>
        </ul>
    </div>
);
```

When a micro-frontend picks up an event, React hooks modify the lastPaymentDate variable, which is used to show the last date a user changes its payment method. I recommend using typed event objects as a best practice. This will reduce the risk of typos in the codebase, which is critical because we're sharing strings across multiple teams. If you are not using TypeScript, you can achieve a similar result by creating an object with constant properties, which will help developers use the right contract for communicating or listening to an event in the application:

```
const PaymentEvents = {
    PAYMENT_CHANGED: "paymentMethodChanged";
// other events
}
```

You can then freeze the object (*https://oreil.ly/2QUAg*) to prevent changes to the object structure and prevent adding or removing properties at runtime.

When we have multiple micro-frontends in the same view and they communicate with each other via events, we must ensure that all the events are captured by the interested micro-frontends. For example, imagine we have three micro-frontends in the same view and two of them load immediately, while the third takes a while due to a networking issue. When the first two are emitting events, the third one isn't able to capture any events that occur while it's loading. One possible solution is to create a buffer of events in the application container and replay them when the third micro-frontend is fully loaded. It would require a bit of effort to create something that monitors every micro-frontend's state, gathers all the events in an array or similar data structure, and then replays all of them to one or more micro-frontends without emitting the full list of events to every micro-frontend (which could cause some internal state mismatching). Having multiple micro-frontends in the same view requires some more thoughts on how to handle failure or partial failure states. But we must think about these scenarios because, as AWS's CTO Werner Vogels said, "Everything fails, all the time."

Project Evolution

We don't want to create a project that works just for a short period of time. We want to create one that can evolve over time, eliminating the need to start from scratch in order to advance our organization's business goals. Let's explore, then, some potential ways this project could evolve and how we can create a coherent implementation across different subdomains.

Embedding a Legacy Application

Imagine that we have to add a tool for customizing existing products, like T-shirts, hoodies, and mugs, to our ecommerce project. The tool is a legacy application that was developed several years ago with an old version of Angular. Only one person from the team that developed this solution is still with the company, and she is keeping the lights on for this project, fixing bugs and optimizing the codebase where possible. To reduce the feature's time to market, the business and the tech department decide to integrate the legacy tool with the existing micro-frontend architecture and ship them for a limited time. Later, a new team will take ownership of the project and revamp it to natively embrace micro-frontends. The application is well encapsulated, not requiring any particular information about the environment that is running, and we can pass the configuration needed to render a file to the configurator via a query string. Additionally, we want to minimize possible clashes with other parts of the codebase, such as with the application shell.

We can solve this problem by wrapping the legacy application inside an iframe, as in Figure 5-6, which will prevent any possible clash with the existing micro-frontend system.

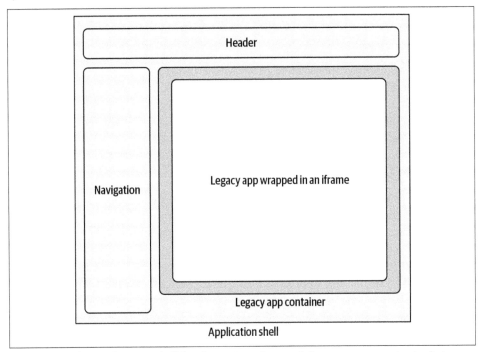

Figure 5-6. The application shell loads a micro-frontend that acts as an adapter between the new and old worlds. The legacy application is wrapped in an iframe to minimize the impact with the existing micro-frontend codebase.

However, if we want to communicate with the legacy application and vice versa, such as with displaying errors across the entire interface instead of only in the iframe, we should create a communication bridge between the legacy application and the application shell in order to reuse the alerting system. We could directly integrate the application shell with the legacy application, but this would mean polluting the application shell codebase. We can implement a better strategy than that. Instead, we will apply an adapter pattern using a micro-frontend as a container for the iframe that contains the legacy application. The micro-frontend will be responsible for orchestrating the iframe using query strings and intercepting any messages from the legacy application, translating it into events emitted in the event bus.

 The *adapter pattern* is a software design pattern (also known as wrapper) that allows an existing class's interface to be used as another interface. It is often used to make existing classes work with others without modifying their source code.

By using a micro-frontend as adapter, we can prepare our project for future evolutions. We can also reduce any refactoring in the application shell, first for integrating the legacy application and then for substituting with the new micro-frontend implementation. Within the application shell, we will maintain a business-unaware logic, since the communication will be translated to events via the event emitter. This process acts as an anticorruption layer between the inner and the outer systems. This pattern also comes in handy when we want to consolidate multiple applications under the same system and slowly but steadily replace every legacy application, with micro-frontends implementing a strangler pattern (*https://oreil.ly/cCGmk*), which allows the micro-frontend application to live alongside the legacy ones.

Developing the Checkout Experience

Let's say the project is finally getting traction inside the organization and Team Nigiri is developing the checkout process. The product owner and the UX team have decided to place a cart inside the application shell's header. The cart should be shown only when a user is authenticated in the shop, so therefore that component should be visible only in certain views. When the cart button is clicked, the new checkout micro-frontend will guide the user to process the order correctly inside the system.

The cart component (see Figure 5-7) has different responsibilities:

- Hide and reveal the cart based on the area a user is navigating to
- Display the total number of items in the cart
- Start the checkout experience

Because the cart component will be present in the application shell, we have to create a logic for hiding it when a user is not authenticated and sharing it when they are. We could have the application shell orchestrate the component's visibility, but the checkout domain logic would leak into the application shell, which could pollute the codebase. Additionally, every time we want to change the visibility logic, we'd need to release a new application shell version. And because the checkout experience and the application shell are owned by different teams, creating such dependencies can only cause more troubles than benefits.

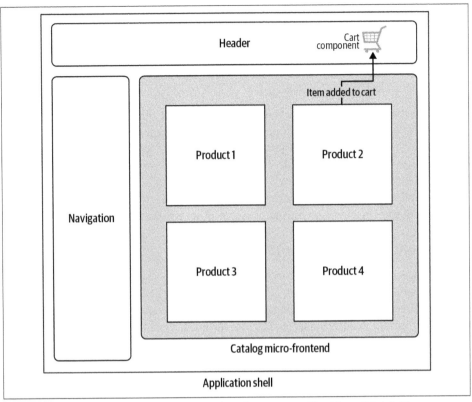

Figure 5-7. The cart component is created and maintained by Team Nigiri. The component is loaded inside the application shell and uses an event emitter for listening for when an object should be added to the cart and showing the total number of elements the user has selected.

A better solution is to ask the team responsible for the application shell to add the component, and the component itself will handle its own visibility based on a set of conditions, such as page URL. In this way, any logic change or improvement will happen inside the component and not leak these implementation details to the application shell. The application shell team will need to upgrade the library used for loading the component if they used a compile time implementation. In the case of Module Federation, they won't need to do anything else because the new component will be loaded at runtime.

To display the total number of items in the cart, we first need to add the product to the cart via an API exposed by the backend and then notify the cart component to update the value displayed in the interface. The best way to achieve this is by emitting an event via the event emitter instance. When the cart component receives the event, it will consume an API to retrieve the number of items currently in the cart (as we explained in Chapter 4).

Finally, when the user starts the checkout experience by clicking on the cart component, all that's required is changing the URL, notifying the application shell to move on to the checkout micro-frontend.

As you can see, investing a bit of time up front to think through the implementation of a simple element like a cart component can make a great difference in the long run. This cart component will maintain strong encapsulation despite living inside a different domain (the application shell). It will receive events from other parts of the system via the event emitter and route the user to the checkout experience. Following the principles of micro-frontends makes us reason in new ways, enhancing our developer experience and avoiding domain leaks in other application areas.

Implementing Dynamic Remotes Containers

In this example, we have seen how to implement remotes specifying their path in the webpack configuration. However, Module Federation allows us to dynamically load remotes directly from JavaScript without having to list every micro-frontend available in the application at compile time. The interesting part of this approach is the possibility of extending our application easily, without recompiling the application shell that contains a list of all the micro-frontends. For instance, we can consume an API or a static JSON for retrieving all the available micro-frontends and compose the global routing system logic in the application shell.

We could also shape the traffic toward a specific version of a micro-frontend to reduce the risk of a new version causing any major bugs in front of a large audience. The possibilities of dynamic remote containers are incredible and can really help introduce advanced logic inside your architecture. To see this implementation in practice, check out the GitHub repository (*https://oreil.ly/J5YsI*) maintained by the webpack team working on Module Federation.

Webpack Lock-in

I bet some of you by now are thinking that going all in with Module Federation may be risky considering Module Federation is fully supported only on webpack 5 at the moment. Let's look more closely at that. Since it was released in Autumn 2020, Module Federation has gained a lot of admirers in the developer community. The frictionless learning curve and the simplicity of implementing it in new and existing projects are definitely its main strengths. Moreover, the fact that it's solving complex challenges like dependencies management and micro-frontend composition is definitely well received by the community.

There is also a framework called Fronts (*https://oreil.ly/KYRSi*), which is used for building micro-frontends using Module Federation or limited features of it without using the webpack plug-in. Many organizations started using Module Federation in production, and frontend frameworks like Angular have started showing interesting examples using Module Federation. It's important to understand whether our fear of relying so heavily on webpack with Module Federation is a real problem or not. How much time will it take to refactor your code using another solution? How long will your project last in production without the possibility of refactoring it? How critical is the project you are developing? In the next three to five years, how likely is a technology change for the project?

One of the strengths of micro-frontends is incremental code refactoring. Micro-frontends are a great solution for evolving your projects from a business and technical perspective, allowing you to try new ideas and solutions and then incrementally improving your codebase. When you choose to avoid a framework or a technology that provides some level of lock-in, you have to think about what you are going to lose and when you decide to build it in house, and you have to estimate how much effort building and, more importantly, maintaining that solution would cost instead of having an open source project maintained and evolved by the community. Sometimes the fear of lock-in is mitigated when you run proper due diligence and see what the alternative paths are.

Summary

In this chapter, we have seen the micro-frontend decisions framework in action. Every team identified the right approach to achieve the requirements presented by the product teams. They maintained a decoupled approach, knowing that this path will guarantee independence and faster response time to any business shift. During this journey, we have also seen a technical implementation of a micro-frontend architecture using webpack and Module Federation.

This is one of the many approaches mentioned in Chapter 4. Every framework and technology will have its own implementation challenges; walking you through the reasoning behind certain decisions is far more valuable than evaluating each implementation. With this approach, you will have a mental model that allows you to move from one framework to another easily, just by following what you learned during this journey.

CHAPTER 6

Build and Deploy Micro-Frontends

In this chapter, we discuss another key topic for distributed systems like micro-frontends: the importance of a solid automation strategy. The microservices architecture adds great flexibility and scalability to our architecture, allowing our APIs to scale horizontally based on the traffic our infrastructure receives and allowing us to implement the right pattern for the right job instead of having a common solution applied to all our APIs, as in a monolithic architecture. Despite these great capabilities, microservices increase the complexity of managing the infrastructure, requiring an immense number of repetitive actions to build and deploy them. Any company embracing the microservices architecture, therefore, must invest a considerable amount of time and effort on their *continuous integration* (CI) or *continuous deployment* (CD) pipelines (more on these to come). Given how fast a business can drift direction nowadays, improving a CI/CD pipeline is not only a concern at the beginning of a project; it's a constant incremental improvement throughout the entire project life cycle. One of the key characteristics of a solid automation strategy is that it creates confidence in artifacts' replicability and provides fast feedback loops for developers.

This is also true for micro-frontends. Having solid automation pipelines will allow our micro-frontend projects to be successful, creating a reliable solution for developers to experiment, build, and deploy. In fact, for certain projects, micro-frontends could proliferate in such a way that it would become nontrivial to manage them. One of the key decisions listed in the micro-frontend decisions framework, discussed in Chapter 3, is the possibility to compose multiple micro-frontends in the same view (horizontal split) or having just one micro-frontend at a time (vertical split). With the horizontal split, we could end up with tens or even hundreds of artifacts to manage in our automation pipelines. Therefore, we have to invest in solutions to manage such scenarios. Vertical splits also require work but are close to the traditional way to set up automation for single-page applications (SPAs). The major difference is you'll have more than one artifact and potentially different ways to build and optimize your code.

We will dive deep into these challenges in this chapter, starting with the principles behind a solid and fast automation strategy and how we can improve the developer experience with some simple but powerful tools. Then we'll analyze best practices for continuous integration and micro-frontend deployment. Finally, we conclude with an introduction to fitness functions for automating and testing architecture characteristics during different stages of the pipelines.

Automation Principles

Working with micro-frontends requires constantly improving the automation pipeline. Skipping this work may hamper the delivery speed of every team working on the project and decrease their confidence to deploy in production or, worse, frustrate the developers as well as the business when the project fails. Nailing the automation part is fundamental if you're going to have a clear idea of how to build a successful continuous integration, continuous delivery, or continuous deployment strategy.

Continuous Integration Versus Continuous Delivery Versus Continuous Deployment

An in-depth discussion about continuous integration, continuous delivery, and continuous deployment is beyond the scope of this book. However, it's important to understand the differences between these three strategies. Continuous integration defines a strategy where an automation pipeline kicks in for every merge into the main branch, extensively testing the codebase before the code is merged in the release branch. Continuous delivery is an extension of continuous integration where, after the tests, we generate the artifact ready to be deployed with a simple click from a deployment dashboard. Continuous deployment goes one step further, deploying in production the artifacts built after the code is committed in the version control system. If you are interested in learning more, I recommend reading *Continuous Delivery* by David Farley and Jez Humble (Addison-Wesley Professional).

To get automation speed and reliability right, we need to keep the following principles in mind:

- Keep the feedback loop as fast as possible.
- Iterate often to enhance the automation strategy.
- Empower your teams to make the right decisions for the micro-frontends they are responsible for.

- Identify some boundaries, also called guardrails, where teams operate and make decisions while maintaining tools standardization.
- Define a solid testing strategy.

Let's discuss these principles to get a better understanding of how to leverage them.

Keep a Feedback Loop Fast

One of the key features for a solid automation pipeline is fast execution. Every automation pipeline provides feedback for developers. Having a quick turnaround on whether our code has broken the codebase is essential for developers for creating confidence in what they have written. Good automation should run often and provide feedback in a matter of seconds or minutes, at the most. It's important for developers to receive constant feedback so they will be encouraged to run the tests and checks within the automation pipeline more often. It's essential, then, to analyze which steps may be parallelized and which are serialized. A technical solution that allows both is ideal. For example, we may decide to parallelize the unit testing step so we can run our tests in small chunks instead of waiting for hundreds, if not thousands, of tests to pass before moving to the next step. Yet some steps cannot be parallelized. So we need to understand how we can optimize these steps to be as fast as possible.

Working with micro-frontends, by definition, should simplify optimizing the automation strategy. Because we are dividing an entire application into smaller parts, there is less code to test and build, for instance, and every stage of a CI should be very fast. However, there is a complexity factor to consider. Due to maintaining many similar automation pipelines, we should embrace infrastructure as code (IaC) principles for spinning new pipelines without manually creating or modifying several pipelines.

Infrastructure as Code

Infrastructure as code represents the management of infrastructure (networks, virtual machines, load balancers, and so on) in a descriptive model. It uses the same principles of source code but applied to infrastructure. Like the principle that the same source code generates the same binary, an IaC model generates the same environment every time it is applied. For instance, AWS CDK allows the use of TypeScript or JavaScript for defining a project infrastructure in an AWS account. Let's take as an example this code snippet, which shows how to create an Amazon CloudFront distribution with an Amazon S3 bucket as an origin associated to it:

```
const cdk = require('@aws-cdk/core');
const cf = require('@aws-cdk/aws-cloudfront');
const origins = require('@aws-cdk/aws-cloudfront-origins');
const s3 = require('@aws-cdk/aws-s3');
```

```
class CfcliStack extends cdk.Stack {

  constructor(scope, id, props) {
    super(scope, id, props);

    const bucket = new s3.Bucket(this, "my-unique-bucket", {
      websiteIndexDocument: 'index.html'
    });
    const distribution = new cf.Distribution(this, "my-CF-distro", {
        defaultBehavior:{
          origin: new origins.S3Origin(bucket)
        }
    })
  }
}
```

In this way, we describe our infrastructure that is replicable in multiple AWS accounts or development environments without the need of manual configurations. When we are defining our automation pipelines for micro-frontends, using IaC as a mechanism for replicating consistent pipelines across teams is an essential task for making sure every team is following the infrastructure-recommended practices defined by the organization, and they speed up the configuration of their infrastructure instead of reinventing it for every new micro-frontend.

In fact, IaC leverages the concept of automation for configuring and provisioning infrastructure in the same way we do for our code. In this way, we can reliably create an infrastructure without the risk of forgetting a configuration or misconfiguring part of our infrastructure. Everything is mapped inside configuration files, or code, providing us with a concrete way to generate our automation pipelines when they need to be replicated. This becomes critical when you work with large teams and especially with distributed teams, because you can release modules and scripts that are reusable between teams.

Iterate Often

An automation pipeline is not a piece of infrastructure that, once defined, remains as it is until the end of a life cycle project. Every automation pipeline has to be reviewed, challenged, and improved. It's essential to maintain a very quick automation pipeline to empower our developers to get fast feedback loops. In order to constantly improve, we need to visualize our pipelines. Screens near the developers' desks can show how long building artifacts take, making clear to everyone on the team how healthy the pipelines are (or aren't) and immediately letting everyone know if a job failed or succeeded. When we notice our pipelines taking more than 8 to 10 minutes, it's time to review them and see if we can optimize certain practices of an automation strategy. Review the automation strategy regularly: monthly if the pipelines are running slowly, and then every three to four months once they're healthy. Don't stop reviewing your pipelines after defining the automation pipeline. Continue to improve and pursue better performance and a quicker feedback loop; this investment in time and effort will pay off very quickly.

Empower Your Teams

At several companies I worked for, the automation strategy was kept out of capable developers' hands. Only a few people inside the organization were aware of how the entire automation system worked and even fewer were allowed to change the infrastructure or take steps to generate and deploy an artifact. This is the worst nightmare of any developer working in an organization with one or more teams. The developer job shouldn't be just writing code; it should include a broad range of tasks, including how to set up and change the automation pipeline for the artifacts they are working on, whether it's a library, a micro-frontend, or the entire application.

Empowering our teams when we are working with micro-frontends is essential because we cannot always rely on all the micro-frontends having the same build pipeline due to the possibility of maintaining multiple stacks at the same time. Certainly, the deployment phase will be the same for all the micro-frontends in a project. However, the build pipeline may use different tools or different optimizations, and centralizing these decisions could result in a worse final result than one from enabling the developers to work in the automation pipeline.

Ideally, the organization should provide some guardrails for the development team. For instance, the CI/CD tool should be the company's responsibility, but all the scripts and steps to generate an artifact should be owned by the team because they know the best way to produce an optimized artifact with the code they have written. This doesn't mean creating silos between a team and the rest of the organization but empowering them to make certain decisions that would result in a better outcome.

Last but not least, encourage a culture of sharing and innovation by creating moments for the teams to share their ideas, proof of concepts, and solutions. This is especially important when you work in a distributed environment. Remote meetings lack everyday casual work conversations we have around the coffee machine. Creating a virtual moment for enjoying these conversations again may seem an overkill at the beginning, but it helps the morale and the connections between team members.

Define Your Guardrails

An important principle for empowering teams and having a solid automation strategy is creating some guardrails for them, so we can make sure they are heading in the right direction.

Guardrails for the automation strategy are boundaries identified by tech leadership, in collaboration with architects and/or platform or cloud engineers, between which teams can operate and add value for the creation of micro-frontends.

In this situation, guardrails might include the tools used for running the automation strategy, the dashboard used for deployment in a continuous delivery strategy, or the fitness functions for enforcing architecture characteristics that we discuss extensively during this chapter.

Introducing guardrails won't mean reducing developers' freedom. Instead, it will guide them toward using the company's standards, abstracting them as much as we can from their world, and allowing the team to innovate inside these boundaries. We need to find the right balance when we define these guardrails, and we need to make sure everyone understands the *why* of them more than the *how*. Usually, creating documentation helps to scale and spread the information across teams and new employees. As with other parts of the automation strategy, guardrails shouldn't be static. They need to be revised, improved, or even removed, as the business evolves.

Define Your Test Strategy

Investing time on a solid testing strategy is essential, specifically end-to-end testing, for instance, when we have multiple micro-frontends per view with multiple teams contributing to the final results and we want to ensure our application works end to end. In this case, we must also ensure that the transition between views is covered and works properly before deploying our artifacts in production.

While unit and integration testing are important, with micro-frontends there aren't particular challenges to face. Instead end-to-end testing has to be revised for applying it to this architecture. Because every team owns a part of the application, we need to make sure the critical path of our applications is extensively covered and we achieve our final desired result. End-to-end testing will help ensure those things.

Developer Experience

A key consideration when working with micro-frontends is the developer experience (DX). While not all companies can support a DX team, even a virtual team across the organization can be helpful. Such a team is responsible for creating tools and improving the experience of working with micro-frontends to prevent frictions in developing new features.

At this stage, it should be clear that every team is responsible for part of the application and not for the entire codebase. Creating a frictionless developer experience will help our developers feel comfortable building, testing, and debugging the part of the application they are responsible for. We need to guarantee a smooth experience for testing a micro-frontend in isolation, as well as inside the overall web application, because there are always touch points between micro-frontends, no matter which architecture we decide to use. A bonus would be creating an extensible experience that isn't closed to the possibility of embracing new or different tools during the project life cycle.

What Does Developer Experience Mean?

DX is usually one or more teams dedicated to studying, analyzing, and improving how developers get their work done. Specifically, such teams observe which tools and processes developers use to accomplish their daily work providing support for improving the development life cycle across the entire organization. One of DX's main goals is to simplify the development and process of building, testing, and deploying artifacts in different environments.

Many companies have created end-to-end solutions that they maintain alongside the projects they are working on, which more than fills the gaps of existing tools when needed. This seems like a great way to create the perfect developer experience for our organization, although businesses aren't static, nor are tech communities. As a result, we need to account for the cost of maintaining our custom developers' experience, as well as the cost of onboarding new employees. It may still be the right decision for your company, depending on its size or the type of the project you are working on, but I encourage you to analyze all the options before committing to building an in-house solution to make sure you maximize the investment.

Horizontal Versus Vertical Split

The decision between a horizontal and vertical split with your new micro-frontends project will definitely impact the developer's experience. A vertical split will represent the micro-frontends as single HTML pages or SPAs owned by a single team, resulting in a developer experience very similar to the traditional development of an SPA. All the tools and workflows available for SPA will suit the developers in this case. You may want to create some additional tools specifically for testing your micro-frontend under certain conditions as well. For instance, when you have an application shell loading a vertical micro-frontend, you may want to create a script or tool for testing the application shell version available on a specific environment to make sure your micro-frontend works with the latest or a specific version.

The testing phases are very similar to a normal SPA, where we can set unit, integration, and end-to-end testing without any particular challenges. Therefore, every team can test its own micro-frontends, as well as the transition between micro-frontends, such as when we need to make sure the next micro-frontend is fully loaded. However, we also need to make sure all micro-frontends are reachable and loadable inside the application shell. One solution I've seen work very well is having the team that owns the application shell do the end-to-end testing for routing between micro-frontends so they can perform the tests across all the micro-frontends.

Horizontal splits come with a different set of considerations. When a team owns multiple micro-frontends that are part of one or more views, we need to provide tools for testing a micro-frontend inside the multiple views assembling the page at runtime. These tools need to allow developers to review the overall picture, potential dependencies clash, the communication with micro-frontends developed by other teams, and so on. These aren't standard tools, and many companies have had to develop custom tools to solve this challenge. Keep in mind that the right tools will vary, depending on the environment and context we operate in, so what worked in one company may not fit in another. Some solutions associated with the framework we decided to use will work, but more often than not, we will need to customize some tools to provide our developers with a frictionless experience.

Another challenge with a horizontal split is how to run a solid testing strategy. We will need to identify which team will run the end-to-end testing for every view and how specifically the integration testing will work, given that an action happening in a micro-frontend may trigger a reaction with another. We do have ways to solve these problems, but the governance behind them may be far from trivial. The developer experience with micro-frontends is not always straightforward. The horizontal split in particular is challenging because we need to answer far more questions and make sure our tools are constantly up to date to simplify the life of our developers.

Frictionless Micro-Frontends Blueprints

The micro-frontend developer experience isn't only about development tools; we must also consider how the new micro-frontends will be created. The more micro-frontends we have and the more we have to create, the more speeding up and automating this process will become mandatory. Creating a command-line tool for scaffolding a micro-frontend will not only cover implementation, allowing a team to have all the dependencies for starting to write code, but also take care of collecting and providing best practices and guardrails inside the company. For instance, if we are using a specific library for observability or logging, adding the library to the scaffolding can speed up creating a micro-frontend—and it guarantees that your company's standards will be in place and ready to use.

Another important item to provide out of the box would be a sample of the automation strategy, with all the key steps needed for building a micro-frontend. Imagine that we have decided to run static analysis and security testing inside our automation strategy. Providing a sample of how to configure it automatically for every micro-frontend would increase developers' productivity and help get new employees up to speed faster. This scaffolding would need to be maintained in collaboration with developers learning the challenges and solutions directly from the trenches. A sample can help communicate new practices and specific changes that arise during the development of new features or projects, further saving your team time and helping them work more efficiently.

Environments Strategies

Another important consideration for the DX is enabling teams to work within the company's environments strategy. The most commonly used strategy across midsize to large organizations is a combination of testing, staging, and production environments. The testing environment is often the most unstable of the three because it's used for quick attempts made by the developers. As a result, staging should resemble the production environment as much as possible, the production environment should be accessible only to a subset of people, and the DX team should create strict controls to prevent manual access to this environment and provide a swift solution for promoting or deploying artifacts in production.

An interesting twist to the classic environment strategy is spinning up environments with a subset of a system for testing of any kind (end-to-end or visual regression, for instance) and then tearing them down when an operation finishes. This particular strategy of on-demand environments is a great addition for the company because it helps not only with micro-frontends but also with microservices for testing in isolation end-to-end flows. With this approach we can also think about end-to-end testing in isolation of an entire business subdomain, deploying only the microservices needed and having multiple on-demand environments, saving a considerable amount of money.

Another feature provided by on-demand environments is the possibility to offer the business or a product owner a preview of an experiment or a specific branch containing a feature. Nowadays, many cloud providers like AWS can provide great cost savings using spot instances (*https://aws.amazon.com/ec2/spot*) for a middle-of-the-road approach, where the infrastructure is more cost effective than the normal offering because of the spare capacity borrowed by customers for a limited amount of time. Spot instances are a perfect fit for on-demand environments.

Version Control

When we start to design an automation strategy, selecting a version control and branching strategy to adopt is a mandatory step. Although there are valid alternatives, like Mercurial, Git is the most popular for a version control system. I'll use Git as a reference in my examples below, but know that all the approaches are applicable to Mercurial as well. Working with version control means deciding which approach to use in terms of repositories. Usually, the debate is between monorepo and polyrepo, also called multirepo. There are benefits and pitfalls in both approaches. You can employ both, though, in your micro-frontend project, to use the right technique for your context.

Monorepo

Monorepo (see Figure 6-1) is based on the concept that all the teams are using the same repository, so therefore all the projects are hosted together.

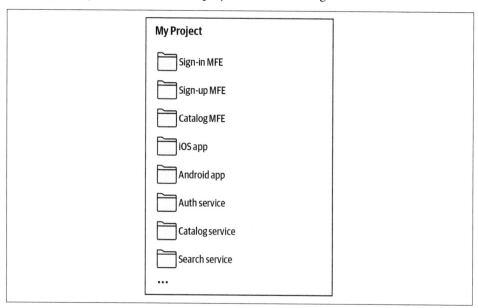

Figure 6-1. Monorepo example where all the projects live inside the same repository

The main advantages of using monorepo are:

Code reusability
> Sharing libraries becomes very natural with this approach. Because all of a project's codebase lives in the same repository, we can smoothly create a new project, abstracting some code and making it available for all the projects that can benefit from it.

Easy collaboration across teams
> Because the discoverability is completely frictionless, teams can contribute across projects. Having all the projects in the same place makes it easy to review a project's codebase and understand the functionality of another project. This approach facilitates communication with the team responsible for the maintenance in order to improve or simply change the implementation pointing on a specific class or line of code without kicking off an abstract discussion.

Cohesive codebase with less technical debt
Working with monorepo encourages every team to be up to date with the latest dependencies versions, specifically APIs but generally with the latest solutions developed by other teams, too. This would mean that our project may be broken and would require some refactoring when there is a breaking change, for instance. Monorepo forces us to continually refactor our codebase, improving the code quality and reducing our tech debt.

Simplified dependencies management
With monorepo, all the dependencies used by several projects are centralized, so we don't need to download them every time for all our projects. And when we want to upgrade to the next major release, all the teams using a specific library will have to work together to update their codebase, reducing the technical debt that in other cases a team may accumulate. Updating a library may cost a bit of coordination overhead, especially when you work with distributed teams or large organizations.

Large-scale code refactoring
Monorepo is very useful for large-scale code refactoring. Because all the projects are in the same repository, refactoring them at the same time is trivial. Teams will need to coordinate or work with technical leaders, who have a strong high-level picture of the entire codebase and are responsible for refactoring or coordinating the refactor across multiple projects.

Easier onboarding for new hires
With monorepo, a new employee can quickly find code samples from other repositories. Additionally, a developer can find inspiration from other approaches and quickly shape them inside the codebase.

Despite the undoubted benefits, embracing monorepo also brings some challenges:

Constant investment in automation tools
Monorepo requires a constant, critical investment in automation tools, especially for large organizations. There are plenty of open source tools available, but not all are suitable for monorepo, particularly after some time on the same project, when the monorepo starts to grow exponentially. Many large organizations must constantly invest in improving their automation tools for monorepo to avoid their entire workforce being slowed down by intermittent commitment on improving the automation pipelines and reducing the time of this feedback loop for the developers.

Scaling tools when the codebase increases
Another important challenge is that automation pipelines must scale alongside the codebase. Many whitepapers from Google, Facebook, and Twitter claim that after a certain threshold, the investment in having a performant automation

pipeline increases until the organization has several teams working exclusively on it. Unsurprisingly, every company aforementioned has built its own version of build tools and released it as open source to deal with the unique challenges they face with thousands of developers working in the same repository.

Projects are coupled together

Given that all the projects are easy to access and, more often than not, they are sharing libraries and dependencies, we risk having tightly coupled projects that can exist only when they are deployed together. We may, therefore, not be able to share our micro-frontends across multiple projects for different customers where the codebase lives in a different monorepo. This is a key consideration to think about before embracing the monorepo approach with micro-frontends.

Trunk-based development

Trunk-based development (*https://oreil.ly/MhU6v*) is the only option that makes sense with monorepo. This branching strategy is based on the assumption that all the developers commit to the same branch, called a trunk. Considering that all the projects live inside the same repository, the trunk main branch may have thousands of commits per day, so it's essential to commit often with small commits instead of developing an entire feature per day before merging. This technique should force developers to commit smaller chunks of code, avoiding the "merge hell" of other branching strategies. Although I am a huge fan of trunk-based development, it requires discipline and maturity across the entire organization to achieve good results.

Disciplined developers

We must have disciplined developers in order to maintain the codebase in a good state. When tens, or even hundreds, of developers are working in the same repository, the Git history, along with the codebase, could become messy very quickly. Unfortunately, it's almost impossible to have senior developers inside all the teams, and that lack of knowledge or discipline could compromise the repository quality and extend the blast radius from one project inside the monorepo to many, if not all, of them.

Using monorepo for micro-frontends is definitely an option, and tools like Lerna (*https://lerna.js.org*) help with managing multiple projects inside the same repository. In fact, Lerna can install and hoist (*https://oreil.ly/aV6O5*), if needed, all the dependencies across packages together and publish a package when a new version is ready to be released. However, we must understand that one of the main monorepo strengths is its code-sharing capability. It requires a significant commitment to maintain the quality of the codebase, and we must be careful to avoid coupling too many of our micro-frontends because we risk losing their nature of independent deployable artifacts.

Git has started to invest in reducing the operations time when a user invokes commands like Git history or Git status in large repositories. And as monorepo has become more popular, Git has been actively working on delivering additional functionalities for filtering what a user wants to clone to their machine without needing to clone the entire Git history and all the project's folders.

Obviously, these enhancements will also be beneficial for our CI/CD, where we can overcome one of the main challenges of embracing a monorepo strategy.

Sparse-Checkout

In Q1 2020, Git introduced the `sparse-checkout` command (for v2.25 and later) for cloning only part of a repository instead of all the files and history of a repository. Reducing the amount of data to clone for running fast automation pipelines would solve one of the main challenges of embracing the monorepo approach.

We need to remember that using the monorepo approach would mean investing in our tools, evangelizing and building discipline across our teams, and finally accepting a constant investment in improving the codebase. If these characteristics suit your organization, monorepo would likely allow you to successfully support your projects. Many companies are using monorepo, specifically large organizations like Google and Facebook, where the investment in maintaining this paradigm is totally sustainable. One of the most famous papers on monorepo (*https://oreil.ly/JkTin*) was written by Google's Rachel Potvin and Josh Levenberg. In their concluding paragraph, they write:

> Over the years, as the investment required to continue scaling the centralized repository grew, Google leadership occasionally considered whether it would make sense to move from the monolithic model. Despite the effort required, Google repeatedly chose to stick with the central repository due to its advantages.
>
> The monolithic model of source code management is not for everyone. It is best suited to organizations like Google, with an open and collaborative culture. It would not work well for organizations where large parts of the codebase are private or hidden between groups.

Polyrepo

The opposite of a monorepo strategy is the polyrepo (see Figure 6-2), or multirepo, where every single application lives in its own repository.

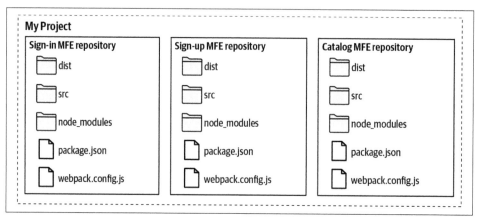

Figure 6-2. Polyrepo example where we split the projects among multiple repositories

Some benefits of a polyrepo strategy are:

Different branching strategy per project
> With monorepo, we should use trunk-based development, but with a polyrepo strategy, we can use the right branching strategy for the project we are working on. Imagine, for instance, that we have a legacy project with a different release cadence than other projects that are in continuous deployment. With a polyrepo strategy, we can use Git flow (*https://oreil.ly/iASL8*) in just that project, providing a branching strategy specific for that context.

No risk of blocking other teams
> Another benefit of working with a polyrepo is that the blasting radius of our changes is strictly confined to our project. There isn't any possibility of breaking other teams' projects or negatively affecting them because they live in another repository.

Encourages thinking about contracts
> In a polyrepo environment, the communication across projects has to be defined via APIs. This forces every team to identify the contracts between producers and consumers and to create governance for managing future releases and breaking changes.

Fine-grained access control
> Large organizations are likely to work with contractors who should see only the repositories they are responsible for, or to have a security strategy in place where only certain departments can see and work on a specific area of the codebase. Polyrepo is the perfect strategy for achieving that fine-grained access control on different codebases, introducing roles, and identifying the level of access needed for every team or department.

Less upfront and long-term investment in tooling

With a polyrepo strategy, we can easily use any tool available out there. For instance, using managed solutions like CircleCI or Drone.io would be more than enough due to the contained size of a micro-frontend repository. Usually, the repositories are not expanding at the same rate as monorepo repositories because fewer developers are committing to the codebase. That means your investment up front and in maintaining the build of a polyrepo environment is far less, especially when you automate your CI/CD pipeline using infrastructure as code or command-line scripts that can be reused across different teams.

Polyrepo also has some caveats:

Difficulties with project discoverability

By its nature, polyrepo makes it more difficult to discover other projects because every project is hosted in its own repository. Creating a solid naming convention that allows every developer to discover other projects easily can help mitigate this issue. Unquestionably, however, polyrepo can make it difficult for new employees or for developers who are comparing different approaches to find other projects suitable for their research.

Code duplication

Another disadvantage of polyrepo is code duplication. For example, a team creates a library that will be used by other teams for standardizing certain approaches, but the tech department is not aware of that library. Often, there are libraries that should be used across several micro-frontends, like logging or observability integration, but a polyrepo strategy doesn't facilitate code sharing if there isn't good governance in place. It's helpful, then, to identify the common aspects that may be beneficial for every team and coordinate the code-sharing effort across teams. Architects and tech leaders are in the perfect position to do this, since they work with multiple teams and have a high-level picture of how the system works and what it requires.

Naming convention

In polyrepo environments, I've often seen a proliferation of names without any specific convention; this quickly compounds the issue of tracking what is available and where. Regulating a naming convention for every repository is critical in a polyrepo system because working with micro-frontends, and maybe with microservices as well, could result in a huge number of repositories inside our version control system.

Best practice maintenance

In a monorepo environment, we have just one repository to maintain and control. In a polyrepo environment, it may take a while before every repository is in line with a newly defined best practice. Again, communication and process may mitigate this problem, but polyrepo requires you to think this through up front because finding out these problems during development will slow down your team's throughput.

Polyrepo is definitely a viable option for micro-frontends, though we risk having a proliferation of repositories. This complexity should be handled with clear and strong governance around naming conventions, repository discoverability, and processes. Micro-frontend projects with a vertical split have far fewer issues using polyrepo than those with a horizontal split, where our application is composed of tens, if not hundreds, of different parts. In the context of micro-frontends, polyrepo also makes it possible to use different approaches from a legacy project. In fact, we may introduce new tools or libraries just for the micro-frontend approach while keeping the same one for the legacy project without the need of polluting the best practices in place in the legacy platform. This flexibility has to be gauged against potential communication overhead and governance that has to be defined inside the organization; therefore, if you decide to use polyrepo, be aware of where your initial investment should be: communication flows across teams and governance.

A Possible Future for a Version Control System

Any of the different paths we can take with a version control system won't be a perfect solution, just the solution that works better in our context. It's always a trade-off. However, we may want to try a hybrid approach (see Figure 6-3), where we can minimize the pitfalls of both approaches and leverage their benefits. Because micro-frontends and microservices should be designed using domain-driven design, we may follow the subdomain and bounded context divisions for bundling all the projects that are included on a specific subdomain.

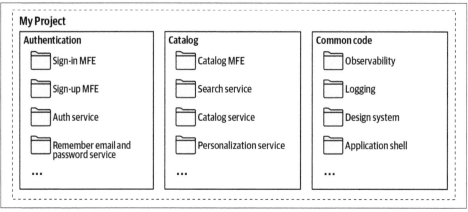

Figure 6-3. A hybrid repositories approach, where we can combine monorepo and polyrepo strengths in a unique solution

In this way, we can enforce the collaboration across teams responsible for different bounded contexts and work with contracts while benefiting from monorepo's strengths across all the teams working in the same subdomain. This approach might result in new practices, new tools to use or build, and new challenges, but it's an interesting solution worth exploring for microarchitectures.

Continuous Integration Strategies

After identifying the version control strategy, we have to think about the continuous integration method. Different CI implementations in different companies are the most successful and effective when owned by the developer teams rather than by an external guardian of the CI machines.

A lot of things have changed in the past few years. For one thing, developers, including frontend developers, have to become more aware of the infrastructure and tools needed for running their code because, in reality, building the application code in a reliable and quick pipeline is part of their job. In the past, I've seen many situations where the CI was delegated to other teams in the company, denying the developers a chance to change anything in the CI pipeline. As a result, the developers treated the automation pipeline as a black box—impossible to change but needed for deploying their artifacts to an environment. More recently, thanks to the DevOps culture spreading across organizations, these situations are becoming increasingly rare.

About DevOps

DevOps is the combination of cultural philosophies, practices, and tools that increases an organization's ability to deliver applications and services at high velocity. Under a DevOps model, development and operations teams are no longer siloed. Sometimes, they're merged into a single team, where the engineers work across the entire application life cycle, from development and test to deployment and operations, and develop a range of skills that aren't limited to a single function.

Nowadays, many companies are giving developers ownership of automation pipelines. That doesn't mean developers should be entitled to do whatever they want in the CI, but they definitely should have some skin in the game because how fast the feedback loop is closed depends mainly on them. The tech leadership team (architects, platform team, DX, tech leaders, engineers, managers, and so on) should provide the guidelines and the tools where the teams operate, while also providing certain flexibility inside those defined boundaries.

In a micro-frontend architecture, the CI is even more important because of the number of independent artifacts we need to build and deploy reliably. The developers, however, are responsible for running the automation strategy for their micro-frontends, using the right tool for the right job. This approach may seem like overkill considering that every micro-frontend may use a different set of tools. However, we usually end up having a couple of tools that perform similar tasks, and this approach also allows a healthy comparison of tools and approaches, helping teams to develop best practices.

More than once I would be walking the corridors and overhear conversations between engineers about how building tools like Rollup have some features or performances that the webpack tool didn't have in certain scenarios and vice versa. This, for me, is a sign of a great confrontation between tools tested in real scenarios rather than in a sandbox.

It's also important to recognize that there isn't a unique CI implementation for micro-frontends; a lot depends on the project, company standards, and the architectural approach. For instance, when implementing micro-frontends with a vertical split, all the stages of a CI pipeline would resemble normal SPA stages. End-to-end testing may be done before the deployment, if the automation strategy allows the creation of on-demand environments, and after the test is completed, the environment can be turned off. However, a horizontal split would require more thought on the right moment for performing a specific task. When performing end-to-end testing, we'd have to perform this phase in staging or production; otherwise, every single pipeline would need to be aware of the entire composition of an application, retrieving every latest version of the micro-frontends and pushing to an ephemeral environment—a solution very hard to maintain and evolve.

Testing Micro-Frontends

Plenty of books discuss the importance of testing our code and catching bugs or defects as early as possible, and the micro-frontends approach is no different.

Testing Strategies

I won't cover all the different possible testing strategies, such as unit testing, integration testing, or end-to-end testing. Instead, I'll cover the differences from a standard approach we are used to implementing in any frontend architecture. If you would like to become more familiar with different testing strategies, I recommend studying the materials shared by incredible authors like Kent Beck or Robert C. Martin (a.k.a. Uncle Bob), especially Beck's *Test-Driven Development: By Example* (Addison-Wesley Professional) and Martin's *Clean Code* (Pearson).

Working with micro-frontends doesn't mean changing the way we are dealing with frontend testing practices, but they do create additional complexity in the CI pipeline when we perform end-to-end testing. Since unit testing and integration testing are not changing compared to other frontend architectures, we'll focus here on end-to-end testing, as this is the biggest challenge for testing micro-frontends.

End-to-end testing

End-to-end testing is used to test whether the flow of an application from start to finish is behaving as expected. We perform tests to identify system dependencies and ensure that data integrity is maintained between various system components and systems. End-to-end testing may be performed before deploying our artifacts in production in an on-demand environment created at runtime just before tearing the environment down. Alternatively, when we don't have this capability in-house, we should perform end-to-end tests in existing environments after the deployment or promotion of a new artifact. In this case, the recommendation would be embracing testing in production when the application has implemented feature flags, allowing toggling of a feature on and off and granting access to test for a set of users.

Testing in production brings its own challenges, especially when a system is integrating with third-party APIs. However, it will save a lot of money on environment infrastructure, maintenance, and developers' resources because we don't have to configure and maintain multiple environments simultaneously. I'm conscious not all companies or projects are suitable for this practice; therefore, using the environments you have available is the last resort. When you start a new project or you have the possibility to change an existing one, take into consideration the possibility of introducing feature flags not only for reducing the risk of bugs in front of users but also for testing purposes.

Finally, some of the complexity brought in by micro-frontends may be mitigated with some good coordination across teams and solid governance overarching the testing process. As discussed multiple times in this book, the complexity of end-to-end testing varies depending on whether we embrace a horizontal or vertical split for our application.

Vertical-split end-to-end testing challenges

When we work with a vertical split, one team is responsible for an entire business subdomain of the application. In this case, testing all the logic paths inside the subdomain is not far from what you would do in an SPA. But we have some challenges to overcome when we need test use cases outside of the team's control, such as the scenario in Figure 6-4.

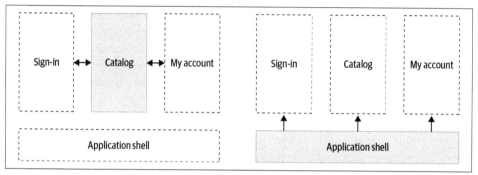

Figure 6-4. An end-to-end testing example with a vertical split architecture

The catalog team is responsible for testing all the scenarios related to the catalog. However, some scenarios involve areas not controlled by the catalog team, like when the user signs out from the application and should be redirected to the "Sign-in" micro-frontend or when a user wants to change something in their profile and should be redirected to the "My account" micro-frontend. In these scenarios, the catalog team will be responsible for writing tests that cross their domain boundary and ensuring that the specific micro-frontend the user should be redirected to loads correctly. In the same way, the teams responsible for the "Sign-in" and "My account" micro-frontends will need to test their business domain and verify that the catalog correctly loads as the user expects.

Another challenge is making sure our application behaves in cases of deep-linking requests or when we want to test different routing scenarios. It always depends on how we have designed our routing strategy, but let's take the example of having the routing logic in the application shell, as in Figure 6-4. The application shell team should be responsible for these tests, ensuring that the entire route of the application loads correctly, that the key behaviors like signing in or out work as expected, and that the application shell is capable of loading the right micro-frontend when a user requests a specific URL.

Horizontal-split end-to-end testing challenges

Using a horizontal split architecture raises the question of who is responsible for end-to-end testing of the final solution. Technically speaking, what we have discussed for the vertical-split architecture still stands, but we have a new level of complexity to manage. For instance, if a team is responsible for a micro-frontend present in multiple views, is the team responsible for end-to-end testing all the scenarios where their micro-frontends are present? Let's try to shed some light on this with the example in Figure 6-5.

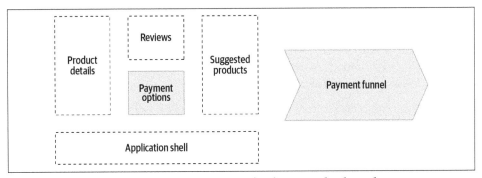

Figure 6-5. An end-to-end testing example with a horizontal-split architecture

The payments team is responsible for providing all the micro-frontends needed for performing a payment inside the project. In the horizontal-split architecture, their micro-frontends are available on multiple views. In Figure 6-5, we can see the payment option micro-frontend that will lead the user to choose a payment method and finalize the payment when they're ready to check out. Therefore, the payment team is responsible for making sure the user will be able to pick a payment option and finalize the checkout, showing the interface needed for performing the monetary transaction with the selected payment option in the following view. In this case, the payment team can perform the end-to-end test for this scenario, but we will need a lot of coordination and governance for analyzing all the end-to-end tests needed and then assigning them to the right teams to avoid duplication of intent, which is even more difficult to maintain in the long run.

The end-to-end tests also become more complex to maintain since different teams are contributing to the final output of a view, and some tests may become invalid or broken the moment other teams are changing their micro-frontends. That doesn't mean we aren't capable of doing end-to-end testing with a horizontal split, but it does require better organization and more thought before implementing.

Testing technical recommendations

For technically implementing end-to-end tests successfully for horizontal- or vertical-split architecture, we have three main possibilities. The first one is running all the end-to-end tests in a stable environment where all the micro-frontends are present. We delay the feedback loop if our new micro-frontend works as expected, end to end.

Another option is using on-demand environments where we pull together all the resources needed for testing our scenarios. This option may become complicated in a large application, however, especially when we use a horizontal-split architecture. This option may also cost us a lot when it's not properly configured (as described earlier).

Finally, we may decide to use a proxy server that will allow us to end-to-end test the micro-frontend we are responsible for. When we need to use any other part of the application involved in a test, we'll just load the parts needed from an environment, either staging or production—in this case, the micro-frontends and the application shell not developed by our team.

In this way, we can reduce the risk of unstable versions or optimization for generating an on-demand environment. The team responsible for the end-to-end testing won't have any external dependency to manage, either, but they will be completely able to test all the scenarios needed for ensuring the quality of their micro-frontend.

Webpack Dev Server Proxy Configuration

For completeness of information, webpack, as with many other building tools, allows us to configure a proxy server that retrieves external resources from specific URLs, like static files, or even consume APIs in a specific environment. This feature may be useful for setting up our end-to-end testing in a scenario where we want to run it during the CI pipeline. The configuration is trivial, as you can see in the following example:

```
// In webpack.config.js
{
  devServer: {
    proxy: {
      '/catalog-mfe': {
        target: 'https://other-server.example.com',
        secure: false
      }
    }
  }
}

// Multiple entry
proxy: [
  {
    context: ['/catalog-mfe/**', '/myaccount-mfe/**'],
    target: 'https://other-server.example.com',
    secure: false
  }
]
```

Additional information about the webpack proxy setup is available in the webpack documentation (*https://oreil.ly/9hcdL*).

When the tool used for running the automation pipeline allows it, you can also set up your CI to run multiple tests in parallel instead of in sequence. This will speed up the results of your tests specifically when you are running many of them at once; it can also be split in parts and grouped in a sensible manner. If we have a thousand unit tests to run, for example, splitting the effort into multiple machines or containers may save us time and get us results faster. This technique may also be applied to other stages of our CI pipeline. With just a little extra configuration by the development team, you can save time testing your code and gain confidence in it sooner. Even tools that work well for us can be improved, and systems evolve over time. Be sure to analyze your tools and any potential alternatives regularly to ensure you have the best CI tools for your purposes.

Fitness Functions

Considering the inherent complexity of distributed systems where multiple modules make up an entire platform, the architecture team should have a way to measure the impact of their architecture decisions and make sure these decisions are followed by all teams, whether they are colocated or distributed. In the book *Building Evolutionary Architecture* (O'Reilly), Neal Ford, Rebecca Parsons, and Patrick Kua discuss how to test an architecture's characteristics in CI with fitness functions. They state that a fitness function "provides an objective integrity assessment of some architectural characteristic(s)."

Many of the steps defined inside an automation pipeline are used to assess architecture characteristics such as static analyses in the shape of cyclomatic complexity or the bundle size in the micro-frontend use case. Having a fitness function that assesses the bundle size of a micro-frontend is a good idea when a key characteristic of your micro-frontend architecture is the size of the data downloaded by users. The architecture team may decide to introduce fitness functions inside the automation strategy, guaranteeing the agreed-upon outcome and trade-off that a micro-frontend application should have. Here are some key architecture characteristics to pay attention to when designing the automation pipeline for a micro-frontend project:

Bundle size
Allocate a budget size per micro-frontend and analyze when this budget is exceeded and why. In the case of shared libraries, also review the size of all the libraries shared, not only the ones built with micro-frontends.

Performance metrics
Tools like Lighthouse and WebPageTest allow us to validate whether a new version of our application has the same or higher standards than the current version.

Static analysis
There are plenty of tools for static analysis in the JavaScript ecosystem, with SonarQube probably being the most well-known. Implemented inside an automation pipeline, this tool will provide us insights such as the cyclomatic complexity of a project (in our case, a micro-frontend). We may also want to enforce

a high code-quality bar when setting a cyclomatic complexity threshold over which we don't allow the pipeline to finish until the code is refactored.

Code coverage
Another example of a fitness function is making sure our codebase is tested extensively. Code coverage provides a percentage of tests run against our project, but bear in mind that this metric doesn't provide us with the quality of the test, just a snapshot of tests written for public functions.

Security
Finally, we want to ensure our code won't violate any regulation or rules defined by the security or architecture teams.

These are some architecture characteristics that we may want to test in our automation strategy when we work with micro-frontends. In a distributed architecture like this one, these metrics become fundamental for architects and tech leads to understand the quality of the product developed, to understand where the tech debt lies, and to enforce key architecture characteristics without having to chase every team or be part of any feature development.

Introducing and maintaining fitness functions inside the automation strategy will provide several benefits for helping the team provide a fast feedback loop on architecture characteristics and helping the company achieve better code quality standards.

Micro-Frontend-Specific Operations

Some automation pipelines for micro-frontends may require additional steps compared to traditional frontend automation pipelines. The first one worth a mention would be checking that every micro-frontend is integrating specific libraries flagged as mandatory for every frontend artifact by the architecture team. Let's assume that we have developed a design system and we want to enforce that all our artifacts must contain the latest major version. In the CI pipeline, we should have a step for verifying the *package.json* file, making sure the design system library contains the right version. If it doesn't, it should notify the team or even block the build, failing the process.

The same approach may be feasible for other internal libraries we want to make sure are present in every micro-frontend, like analytics and observability. Considering the modular nature of micro-frontends, this additional step is highly recommended—no matter the architecture style we decide to embrace in this paradigm—for guaranteeing the integrity of our artifacts across the entire organization.

Another interesting approach, mainly available for vertical-split architecture, is the possibility of a server-side render at compile time instead of runtime when a user requests the page. The main reason for doing this is saving computation resources and costs, such as when we have to merge data and user interfaces that don't change very often. Another reason is to provide a highly optimized and fast-loading page with inline CSS and maybe even some JavaScript.

When our micro-frontend artifact results in an SPA with an HTML page as the entry point, we can generate a page skeleton with minimal CSS and HTML nodes inlined to suggest how a page would look, providing immediate feedback to the user while we are loading the rest of the resources needed for interacting with micro-frontends. This isn't an extensive list of possibilities an organization may want to evaluate for micro-frontends, because every organization has its own gotchas and requirements. However, these are all valuable approaches that are worth thinking about when we are designing an automation pipeline.

Deployment Strategies

The last stage of any automation strategy is the delivery of the artifacts created during the build phase. Whether we decide to deploy our code via continuous deployment, shell script running on premises, in a cloud provider, or via a user interface, understanding how we can deploy micro-frontends independently from each other is fundamental.

By their nature, micro-frontends should be independent. The moment we have to coordinate a deployment with multiple micro-frontends, we should question the decisions we made identifying their boundaries. Coupling risks jeopardize the entire effort of embracing this architecture, generating more issues than value for the company. With microarchitectures, we deploy only a small portion of code without impacting the entire codebase. As with micro-frontends and microservices, we may decide to move forward to avoid the possibility of breaking the application and, therefore, the user experience. We'll present the new version of a micro-frontend to a smaller group of users instead of doing a big-bang release to all our users. For this scope, the microservices world uses techniques like blue-green deployment and canary releases, where a portion of the traffic is redirected to a new microservice. Adapting these key techniques in any micro-frontend deployment strategy is worth considering.

Blue-Green Deployment Versus Canary Releases

Blue-green deployment starts with the assumption that the last stage of our tests should be done in the production environment we are running for the rest of our platform. After deploying a new version, we can test our new code in production without redirecting users to the new version while getting all the benefits of testing in the production environment. When all the tests pass, we are ready to redirect 100% of our traffic to the new version of our micro-frontend.

This strategy reduces the risk of deploying new micro-frontends because we can do all the testing needed without impacting our user base.

Another benefit of this approach is that we may decide to provision only two environments, testing and production; considering that all the tests are running in production with a safe approach, we're cutting infrastructure costs without having to support the staging environment. As you can see in Figure 6-6, we have a router that should aim for shaping the traffic toward the right version.

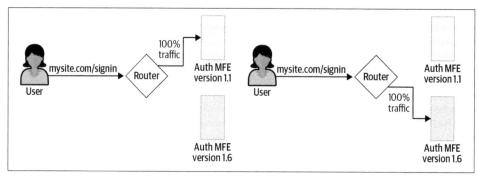

Figure 6-6. Blue-green deployment

In canary releases, we don't switch all of the traffic to a new version after all tests pass. Instead, we gradually ease the traffic to a new micro-frontend version. As we monitor the metrics from the live traffic consuming our new frontend, such as increased error rates or less user engagement), we may decide to increase or decrease the traffic accordingly (see Figure 6-7).

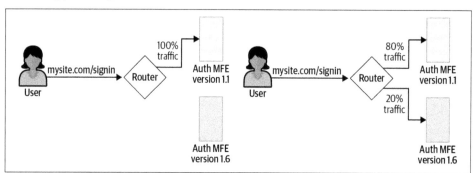

Figure 6-7. Canary release

In both approaches, we need to have a router that shapes the traffic (for a canary release) or switches the traffic from one version to another (blue-green deployment). The router could be some logic handled on the client side, server side, or edge side, depending on the architecture chosen. We summarize the options available in Table 6-1.

Table 6-1. Router options available for canary releases and blue-green deployments

	Blue-green deployment or canary release mechanism
Client-side routing	Application shell
	Configuration passed via static JSON or backend APIs
Edge-side routing	Logic running at the edge (e.g., AWS Lambda@Edge)
Server-side routing	Application server logic
	API gateway
	Load balancer

Let's explore some scenarios for leveraging these techniques in a micro-frontend architecture.

When we compose our micro-frontends at a client-side level using an application shell, for instance, we may extend the application shell logic, loading a configuration containing the micro-frontend versions available and the percentage of traffic to be presented with a specific version. For instance, we may want to load a configuration similar to the following example for shaping the traffic, issuing a cookie or storing in web storage the version the user was assigned to and changing it to a different version when we are sure our micro-frontend doesn't contain critical bugs:

```
{
    "homepage":{
        "v.1.1.0": {
            "traffic": 20,
            "url": "acme.com/mfes/homepage-1_1_0.html"
        },
        "v.1.2.2": {
            "traffic": 80,
            "url": "acme.com/mfes/homepage-1_2_2.html"
        }
    },
    "signin":{
        "v.4.0.0": {
            "traffic": 90,
            "url": "acme.com/mfes/signin-4_0_0.html"
        },
        "v.4.1.5": {
            "traffic": 10,
            "url": "acme.com/mfes/signin-4_1_5.html"
        }
    }

    ...
}
```

As you can see in this configuration example, we have defined the micro-frontends associated to a given route, the micro-frontend version, and the traffic we want to route toward a specific version.

For another project, we may decide that introducing a canary release mechanism inside the application shell logic is not worth the effort, moving this logic to the edge using Lambda@Edge, executing the lambda function in AWS locations closer to the user. In the canary release mechanism to the edge, the decision of which version to serve the user is made to the closest AWS region so latency is reduced. In addition, architecturally speaking, we are decoupling an infrastructure duty from the codebase of our application shell.

Lambda@Edge Canary Releases

During AWS re:Invent 2019, I had the opportunity to be part of a talk about the implementation done inside DAZN for handling canary releases, strangler pattern, and dynamic rendering. That talk is available on YouTube (*https://youtu.be/ fT-5RHTtFNg*), if you are interested in the details of how to implement a similar solution using edge computing.

With a horizontal-split implementation, where we assemble at runtime different micro-frontends, introducing either blue-green or canary should be performed at the application server level when we compose the page to be served. We may decide to do it at the client-side level as well. However, as you can imagine, the number of micro-frontends to handle may matter, and mapping all of them may result in a large configuration to be loaded client side. So we create a system for serving just the configuration needed for a given URL to the client side. Other options include releasing different composition logic and testing them using an API gateway or a load balancer for shaping the traffic toward a server cluster hosting the new implementation and the one hosting the previous version. In this way, we rely on the infrastructure to handle the logic for canary release or blue-green deployment instead of implementing, and maintaining, logic inside the application server.

As you can see, the concept of the router present in Figures 6-6 and 6-7 may be expressed in different ways based on the architecture embraced and the context you are operating in.

Moreover, the context should drive the decision; there may be strong reasons for implementing the canary releases at a different infrastructure layer based on the environment we operate in.

Strangler Pattern

Blue-green deployment and canary releases help when we have a micro-frontend architecture deployed in production. But what if we are scaling an existing web application introducing micro-frontends? In this scenario, we have two options: we either wait until the entire application is rewritten with micro-frontends or we can apply the microservices ecosystem's well-known strangler pattern (*https://oreil.ly/cCGmk*) to our frontend application. The strangler pattern comes from the idea of generating incremental value for the business and the user by releasing parts of the application instead of waiting for the wholly new application to be ready.

Basically, with micro-frontends, we can tackle an area of the application where we think we may generate value for the business, build with micro-frontends, and deploy them in the production environment living alongside the legacy application. In this way, we can provide value steadily, while the frequent releases allow you to monitor progress more carefully, drifting toward the right direction for our business and our final implementation. Using the strangler pattern is very compelling for many businesses, mainly because it allows them to experiment and gather valuable data directly from production without relying solely on projections. The initial investment for the developer's teams is pretty low and can immediately generate benefit for the final user. Moreover, this approach becomes very useful for the developers for understanding whether the reasoning behind releasing the first micro-frontends was correct or needs to be tweaked, because it forces the team to think about a problem smaller than the entire application and try the approach out end to end, from conception to release, learning along the way which stage they should improve, if any.

As we can see in Figure 6-8, when a user requests a page living in the micro-frontend implementation, a router is responsible for serving it. When an area of the application is not yet ready for micro-frontends, the router would redirect the user to the legacy platform.

Every time we develop a new part of the application, it will replace another part of the legacy application until the whole legacy application is completely replaced by the micro-frontend platform. Implementing the strangler pattern has some challenges, of course. You'll need to make some changes in the legacy application to make this mechanism work properly, particularly when the micro-frontend application isn't living alongside the legacy application infrastructure but may live in a different subdomain. For instance, the legacy application should be aware that the area covered by the micro-frontend implementation shouldn't be served anymore from its codebase but should redirect the user to an absolute URL so the router logic will kick in again for redirecting the user to the right part of the application.

Another challenge is finding a way to quickly redirect users from micro-frontends to another version in case of errors. A technique we used for rolling out our new micro-frontend platform was to maintain three versions of our application for a period of time: the legacy, the legacy modified for coexisting with the micro-frontends (called the hybrid), and the micro-frontend platform. With this approach, we could always serve the hybrid and the micro-frontend platform, and in the extreme case of an issue we weren't able to fix quickly, we were able to redirect all the traffic to the legacy platform.

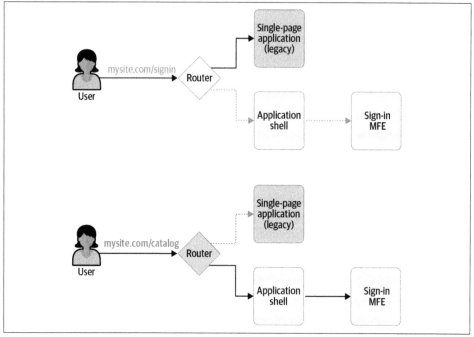

Figure 6-8. A strangler pattern where the micro-frontends live alongside the legacy application so that we can create immediate value for the users and the company instead of waiting for the entire application to be developed

This configuration was maintained for several months until we were ready with other micro-frontends. During that time, we were able to improve the platform as expected by the business.

In some situations, this may look like an over-engineered solution, but our context didn't allow us to have downtime in production, so we had to find a strategy for providing value for our users as well for the company. The strangler pattern let us explore the risks our company was comfortable taking and then, after analyzing them, design the right implementation.

Observability

The last important part to take into consideration in a successful micro-frontend architecture is the observability of our micro-frontends. Moreover, observability closes the feedback loop when our code runs in a production environment; otherwise, we would not be able to react quickly to any incidents happening during prime time. In the last few years, many observability tools started to appear for the frontend ecosystem, such as Sentry, New Relic, or LogRocket. These tools allow us to individuate the user journey before encountering a bug that may or may not prevent the user from completing the action. Observability is a must-have feature; nowadays, it should be part of any releasing strategy and is even more important when we are implementing distributed architectures such as micro-frontends.

Every micro-frontend should report errors—custom and generic—for providing visibility when a live issue happens. In that regard, Sentry, New Relic, or LogRocket can help in this task by providing the visibility needed. In fact, these tools are retrieving the user journey, collecting the JavaScript stack trace of an exception, and clustering into groups. We can configure the alerting of every type of error or warning in these tools dashboards and even plug these tools with alerting systems like PagerDuty.

It's very important to think about observability at a very early stage of the process because it plays a fundamental role in closing the feedback loop for developers, especially when we are dealing with multiple micro-frontends composing the same view. These tools will help us to debug and understand in which part of our codebase the problem is happening and quickly drive a team to the resolution, providing some user's context information like browser used, operating system, user's country, and so on. All this information, in combination with the stack trace, provides a clear investigation path for any developer to resolve the problem without spending hours trying to reproduce a bug in the developer's machine or in a testing environment.

Summary

We've covered a lot of ground here, so a recap is in order. First, we defined the principles we want to achieve with automation pipelines, focusing on fast feedback and constant review based on the evolution of both tech and the company. Then we talked about the developer experience. If we aren't able to provide a frictionless experience, developers may try to game the system or use it only when it's strictly necessary, reducing the benefits they can have with a well-designed CI/CD pipeline. We next discussed implementing the automation strategy, including all the best practices, such as unit, integration, and end-to-end testing; bundle-size checks; fitness functions; and many others that could be implemented in our automation strategy for guiding developers toward the right software quality. After building our artifact and performing some additional quality reviews, we are ready to deploy our micro-frontends. We addressed testing the final results in production using canary or blue-green deployment to reduce the risk of presenting bugs to the users and releasing as quickly and as often as possible without fear of breaking the entire application.

Finally, we discussed using the strangler pattern when we have an existing application and want to provide immediate value to our business and users. Such a pattern will steadily reduce the functionalities served to the user by a legacy application and increase the one in our micro-frontend platform.

Automation is a very interesting topic, especially when we are implementing micro-architectures. There are plenty of additional topics we could cover, but if you are capable of covering these inside your automation strategy, you will be in really great shape, and you can always extend and evolve based on the business and technical needs. The main takeaway is that automation is not a one-off action but an iterative process that has to be reviewed and improved with the life cycle of a product.

CHAPTER 7

Automation Pipeline for Micro-Frontends: A Case Study

Now that we've discussed the theory of a micro-frontend automation pipeline, let's review a use case example, including the different steps that should be taken into consideration based on the topics we covered. Let's keep in mind that not all the steps or the configuration described in this example have to be present in every automation strategy, because companies and projects are different.

Setting the Scene

ACME Inc., a video-streaming service, empowers its developers and trusts them to know better than anyone else in the organization which tools they should use for building the micro-frontends needed for the project. Every team is responsible for setting up a micro-frontend build, so the developers are encouraged to choose the tools needed based on the technical needs of micro-frontends and on some boundaries, or guardrails, defined by the company.

The company uses a custom cloud automation pipeline based on docker containers, and the cloud team provides the tools needed for running these pipelines. The project is structured using micro-frontends with a vertical-split architecture, where micro-frontends are technically represented by an HTML page, a JavaScript file, and a CSS file. Every development team in the organization works with unit, integration, and end-to-end testing, a decision made by the tech leaders and the head of engineering to ensure the quality and reliability of code deployed in production.

The architecture team, which is the bridge between product and engineers, requests using fitness functions within the pipeline to ensure the artifacts delivered in the production environment contain the architecture characteristics they desire. The team will be responsible for translating product people's business requirements to technical ones the techies can create.

The development teams decide to use a monorepo strategy, so all the micro-frontends will be present in the same repository. The team will use trunk-based development for its branching strategy and release directly from the main branch instead of creating a release branch.

The project won't use feature flags. The team decides to defer this decision for having fewer moving parts to take care of, so manual and automated testing will be performed in existing environments already created by the DX team.

Finally, for bug fixing, the teams will use a fix-forward strategy, where they will fix bugs in the trunk branch and then deploy. The environment strategy present in the company is composed of three environments: development (DEV), staging (STAGE), and production (PROD), as we can see in Figure 7-1.

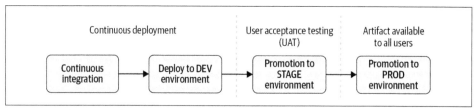

Figure 7-1. An example of an environments strategy

The DEV environment is in continuous deployment so that the developers can see the results of their implementations as quickly as possible. When a team feels ready to move to the next step, it can promote the artifact to user acceptance testing (UAT). At this stage, the UAT team will make sure the artifact respects all the business requirements before promoting the artifact to production, where it will be consumed by the final user. Based on all this, Figure 7-2 illustrates the automation strategy for our use case project up to the DEV environment. It's specifically designed for delivering the micro-frontends at the desired quality.

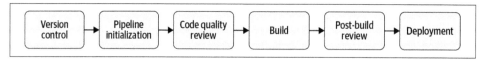

Figure 7-2. High-level automation strategy design

A dashboard built in-house will promote artifacts across environments. In this way, the developers and quality assurance have full control of the different steps for reviewing an artifact before it is presented to users. Such an automation strategy will create a constant, fast feedback loop for the developers, catching potential issues as soon as possible during the continuous integration phase instead of further down the line, making the bug fixing as cheap as possible.

Defect Costs Rise over Time

Remember, the cost of detecting and fixing defects in software increases exponentially over time in the software development workflow. That's because when a developer is working on a feature, the code developed is fresh in their mind; a code change is fairly trivial. When a developer catches bugs in production, months may have passed since the developer worked on that code. In the meantime, the developer will have worked on several other projects or features, so remembering the team's entire logic and approach will take time. Finding bugs in production costs you more than just time. It hurts the company's credibility and costs more money than just investing in a fast feedback loop at the beginning. The National Institute of Standards and Technology estimates the cost of fixing bugs in production (*https://oreil.ly/2HEGi*) to be 25 times more expensive than catching them during the development phase.

The automation strategy in this project is composed of six key areas, within which there are multiple steps:

1. Version control
2. Pipeline initialization
3. Code-quality review
4. Build
5. Post-build review
6. Deployment

Let's explore these areas in detail.

Version Control

The project will use monorepo for version control, so the developers decided to use Lerna (*https://lerna.js.org*), which enables them to manage all the different micro-frontend dependencies at the same time. Lerna also allows hoisting all the shared modules across projects in the same node_modules folder in the root directory, so that if a developer has to work on multiple projects, they can download a resource for multiple micro-frontends just once. Dependencies will be shared, so a unique bundle can be downloaded once by a user and will have a high time-to-live time at CDN level. Considering the vendors aren't changing as often as the application's business logic, we'll avoid an increase of traffic to the origin.

ACME Inc. uses GitHub as a version control system, partially because there are always interesting automation opportunities in a cloud-based system like GitHub. In fact, GitHub has a marketplace (*https://oreil.ly/qoq1a*) with many scripts available to be run at different branching life cycles. For instance, we may want to apply linting rules at every commit or when someone is opening a pull request. We can also decide to run our own scripts if we have particular tasks to apply in our codebase during an opening of a pull request, like scanning the code to avoid any library secrets being presented or for other security reasons.

Pipeline Initialization

The pipeline initialization stage includes several common actions to perform for every micro-frontend, including:

- Cloning the micro-frontend repository inside a container
- Installing all the dependencies needed for the following steps

In Figure 7-3, we can see the first part of our automation pipeline where we perform two key actions: cloning the micro-frontend repository and installing the dependencies via yarn or npm command, depending on each team's preference.

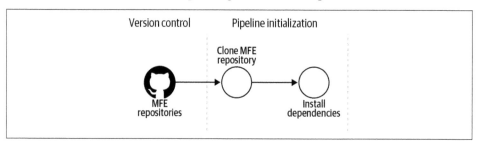

Figure 7-3. Pipeline initialization stage, showing two actions: cloning the repository and installing the dependencies

The most important thing to remember is to make the repository cloning as fast as possible. We don't need the entire repository history for a CI process, so it's a good practice to use the command depth for retrieving just the last commit, especially when we use a monorepo approach, considering the repository may grow in size very quickly. The cloning operation will speed up in particular when we are dealing with repositories with years of history tracked in the version control system:

```
git clone --depth [depth] [remote-url]
```

An example would be:

```
git clone --depth 1 https://github.com/account/repository
```

Code-Quality Review

During this phase, we are performing all the checks to make sure the code implemented respects the company standards. Figure 7-4 shows several stages, from static analysis to visual tests. For this project, the company decided not only to cover unit and integration testing but also to ensure that the code was maintainable in the long term, the user interface integration respects the design guidelines from the UX team, and the common libraries developed are present inside the micro-frontends and respect the minimum implementations.

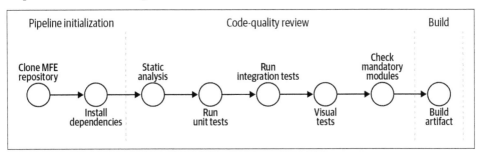

Figure 7-4. Code-quality checks like unit testing, static analysis, and visual regression tests

For static analysis, ACME Inc. uses SonarQube (*https://oreil.ly/Y0BN4*) with the Java-Script plug-in. SonarQube is a tool for static analysis, and it retrieves many metrics, including cyclomatic complexity (CYC), which tech leaders and architects who aren't working every day in the codebase need in order to understand the code quality produced by a team. Often underestimated, CYC can provide a lot of useful information about how healthy your project is. It provides a score on the code complexity based on the number of branches inside every function, which is an objective way to understand if the micro-frontend is simple to read but harder to maintain in the long run.

Let's consider this example:

```
const myFunc = (someValue) =>{
    // variable definitions

    if(someValue === "1234-5678"){ //CYC: 1 - first branch
// do something
} else if(someValue === "9876-5432"){ //CYC: 2 - second branch
    // do something else
} else { //CYC: 3 - third branch
    // default case
}

// return something
}
```

This function has a CYC score of 3, which means we will need at least three unit tests for this function. It may also indicate that the logic managed inside the function starts to become complex and harder to maintain.

By comparison, a CYC score of 10 means a function definitely requires some refactoring and simplification; we want to keep our CYC score as low as possible so that any change to the code will be easier for us but also for other developers inside or outside our team.

Unit and integration testing are becoming more important every day, and the tools for JavaScript are becoming better. Developers, as well as their companies, must recognize the importance of automated testing before deploying in production. With micro-frontends, we should invest in these practices mainly because the area to test per team is far smaller than a normal single-page application and the related complexity should be lower. Considering the size of the business logic as well, testing micro-frontends should be very quick. There aren't any excuses for avoiding this step.

ACME Inc. decided to use Jest (*https://jestjs.io*) for unit and integration testing, which is standard within the company. Since there isn't a specific tool for testing micro-frontends, the company's standard tool will be fine for unit and integration tests.

The final step is specific to a micro-frontend architecture: checking on implementing specific libraries, like logging or observability, across all the micro-frontends inside a project. When we develop a micro-frontend application, there are some parts we want to write once and put in all our micro-frontends. A check on the libraries present in every micro-frontend will help enforce these controls, making sure that all the micro-frontends respect the company's guidelines and we aren't reinventing the wheel. Controlling the presence inside the *package.json* file present in every JavaScript project is a simple way to do this; however, we can go a step further by implementing more complex reviews, like library versions, analysis on the implementation, and so on. It's very important to customize an automation pipeline introducing these kinds of fitness functions to ensure the architectural decisions are respected despite the nature of this architecture. Moreover, with micro-frontends where sharing code across them may result in way more coordination than a monolithic codebase, these kinds of steps are fundamental for having a positive end result.

Build

The artifact is created during the build stage. For this project, the teams are using webpack (*http://webpack.js.org*) for performing any code optimizations (like minifying). Micro-frontends allow us to use different tools for building our code; in fact, it may be normal to use webpack for building and optimizing certain micro-frontends and using another tool for others. The important thing to remember is to provide freedom to the teams inside certain boundaries. If you have any particular requirements that should be applied at build time, raise them with the teams and make sure when a new tool is introduced inside the build phase—and generally inside the automation pipeline—it has the capabilities required for maintaining the boundaries. Introducing a new build tool is not a problem per se, because we can experiment and compare the results from the teams. We may even discover new capabilities and techniques we wouldn't find otherwise. Yet we don't *have* to use different tools. It's perfectly fine if all the teams agree on a set of tools to use across the entire automation pipeline; however, don't block innovation. Sometimes we discover interesting results from an approach different from the one agreed to at the beginning of the project.

Post-Build Review

The post-build stage (shown in Figure 7-5) is the last opportunity to confirm our artifact has all the performance characteristics and requirements ready to be deployed in production.

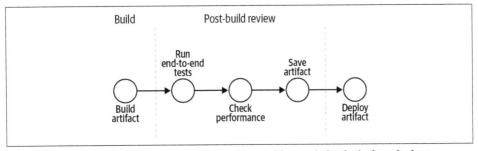

Figure 7-5. In the post-build review, we perform additional checks before deploying an artifact to an environment

A key step is storing the artifact in an artifacts repository, like Nexus or Artifactory. You may also decide to use a simpler storage solution, like an Amazon Web Services (AWS) S3 bucket. The important thing is to have a unique source of truth where all your artifacts are stored.

ACME Inc. decided to introduce additional checks during this stage: end-to-end testing and performance review. Whether these two checks are performed at this stage depends on the automation strategy we have in place and the capability of the system. In this example, we are assuming that the company can spin up a static environment for running end-to-end testing and performance checks and then tear it down when these tests are completed.

End-to-end testing is critical for micro-frontends. In this case where we have a vertical split and the entire user experience is inside the same artifact, testing the entire micro-frontend like we usually do for single-page applications is natural. However, if we have multiple micro-frontends in the same view with a horizontal split, we should postpone end-to-end testing to a later stage in order to test the entire view.

When we cannot afford to create and maintain on-demand environments, we might use web servers that are proxying the parts not related to a micro-frontend. For instance, webpack's dev server plug-in can be configured to fetch all the resources requested by an application during end-to-end tests locally or remotely, specifying from which environment to pull the resources when not related to the build artifact. If a micro-frontend is used in multiple views, we should check whether the code will work end to end in every view the micro-frontend is used.

Although end-to-end testing is becoming more popular in frontend development, there are several schools of thought about when to perform the test. You may decide to test in production—as long as all the features needed to sustain testing in that environment are present. Therefore, be sure to include feature flags, potential mock data, and coordination when integrating with third parties to avoid unexpected and undesirable side effects.

Performance checks have become far easier to perform within an automation pipeline, thanks to command-line interface (CLI) tools now being available to be wrapped inside a docker container and being easy to integrate into any automation pipeline. There are many alternatives, however. I recommend starting with Lighthouse (*https://oreil.ly/ip4Ap*) CLI or webhint (*https://webhint.io*) CLI. The former is a well-known tool created by Google and present even in Chrome browser, while the latter allows us to create additional performance tests for enhancing the list of tests already available by default.

With one of these two solutions implemented in our automation strategy, we can make sure our artifact respects key metrics, like performance, accessibility, and best practices. Ideally, we should be able to gather these metrics for every artifact in order to compare them during the lifespan of the project. In this way, we can review the improvements and regressions of our micro-frontends and organize meetings with the tech leadership for analyzing the results and determining potential improvements, creating a continuous learning environment inside our organization.

With these steps implemented, we make sure our micro-frontends deployed in production are functioning (through end-to-end testing) and performing as expected when the architectural characteristics are identified.

Deployment

The last step in our example is the deployment of a micro-frontend. An AWS S3 bucket will serve as the final platform to the user, and Cloudfront will be our CDN. As a result, the CDN layer will take the traffic hit, and there won't be any scalability issues to take care of in production, despite the shape of user traffic that may hit the web platform. An AWS Lambda—an event-driven serverless computing platform provided by Amazon as a part of Amazon Web Services—will be triggered to decompress the *tar.gz* file present in the artifacts repository, and then the content will be deployed inside the dev environment bucket. Remember that the company built a deployment dashboard for promoting the artifacts through different environments. In this case, for every promotion, the dashboard triggers an AWS Lambda for copying the files from one environment to another.

ACME Inc. decided to create a very simple infrastructure for hosting its micro-frontends, neatly avoiding additional investments in order to understand how to scale the additional infrastructure needed for serving micro-frontends. Obviously, this is not always the case. But I encourage you to find the cheapest, easiest way for hosting and maintaining your micro-frontends. You'll remove some complexities to be handled in production and have fewer moving parts that may fail.

Automation Strategy Summary

Every area of this automation strategy (shown in Figure 7-6) is composed of one or more steps to provide a feedback loop to the development teams for different aspects of the development process from different testing strategies, like unit testing or end-to-end testing, visual regression, bundle-size check, and many others. All of these controls create confidence in the delivery of high-quality content. This strategy also provides developers with a useful and constant reminder of the best practices leveraged inside the organization, guiding them to delivering what the business wants.

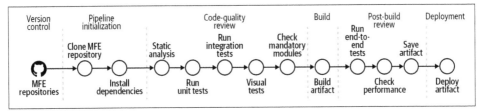

Figure 7-6. The end-to-end automation strategy diagram

The automation strategy shared in this chapter is one of many a company may decide to use. Different micro-frontend architectures will require additional or fewer steps than the ones described here. However, this automation strategy covers the main stages for ensuring a good result for a micro-frontend architecture.

Remember that the automation strategy evolves with the business and the architecture; therefore, after the first implementation, review it often with the development teams and the tech leadership. When automation serves the purpose of your micro-frontends well, implementation has a greater chance to be successful.

As we have seen, an automation strategy for micro-frontends doesn't differ too much from a traditional one used for an SPA. I recommend organizing some retrospectives every other month with architects, tech leaders, and representatives of every team to review and enhance such an essential cog in the software development process. And since every micro-frontend should have its own pipeline, the DX team is perfectly positioned to automate the infrastructure configurations as much as possible in order to have a frictionless experience when new micro-frontends arise. Using containers allows a DX team to focus on the infrastructure, providing the boundaries needed for a team implementing its automation pipeline.

Summary

In this chapter, we have reviewed a possible automation strategy for micro-frontends based on many concepts from the previous chapter. Your organization may benefit from some of these stages, but bear in mind that you need to constantly review the goals you want to achieve in your automation strategy. This is a fundamental step for succeeding with micro-frontends. Avoid it, and you may risk the entire project. The nature of micro-frontends requires an investment in creating a frictionless automation pipeline and enhancing it constantly. When a company starts to struggle to build and deploy regularly, that's a warning that the automation strategy probably needs to be reviewed and reassessed. Don't underestimate the importance of a good automation strategy; it may change the final outcome of your projects.

CHAPTER 8

Backend Patterns for Micro-Frontends

You may think that micro-frontends are a possible architecture only when you combine them with microservices because we can have end-to-end technology autonomy. Maybe you're thinking that your monolith architecture would never support micro-frontends, or even that having a monolith on the API layer would mean mirroring the architecture on the frontend as well. However, that's not the case. There are several nuances to take into consideration, and micro-frontends can definitely be used in combination with microservices and monolith. In this chapter, we review some possible integrations between the frontend and backend layers. In particular, we analyze how micro-frontends can work in combination with a monolith, with microservices, and even with the backend-for-frontend (BFF) pattern. Also, we will discuss the best patterns to integrate with different micro-frontends implementations, such as the vertical split, the horizontal split with a client-side composition, and the horizontal split with server-side composition. Finally, we will explore how GraphQL can be a valid solution for micro-frontends as a single entry point for our APIs.

API Integration and Micro-Frontends

Let's start by defining the different API approaches we may have in a web application. As shown in Figure 8-1, we focus our journey on the most used and well-known patterns. This doesn't mean micro-frontends work only with these implementations. You can devise the right approach for a WebSocket (a two-way computer communication protocol over a single TCP) or hypermedia, for instance, by learning how to deal with BFF, API gateway, or service dictionary patterns. (REST can be used with hypermedia links in the response contents, and the client that consumes the API can dynamically navigate to the appropriate resources by traversing the hypermedia links.)

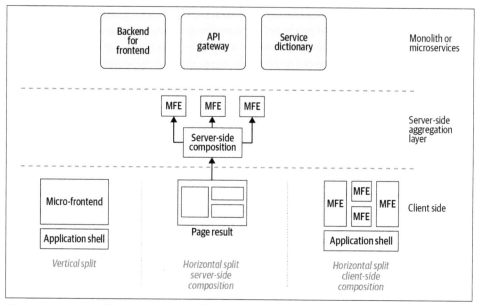

Figure 8-1. Micro-frontends and API layers

The patterns we analyze in this chapter are:

Service dictionary

> The service dictionary is just a list of services available for the client to consume. It's used mainly when we are developing an API layer with a monolith or modular monolith architecture; however, it can also be implemented with a microservices architecture with an API gateway, among other architectures. A service dictionary avoids the need to create shared libraries, environment variables, or configurations injected during the CI process or to have all the endpoints hardcoded inside the frontend codebase. The dictionary is loaded for the first time when the micro-frontend loads, allowing the client to retrieve the URLs to consume directly from the service dictionary.

API gateway

> Well-known in the microservices community, an API gateway is a single entry point for a microservices architecture. The clients can consume the APIs developed inside microservices through one gateway. The API gateway also allows centralizing a set of capabilities, such as:

Token validation

> Validating the signature of a token prior to passing the request on to a microservice.

Visibility and reporting
> We have a centralized way to verify all the inbound and outbound traffic.

Rate-limiting
> API gateway rejects the request after exceeding a specific threshold. For instance, we can set 100 requests per second as a limit from a client. When the limit is exceeded, the API gateway returns errors instead of calling the microservice to fulfill the request.

BFF
> The BFF is an extension of the API gateway pattern, creating a single entry point per client type. For instance, we may have a BFF for the web application, another for mobile, and a third for the Internet of Things (IoT) devices we are commercializing. BFF reduces the chattiness between client and server, aggregating the API responses and returning an easy data structure for the client to be parsed and rendered inside a user interface, allowing a great degree of freedom to shape APIs dedicated to a client, and reducing the round trips between a client and the backend layer.

These patterns are not mutually exclusive, either; they can be combined to work together.

An additional possibility worth mentioning is writing an API endpoints library for the client side shared across multiple micro-frontends. However, I discourage this practice with micro-frontends because we risk embedding an older library version in some of them, and the user interface may have some issues like outdated information or even errors due to dismissal of some APIs. Without strong governance and discipline around this library, we risk having certain micro-frontends using the wrong version of an API.

Domain-driven design (DDD) also influences architecture and infrastructure decisions. Especially with microarchitectures, we can divide an application into multiple business domains, using the right approach for each business domain. For instance, it's not unusual to have part of the application exposing the APIs with a BBF pattern and another part exposing with a service dictionary. This level of flexibility provides architects and developers with a variety of choices not possible before. At the same time, however, we need to be careful not to fragment the client-server communication too much and instead introduce a new pattern when it provides a real benefit for our application.

Working with a Service Dictionary

A service dictionary is nothing more than a list of endpoints available in the API layer provided to a micro-frontend. This allows the API to be consumed without the need to bake the endpoints inside the client-side code to inject them during a continuous integration pipeline or in a shared library. Usually, a service dictionary is provided via a static JSON file or an API that should be consumed as the first request for a micro-frontend (in the case of a vertical-split architecture) or an application shell (in the case of a horizontal split). A service dictionary may also be integrated into existing configuration files or APIs to reduce the round trips to the server and optimize the client startup. In this case, we can have a JSON object containing a list of configurations needed for our clients, where one of the elements is the service dictionary.

Here is an example of service dictionary structure:

```
{
"my_amazing_api": {
        "v1": "https://api.acme.com/v1/my_amazing_api",
        "v2": "https://api.acme.com/v2/my_amazing_api",
        "v3": "https://api.acme.com/v3/my_amazing_api"
    },
    "my_super_awesome_api": {
        "v1": "https://api.acme.com/v1/my_super_awesome_api"
    }
}
```

As you can see, we are listing all the APIs supported by the backend. Thanks to API versioning, we can handle cross-platform applications without introducing breaking changes because each client can use the API version that suits it better. One thing we can't control in such scenarios is the presence of a new version in every mobile device. When we release a new version of a mobile application, updating may take several days, if not weeks, and in some situations, it may take even longer. Therefore, versioning the APIs is important to ensure we don't harm our user experience. Reviewing the cadence of when to dismiss an API version, then, is important.

One of the main reasons is that potential attacks may harm our platform's stability. Usually, when we upgrade an API to a new version, we are improving not only the business logic but also the security. But unless this change can be applicable to all the versions of a specific API, it would be better to assess whether the APIs are still valid for legitimate users and then decide whether to dismiss the support of an API. To create a frictionless experience for our users, implementing a forced upgrade in every application released via an executable (mobile, smart TVs, or consoles) may be a solution, preventing the user from accessing older applications due to drastic updates in our APIs or even in our business model. Therefore, we must think about how to mitigate these scenarios in order to create a smooth user experience for our customers.

Endpoint discoverability is another reason to use a service dictionary. Not all companies work with cross-functional teams; many still work with components teams, with some teams fully responsible for the frontend of an application and others for the backend. Using a service dictionary allows every frontend team to be aware of what's happening in other teams. If a new version of an API is available or a brand-new API is exposed in the service dictionary, the frontend team will be aware. This is also a valid argument for cross-functional teams when we develop a cross-functional application. In fact, it's very unlikely that inside a "two-pizza team" we would be able to have all the knowledge needed for developing web, backend, mobile (iOS and Android), and maybe even smart TVs and console applications, considering many of these devices are supporting HTML and JavaScript.

A Two-Pizza Team

According to Jeff Bezos, CEO of Amazon, if a team can't be fed with two pizzas, it's too big. The introduction of the two-pizza rule in Amazon meant every team should be no larger than eight or nine people, which two pizzas would be enough to feed! The reasoning behind this rule isn't to save money on pizzas. It's based on the number of links between people inside a team. There is a formula for calculating the links between members in a group: $n(n - 1) / 2$, where n corresponds to the number of people. For instance, if a team has 6 people, there will be 15 links between everyone. Double the team to 12 members, and there will be 66 links. Complexity grows exponentially, not linearly, creating a higher risk of missing information across all the team's members.

Using a service dictionary allows every team to have a list of available APIs in every environment just by checking the dictionary. We often think the problem is just a communication issue that can be resolved with better communication. However, look again at the number of links in a 12-person team. Forgetting to update a team regarding a new API version may happen more often than not. A service dictionary helps introduce the discussion with the team responsible for the API, especially in large organizations with distributed teams.

Last but not least, a service dictionary is also helpful for testing micro-frontends with new endpoint versions while in production. A company that uses a testing-in-production strategy can expand that to its micro-frontend architecture, thanks to the service dictionary, all without affecting the standard user experience. We can test new endpoints in production by providing a specific header recognized by our service dictionary service. The service will interpret the header value and respond with a custom service dictionary used for testing new endpoints directly in production. We would choose to use a header instead of a token or any other type of authentication because it covers authenticated and unauthenticated use cases.

Figure 8-2 shows a high-level design of what the implementation would look like. We can see that the application shell consumes the service dictionary API as the first step. But this time, the application shell passes a header with an ID related to the configuration to load. In this example, the ID was generated at runtime by the application shell. When the service dictionary receives the call, it will check whether a header is present in the request and, if so, it will try to load the associated configuration stored inside the database.

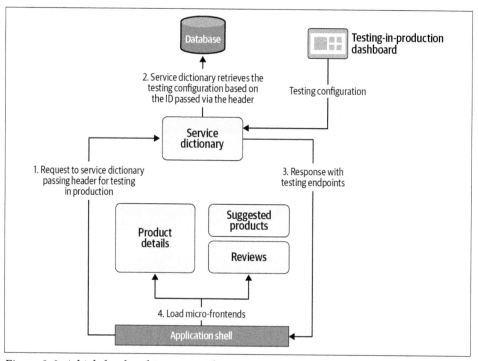

Figure 8-2. A high-level architecture on how to use a service dictionary for testing in production

It then returns the response to the application shell with the specific service dictionary requested. The application shell is now ready to load the micro-frontends to compose the page. Finally, the custom endpoint configuration associated with the client ID is produced via a dashboard (top right corner of the diagram) used only by the company's employees. In this way, we may even extend this mechanism for other use cases inside our backend, providing a great level of flexibility for micro-frontends and beyond.

The service dictionary can be implemented with either a monolith or a modular monolith. The important thing to remember is to allow categorization of the endpoints list based on the micro-frontend that requests the endpoints. For instance, we can group the endpoints related to a business subdomain or a bounded context. This is the strategic goal we should aim for. A service dictionary makes more sense with micro-frontends composed on the client side rather than on the server side. BFFs and API gateways are better suited for the server-side composition, considering the coupling between a micro-frontend and its data layer.

Modular Monolith

A concept from the 1960s, a modular monolith is where the code is actually compartmentalized into separate modules. Moving to a modular monolith may be enough for some companies to continue evolving the API layer instead of doing a full migration to microservices. In his book *Monolith to Microservices* (O'Reilly), Sam Newman provides many insights into migrating a monolithic backend to microservices, and he discusses the concept of the modular monolith as a potential first step for our migration journey.

Let's now explore how to implement the service dictionary in a micro-frontend architecture.

Implementing a service dictionary in a vertical-split architecture

The service dictionary pattern can easily be implemented in a vertical-split micro-frontend architecture, where every micro-frontend requests the dictionary related to its business domain.

However, it's not always possible to implement a service dictionary per domain, such as when we are transitioning from an existing SPA to micro-frontends, where the SPA requires the full list of endpoints because it won't reload the JavaScript logic until the next user session. In this case, we may decide to implement a tactical solution, providing the full list of endpoints to the application shell instead of a business domain endpoints list to every single micro-frontend. With this tactical solution, we assume the application shell exposes or injects the list of endpoints for every micro-frontend. When we are in a position to divide the services list by domain, there will be a minimum effort for removing the logic from the application shell and then moving into every micro-frontend, as displayed in Figure 8-3.

The service dictionary approach may also be used with a monolith backend. If we determine that our API layer will never move to microservices, we can still implement a service dictionary divided by domain per every micro-frontend, especially if we implement a modular monolith.

Taking into account Figure 8-3, we can derive a sample of sequence diagrams like the one in Figure 8-4. Bear in mind, there may be additional steps to perform either in the application shell or in the micro-frontend loaded, depending on the context we operate in. Take the sequence diagram in Figure 8-4 just as an example.

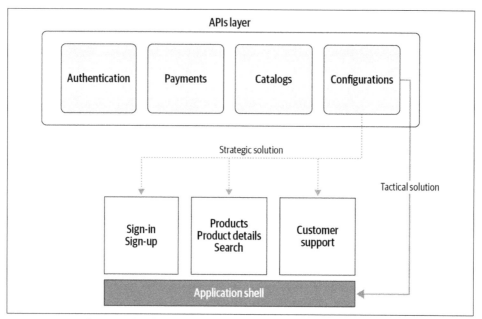

Figure 8-3. With vertical-split architecture, we can retrieve the service dictionary directly inside a micro-frontend from an endpoint—in this case, Configurations. Dividing the endpoints list by business domain allows us to structure our teams accordingly.

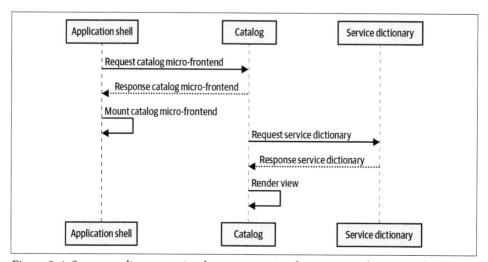

Figure 8-4. Sequence diagram to implement a service dictionary with a vertical-split architecture

As the first step, the application shell loads the micro-frontend requested—in this example, the catalog micro-frontend. After mounting the micro-frontend, the catalog initializes and consumes the service dictionary API for rendering the view. It can consume any additional APIs, as necessary. From this moment on, the catalog micro-frontend has access to the list of endpoints available and uses the dictionary to retrieve the endpoints to call. In this way, we are loading only the endpoints needed for a micro-frontend, reducing the payload of our configuration and maintaining control of our business domain.

Implementing a service dictionary in a horizontal-split architecture

To implement the service dictionary pattern with a micro-frontend architecture using a horizontal split, we have to pay attention to where the service dictionary API is consumed and how to expose it for the micro-frontends inside a single view. When the composition is managed client side, the recommended way to consume a service dictionary API is inside the application shell or host page. Because the container has visibility into every micro-frontend to load, we can perform just one round trip to the API layer to retrieve the APIs available for a given view and expose or inject the endpoints list to every loaded micro-frontend. Consuming the service dictionary APIs from every micro-frontend would negatively impact our applications' performance, so it's strongly recommended to stick the logic in the micro-frontend container, as shown in Figure 8-5.

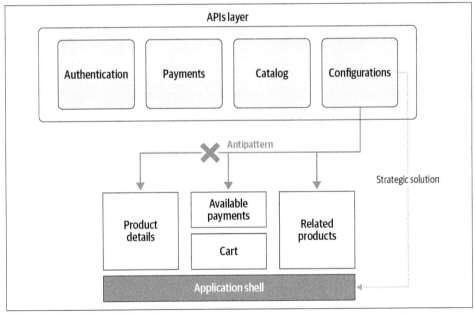

Figure 8-5. The service dictionary should always be loaded from the micro-frontend container in a horizontal-split architecture

The application shell should expose the endpoints list via the window object, making it accessible to all the micro-frontends when the technical implementation allows us to do it. Another option is injecting the service dictionary, alongside other configurations, after loading every micro-frontend. For example, using module federation in a React application requires sharing the data using React context APIs (*https://oreil.ly/ YXLnb*). The context API allows you to expose a context—in our case, the service dictionary—to the component tree without having to pass props down manually at every level. The decision to inject or expose our configurations is driven by the technical implementation.

Let's see how we can express this use case with the sequence diagram in Figure 8-6.

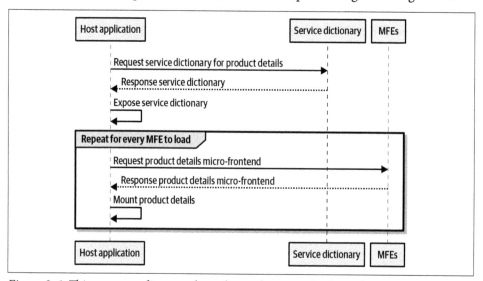

Figure 8-6. This sequence diagram shows how a horizontal-split architecture with client-side composition may consume the service dictionary API

In this sequence diagram, the request from the host application, or application shell, to the service dictionary is at the very top of the diagram. The host application then exposes the endpoints list via the `window` object and starts loading the micro-frontends that compose the view. Again, in real scenarios, we may have a more complex situation. Adapt the technical implementation and business logic to your project needs accordingly. For instance, you may want to create a container, loaded by the application shell, for all your micro-frontends hosted in the same view and fetch the service dictionary from the container instead of from the application shell.

Working with an API Gateway

An API gateway pattern represents a unique entry point for the outside world to consume APIs in a microservices architecture. Not only does an API gateway simplify access for any frontend to consume APIs by providing a unique entry point, but it's also responsible for requests routing, API composition and validation, and other edge functions, namely authorization, logging, rate limiting, and any other centralized functionality we need to have before the API gateway sends the request to a specific microservice. An API gateway also allows us to keep the same communication protocol between clients and the backend, while the gateway routes a request in the background in the format requested by a microservice (see Figure 8-7).

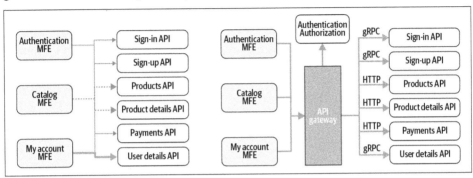

Figure 8-7. An API gateway pattern simplifies the communication between clients and server and centralizes functionalities like authentication and authorization via edge functions

Imagine a microservices architecture composed with HTTP and gRPC protocols. Without implementing an API gateway, the client won't be aware of every API or all the communication protocol details. Instead of using the API gateway pattern, we can hide the communication protocols behind the API gateway and leave the client's implementation dealing with the API contracts and implementing the business logic needed on the user interface. Other capabilities of edge functions are rate limiting, caching, metrics collection, and log requests. Without an API gateway, all these functionalities will need to be replicated in every microservice instead of centralized, as we can do with a single entry point.

Still, the API gateway also has some downsides. As a unique entry point, it could be a single point of failure, so we need to have a cluster of API gateways to add resilience to our application. Another challenge is more operational. In a large organization, where we have hundreds of developers working on the same project, we may have many services behind a single API gateway. We'll need to provide solid governance for adding, changing, or removing APIs in the API gateway to prevent teams being frustrated with a cumbersome flow. Finally, we'll add some latency to the system if we implement an additional layer between the client and the microservice consumed.

The process for updating the API gateway must be as lightweight as possible, making investing in the governance around this process a mandatory step. Otherwise, developers will be forced to wait in line to update the gateway with a new version of their endpoint. The API gateway can work in combination with a service dictionary, adding the benefits of a service dictionary to those of the API gateway pattern. Finally, with microarchitectures, we are opening a new scenario, where it may be possible and easier to manage and control because we are splitting the APIs by domain, having multiple API gateways to gather a group of APIs, for instance.

One API entry point per business domain

Another opportunity to consider is creating one API entry point per business domain instead of having one entry point for all the APIs, as with an API gateway. Multiple API gateways enable you to partition your APIs and policies by solution type and business domain. In this way, we avoid having a single point of failure in our infrastructure. Part of the application can fail without impacting the rest of the infrastructure. Another important characteristic of this approach is that we can use the best entry point strategy per bounded context based on the requirements needed, as shown in Figure 8-8.

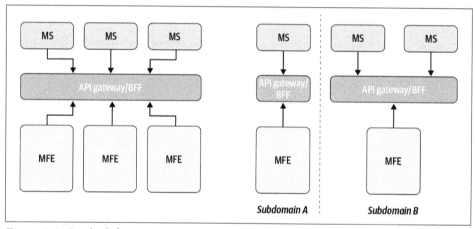

Figure 8-8. On the left is a unique entry point for the API layer; on the right are multiple entry points, one per subdomain

So let's say we have a bounded context that needs to aggregate multiple APIs from different microservices and return a subset of the body response of every microservice. In this case, a BFF would be a better fit for being consumed by a micro-frontend than handing over to the client doing multiple round trips to the server and filtering the APIs' body responses for displaying the final result to the user. But in the same application, we may have a bounded context that doesn't need a BFF. Let's go one step further and say that in this subdomain, we have to validate the user token in every call to the API layer to check whether the user is entitled to access the data. In this case, using an API gateway pattern with validation at the API gateway level will allow you to fulfill the requirements in a simple way.

With infrastructure ownership, choosing different entry points for our API layer means every team is responsible for building and maintaining the entry point chosen, reducing potential external dependencies across teams, and allowing them to own end to end the subdomain they are responsible for. Therefore, potentially we can have a one-to-one relationship between subdomain and entry point. This approach may require more work to build, but it allows a fine-grained control of identifying the right tool for the job instead of experiencing a trade-off between flexibility and functionalities. It also allows the team to really be independent end to end, allowing engineers to change the frontend, backend, and infrastructure without affecting any other business domain.

A client-side composition, with an API gateway and a service dictionary

Using an API gateway with a client-side micro-frontend composition (either vertical or horizontal split) is not that different from implementing the service dictionary in a monolith backend.

In fact, we can use the service dictionary to provide our micro-frontends with the endpoints to consume, using the same suggestions we provided previously. The main difference in this case is that the endpoints list will be provided by a microservice responsible for serving the service dictionary or a more generic client-side configuration, depending on our use case. Another interesting option is that, with an API gateway, authorization may happen at the API-gateway level, removing the risk of introducing libraries at the API level, as we can see in Figure 8-9.

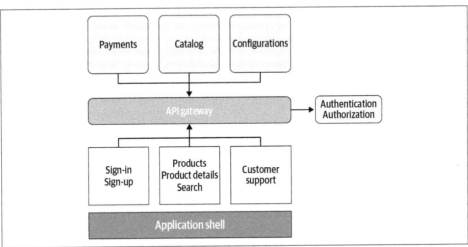

Figure 8-9. A vertical-split architecture with a client-side composition requesting data to a microservice architecture with an API gateway as entry point

Based on the concepts shared with the service dictionary, the backend infrastructure has changes but not the implementation side. As a result, the same implementations applicable to the service dictionary are also applicable in this scenario with the API gateway.

Let's look at one more interesting use case for the API gateway. Some applications allow us to use a micro-frontend architecture to provide different flavors of the same product to multiple customers, such as customizing certain micro-frontends on a customer-by-customer basis. In such cases, we tend to reuse the API layer for all the customers, using part or all of the microservices based on the user entitlement. But in a shared infrastructure, we can risk having some customers consuming more of our backend resources than others. In such scenarios, using API throttling at the API gateway will mitigate this problem by assigning the right limits per customer or per product. At the micro-frontend level, we won't need to do much more than handle the errors triggered by the API gateway for this use case.

A server-side composition with an API gateway

A microservices architecture opens up the possibility of using a micro-frontends architecture with a server-side composition.

Remember that with a server-side composition, we identify our micro-frontends with a horizontal split, not a vertical one.

As we can see in Figure 8-10, after the browser's request to the API gateway, the gateway handles the user authentication/authorization first, then allows the client request to be processed by the UI composition service responsible for calling the microservices needed to aggregate multiple micro-frontends, with their relative content fetched from the microservices layer.

For the microservices layer, we use a second API gateway to expose the API for internal services—in this case, used by the micro-frontend services for fetching the related API. Figure 8-11 illustrates a hypothetical implementation with the sequence diagram related to this scenario.

After the API gateway token validation, the client-side request lands at the UI composition service, which calls the micro-frontend to load. The micro-frontend service is then responsible for fetching the data from the API layer and the relative template for the UI and serving a fragment to the UI composition layer that will compose the final result for the user.

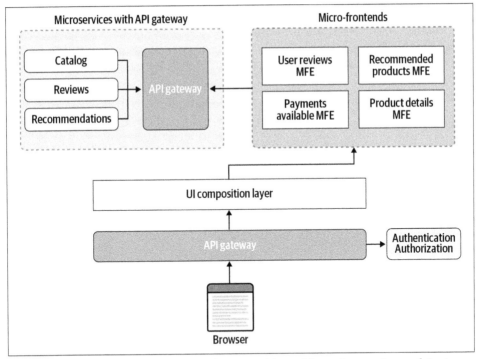

Figure 8-10. An example of a server-side composition with a microservices architecture

The diagram in Figure 8-11 presents an example with a micro-frontend, but it's applicable for all the others that should be retrieved for composing a user interface. Usually, the microservice used for fetching the data from the API layer should have a one-to-one relation with the API it consumes, which allows an end-to-end team's ownership of a specific micro-frontend and microservice.

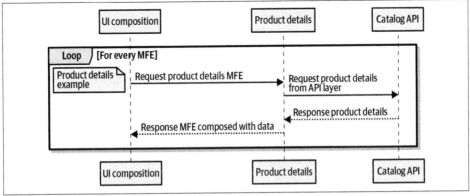

Figure 8-11. An example of server-side composition with API gateway

There are several micro-frontend frameworks with a similar implementation, such as the interface framework from Zalando (*https://oreil.ly/Xl26d*), OpenComponents (*https://oreil.ly/0ETxx*), Project Mosaic (*https://www.mosaic9.org*), and Ara Framework based on Airbnb Hypernova (*https://oreil.ly/buy8G*).

Working with the BFF Pattern

Although the API gateway pattern is a very powerful solution for providing a unique entry point to our APIs, in some situations we have views that require aggregating several APIs to compose the user interface, such as a financial dashboard that may require several endpoints for gathering the data to display inside a unique view. Sometimes, we aggregate this data on the client side, consuming multiple endpoints and interpolating data for updating our view with the diagrams, tables, and useful information that our application should display. Can we do something better than that? BFF comes to the rescue.

Another interesting scenario where an API gateway may not be suitable is in a cross-platform application where our API layer is consumed by web and mobile applications. Moreover, the mobile platforms often require displaying the data in a completely different way from the web application, especially taking into consideration screen size.

In this case, many visual components and relative data may be hidden on mobile in favor of providing a more general high-level overview and allowing a user to drill down to a specific metric or information that interests them instead of waiting for all the data to download.

Finally, mobile applications often require a different method for aggregating data and exposing it in a meaningful way to the user. APIs on the backend are the same for all clients, so, for mobile applications, we need to consume different endpoints and compute the final result on the device instead of changing the API responses based on the device that consumes the endpoint.

In all these cases, BFF, as described by Phil Calçado (*https://oreil.ly/SpqZ9*) (former employee of SoundCloud), comes to the rescue. The BFF pattern develops niche backends for each user experience. This pattern will only make sense if and when you have a significant amount of data coming from different endpoints that must be aggregated for improving the client's performance or when you have a cross-platform application that requires different experiences for the user based on the device used. This pattern can also help solve the challenge of introducing a layer between the API and the clients, as we can see in Figure 8-12.

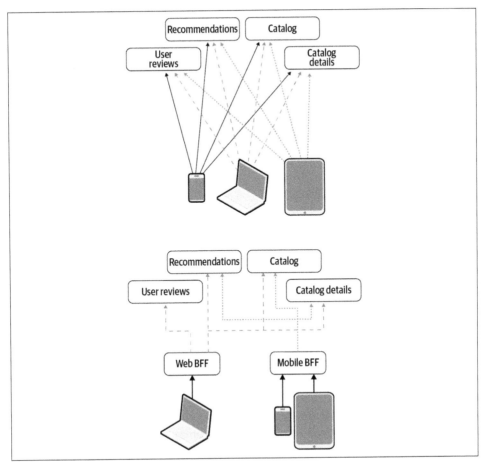

Figure 8-12. On the top, a microservices architecture consumed by different clients; on the bottom, a BBF layer exposing only the APIs needed for a given group of devices—in this case, mobile and web BFF

Thanks to BFF, we can create a unique entry point for a given device group, such as one for mobile and another for a web application. However, this time we also have the option of aggregating API responses before serving them to the client and, therefore, generating less chatter between clients and the backend because the BFF aggregates the data and serves only what is needed for a client with a structure reflecting the view to populate. Interestingly, the microservices architecture's complexity sits behind the BFF, creating a unique entry point for the client to consume the APIs without needing to understand the complexity of a microservices architecture.

BFF can also be used when we want to migrate a monolith to microservices. In fact, thanks to the separation between clients and APIs, we can use the strangler pattern for killing the monolith in an iterative way, as illustrated in Figure 8-13. This technique is also applicable to the API gateway pattern.

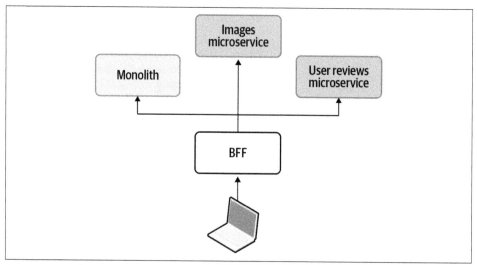

Figure 8-13. The microservices boxes represent services extracted from the monolith and converted to microservices. The BFF layer allows the client to be unaware of the change happening in the backend, maintaining the same contract at the BFF level.

Another interesting use case for the BFF is aggregating APIs by domain, as we have seen for the API gateway. Creating a BFF for a group of devices could lead to multiple BFFs calling the same microservices. When not controlled properly, this can harm platform stability. Obviously, we may decide to introduce caches in different layers for mitigating traffic spikes, but we can mitigate this problem another way. Following our subdomain decomposition, we can identify a unique entry point for each subdomain, grouping all the microservices for a specific domain together instead of taking into consideration the type of device that should consume the APIs. This would allow us to have similar service-level agreements (SLAs) and a commitment between a service provider and a client, inside the same domain; to control the response to the clients in a more cohesive way; and to allow the application to fail more gracefully than having a single layer responsible for serving all the APIs, as in the previous examples.

Figure 8-14 illustrates how we can have two BFFs—one for the catalog and one for the account section—for aggregating and exposing these APIs to different clients. In this way, we can scale the BFFs based on their traffic.

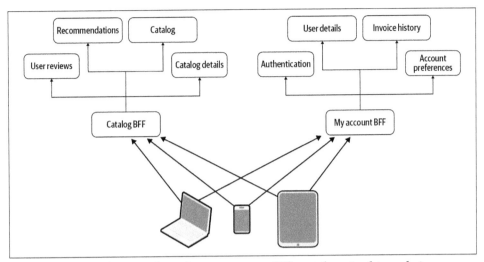

Figure 8-14. This diagram shows how to separate different domain-driven design subdomains

Gathering all the APIs behind a unique layer, however, may lead to an application's popular subdomains requiring a different treatment compared to less-accessed subdomains. Dividing by subdomain, then, would allow us to apply the right SLA instead of generalizing one for the entire BFF layer.

Sometimes BFF raises some concerns due to some inherent pitfalls such as reusability and code duplication. In fact, we may need to duplicate some code for implementing similar functionalities across different BFF, especially when we create one per device family. In these cases, we need to assess whether the burden of having teams implementing similar code twice is greater than abstracting (and maintaining) the code.

A client-side composition, with a BFF and a service dictionary

Because a BFF is an evolution of the API gateway, many of the implementation details for an API gateway are valid for a BFF layer as well, plus we can aggregate multiple endpoints, reducing client chatter with the server. It's important to iterate this capability because it can drastically improve application performance. Yet there are some caveats when we implement either a vertical split or a horizontal one. For instance, in Figure 8-15, we have a "product details" page that has to fetch the data for composing the view.

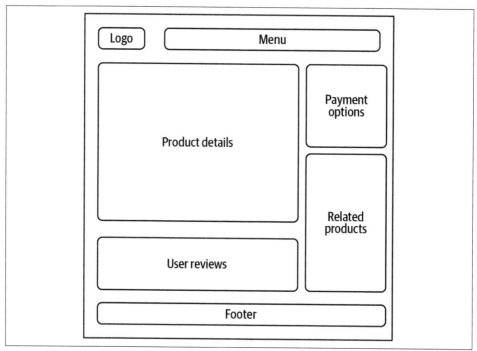

Figure 8-15. A wireframe of a product page

When we want to implement a vertical-split architecture, we may design the BFF to fetch all the data needed for composing this view, as we can see in Figure 8-16.

In this example, we assume the micro-frontend has already retrieved the endpoint for performing the request via a service dictionary and that it consumes the endpoints, leaving the BFF layer to compose the final response. In this use case, we can also easily use a service dictionary for exposing the endpoints available in our BFF to our micro-frontends, similar to the way we do it for the API gateway solution.

However, when we have a horizontal split composed on the client side, things become trickier because we need to maintain the micro-frontends' independence and have the host page domain as unaware as possible. In this case, we need to combine the APIs in a different way, delegating each micro-frontend to consume the related API. Otherwise, we will need to make the host page responsible for fetching the data for all the micro-frontends, which could create a coupling that would force us to deploy the host page with the micro-frontends, breaking the intrinsic characteristic of independence between micro-frontends.

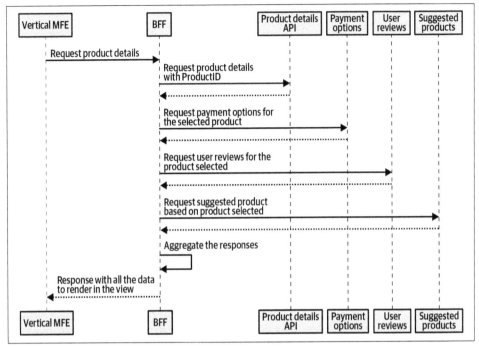

Figure 8-16. Sequence diagram showing the benefits of the BFF pattern used in combination with a vertical split composed on the client side

Taking into consideration that these micro-frontends and the host page may be developed by different teams, this setup would slow down features development rather than leveraging the benefits that this architecture provides us. BFF with a horizontal split composed on the client side could create more challenges than benefits in this case. It's wise to analyze whether this pattern's benefits will outweigh the challenges.

A server-side composition, with a BFF and service dictionary

When we implement a horizontal-split architecture with server-side composition and we have a BFF layer, our micro-frontend implementation resembles the API gateway one. The BFF exposes all the APIs available for every micro-frontend, so using the service dictionary pattern will allow us to retrieve the endpoints for rendering our micro-frontends ready to be composed by a UI composition layer.

Using GraphQL with Micro-Frontends

In a chapter about APIs and micro-frontends, we couldn't avoid mentioning GraphQL (*https://graphql.org*). GraphQL is a query language for APIs and a server-side runtime for executing queries by using a type system you define for your data. GraphQL was created by Facebook and released in 2015. Since then, it has gained a lot of traction within the developer community. Especially for frontend developers, GraphQL represents a great way to retrieve the data needed for rendering a view, decoupling the complexity of an API layer, rationalizing the API response in a graph, and allowing any client to reduce the number of round trips to the server for composing the UI.

Because GraphQL is a client-centric API, the paradigm for designing an API schema should be based on how the view we need to render looks instead of looking at the data exposed by the API layer. This is a very key distinction compared to how we design our database schemas or our REST APIs. Two projects in the GraphQL community—Apollo (*https://www.apollographql.com*) and Relay (*https://relay.dev*)—stand out as providing great support and productivity with the open source tools available. Both projects leverage GraphQL, adding an opinionated view on how to implement this layer inside our application, increasing our productivity thanks to the features available in one or both, including authentication, rate limiting, caching, and schema federations.

GraphQL can be used as an API gateway, acting as a proxy for specific microservices, for instance, or as a BFF, orchestrating the requests to multiple endpoints and aggregating the final response for the client. Remember that GraphQL acts as a unique entry point for your entire API layer. By design, GraphQL exposes a unique endpoint where the clients can perform queries against the GraphQL server. Because of this, we tend to not version our GraphQL entry point, although if the project requires a versioning because we don't have full control of the clients that consume our data, we can version the GraphQL endpoint. Shopify (*https://oreil.ly/kJMAz*) does this by adding the date in the URL and supporting all the versions up to a certain period.

GraphQL simplifies data retrieval for the clients, allows us to query only the fields needed in a view based on client type (e.g., mobile or web), and simplifies the maintenance and evolution of the GraphQL layer compared to more complicated backend ecosystems. The data graph is reachable via a unique endpoint. When a new microservice is added to the graph, the only change for the client to make would be at the query level, also minimizing maintenance.

The schema federation

Schema federation is a set of tools to compose multiple GraphQL schemas (*https://oreil.ly/voSpS*) declaratively into a single data graph. When we work with GraphQL in a midsize to large organization, we risk creating a bottleneck because all the teams are contributing to the same schema. But with a schema federation, we can have individual teams working on their own schemas and exposing them to the client as unique entry points, just like a traditional data graph. Apollo Server exposes a gateway with all associated schemas from other services, allowing each team to be independent and not change the way the frontend consumes the data graph.

This technique comes in handy when we work with microservices, though it comes with a caveat. A GraphQL schema should be designed with the UI in mind, so it's essential to avoid silos inside the organization. We must facilitate the initial analysis engaging with multiple teams and follow all improvements in order to have the best implementation possible. Figure 8-17 shows how a schema federation works, using the gateway as an entry point for all the implementing services and providing a unique entry point and data graph to query for the clients.

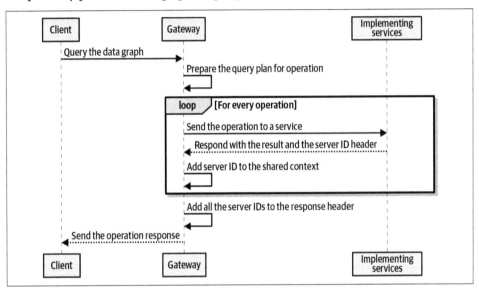

Figure 8-17. A sequence diagram showing how schema federation exposes all the schemas from multiple services

Schema federation represents the evolution of schema stitching (*https://oreil.ly/ XVjL2*), which has been used by many large organizations for similar purposes. It wasn't well designed, however, which led Apollo to deprecate schema stitching in favor of schema federation. More information regarding the schema federation is available on Apollo's documentation website (*https://oreil.ly/XUh0s*).

Using GraphQL with micro-frontends and client-side composition

Integrating GraphQL with micro-frontends is a trivial task, especially after reviewing the implementation of the API gateway and BFF. With schema federations, we can have the teams who are responsible for a specific domain's APIs create and maintain the schema for their domain and then merge all the schemas into a unique data graph for our client applications. This approach allows the team to be independent, maintaining their schema and exposing what the clients would need to consume.

When we integrate GraphQL with a vertical split and a client-side composition, the integration resembles the others previously described: the micro-frontend is responsible for consuming the GraphQL endpoint and rendering the content inside every component present in a view. Applying such scenarios with microservices becomes easier thanks to schema federation, as shown in Figure 8-18.

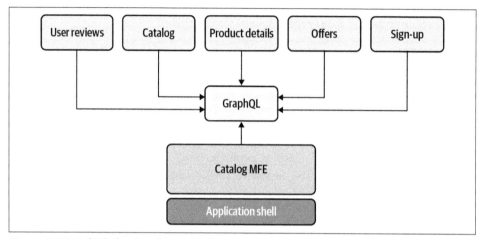

Figure 8-18. A high-level architecture for composing a microservice backend with schema federation. The catalog micro-frontend consumes the graph composed by all the schemas inside the GraphQL server.

In this case, thanks to the schema federation, we can compose the graph with all the schemas needed and expose a unique data graph for a micro-frontend to consume. Interestingly, with this approach, every micro-frontend will be responsible for consuming the same endpoint. Optionally, we may want to split the BFF into different domains, creating a one-to-one relation with the micro-frontend. This would reduce the scope of work and make our application easier to manage, considering the domain scope is smaller than having a unique data graph for all the applications.

Applying a similar backend architecture to horizontal-split micro-frontends with a client-side composition isn't too different from other implementations we have discussed in this chapter.

As we see in Figure 8-19, the application shell exposes or injects the GraphQL endpoint to all the micro-frontends, and all the queries related to a micro-frontend will be performed by every micro-frontend.

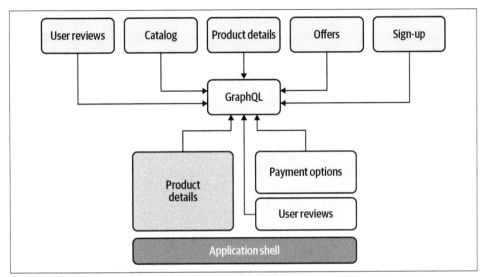

Figure 8-19. A high-level architecture of GraphQL with schema federation. When we implement it with a micro-frontend architecture with horizontal split and a client-side composition, all micro-frontends query the graph layer.

When we have multiple micro-frontends in the same or different view performing the same query, it's wise to look at the query and response cacheability at different levels—like the CDN (*https://oreil.ly/XfHII*) used—and otherwise leverage the GraphQL server-client cache. Caching is a very important concept that has to be leveraged properly; doing so could protect your origin from burst traffic, so spend the time.

Using GraphQL with micro-frontends and a server-side composition

The last approach is using a GraphQL server with a micro-frontend architecture with horizontal split and a server-side composition. When the UI composition requests multiple micro-frontends to their relative microservices, every microservice queries the graph and prepares the view for the final page composition (see Figure 8-20).

In this scenario, every microservice that will query the GraphQL server requires having the unique entry point accessible, authenticating itself, and retrieving the data needed for rendering the micro-frontend requested by the UI composition layer. This implementation overlaps quite nicely with the others we have seen so far on API gateway and BFF patterns.

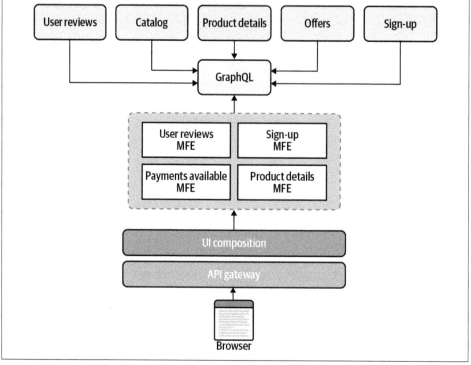

Figure 8-20. A high-level architecture for a micro-frontend architecture with a server-side composition where every micro-frontend consumes the graph exposed by the GraphQL server

Best Practices

After discussing how micro-frontends can fit with multiple backend architectures, we must address some topics that are architecture-agnostic but could help with the successful integration of a micro-frontend architecture.

Multiple micro-frontends consuming the same API

When we work with a horizontal-split architecture, we may end up having similar micro-frontends in the same view consuming the same APIs. In this case, we should challenge ourselves to determine whether maintaining separate micro-frontends brings any value to our system. Would grouping them in a unique micro-frontend be better? Usually, such scenarios should indicate a potential architectural improvement. Don't ignore that signal; instead, try to revisit the decision made at the beginning of the project with the information and the context available, making sure performing the same API request twice inside the same view is acceptable. If not, be prepared to review the micro-frontend boundaries.

APIs come first, then the implementation

Independently of the architecture we will implement in our projects, we should apply API-first principles to ensure all teams are working with the same understanding of the desired result.

An API-first approach means that for any given development project, your APIs are treated as "first-class citizens." As discussed at the beginning of this book, we need to make sure the APIs identified for communicating between micro-frontends or for client-server communication are defined up front to enable our teams to work in parallel and generate more value in a shorter time. In fact, investing time at the beginning for analyzing the API contract with different teams will reduce the risk of developing a solution not suitable for achieving the business goals or a smooth integration within the system.

Gathering all the teams involved in the creation and consumption of new APIs can save a lot of time further down the line when the integration starts. At the end of these meetings, producing an API spec with mock data will allow teams to work in parallel. The team that has to develop the business logic will have clarity on what to produce and can create tests for making sure they will produce the expected result, and the teams that consume this API will be able to start the integration, evolving or developing the business logic using the mocks defined during the initial meeting. Moreover, when we have to introduce a breaking change in an API, sharing a request for comments (RFC) (*https://tools.ietf.org/html/rfc825*) with the teams consuming the API may help to update the contract in a collaborative way. This will provide visibility on the business requirements to everyone and allow them to share their thoughts and collaborate on the solution using a standard document for gathering comments. RFCs are very popular in the software industry. Using them for documenting API changes will allow us to scale the knowledge and reasoning behind certain decisions, especially with distributed teams where it is not always possible to schedule a face-to-face meeting in front of a whiteboard. RFCs are also used when we want to change part of the architecture, introduce new patterns, or change part of the infrastructure.

API consistency

Another challenge we need to overcome when we work with multiple teams on the same project is creating consistent APIs, standardizing several aspects of an API, such as error handling.

API standardization allows developers to easily grasp the core concepts of new APIs, minimizes the learning curve, and makes the integration of APIs from other domains easier. A clear example would be standardizing error handling so that every API returns a similar error code and description for common issues like wrong body requests, service not available, or API throttling. This is true not only for client-server communication but for micro-frontends too. Let's think about the communication between a component and a micro-fronted or between micro-frontends in the same view. Identifying the events schema and the possibility we grant inside our system is fundamental for the consistency of our application and for speeding up the development of new features. There are very interesting insights available online for client-server communication, some of which may also be applicable to micro-frontends. Google (*https://oreil.ly/8CZeL*) and Microsoft (*https://oreil.ly/VmFoN*) API guidelines share a well-documented section on this topic, with many details on how to structure a consistent API inside their ecosystems.

WebSocket and micro-frontends

In some projects, we need to implement a WebSocket connection for notifying the frontend that something is happening, like a video chat application or an online game. Using WebSockets with micro-frontends requires a bit of attention because we may be tempted to create multiple socket connections, one per micro-frontend. Instead, we should create a unique connection for the entire application and inject or make available the WebSocket instance to all the micro-frontends loaded during a user session.

When working with horizontal-split architectures, create the socket connection in the application shell and communicate any message or status change (error, exit, and so on) to the micro-frontends in the same view via an event emitter or custom events for managing their visual update. In this way, the socket connection is managed once instead of multiple times during a user session. There are some challenges to take into consideration, however. Imagine that some messages are communicated to the client while a micro-frontend is loaded inside the application shell. In this case, creating a message buffer may help to replay the last few messages and allow the micro-frontend to catch up once fully loaded.

Finally, if only one micro-frontend has to listen to a WebSocket connection, encapsulating this logic inside the micro-frontend would not cause any harm because the connection will leave naturally inside its subdomain. For vertical-split architectures, the approach is less definitive. We may want to load inside every micro-frontend instead of at the application shell, simplifying the life cycle management of the socket connection.

The right approach for the right subdomain

Thanks to their modularity and the independence offered by their distributed-system nature, micro-frontends and microservices provide a level of flexibility we didn't have before. To leverage this new quality inside our architecture, we need to identify the right approach for the job. For instance, in some parts of an application, we may want to have some micro-frontends communicating with a BFF instead of a regular service dictionary because that specific domain requires an aggregation of data retrievable by existing microservices, but the data should be aggregated in a completely different way. Using microarchitectures, these decisions are easier to embrace, due to the architecture's intrinsic characteristic. To grant this flexibility, we must invest time at the beginning of the project analyzing the boundaries of every business domain and then refine them every time we see complications in API implementation.

In this way, every team will be entitled to use the right approach for the job instead of following a standard approach that may not be applicable for the solution they are developing. This is not a one-off decision, but it has to evolve and revise with a regular cadence to support the business evolution.

Designing APIs for cross-platform applications

Nowadays, we are developing cross-platform applications more often than not. Mobile devices are part of our routine. They help us accomplish our daily tasks, and a tablet may have already replaced our laptop for working. When we approach a cross-platform application and we aren't using a BFF layer to aggregate the data model for every device we target, we need to remember a simple rule: move the configurations as much as you can on the API layer. With this approach, we will be able to abstract and control certain behaviors without the need to build a new release of our mobile application and wait for the penetration in the market. For example, let's say you need to create a polling strategy for consuming an API and react to the response every few minutes. Usually, we would just define the interval in the client application. However, in some use cases, this implementation may become risky, such as when you have very bursty traffic and you want to create a mechanism to back off your requests to the server instead of throttling or slowing down the communication between server and client. In this case, moving the interval value to the body response of the API to pull would allow you to manage situations like that without distributing a new version of the mobile application. This also applies to micro-frontends, where we may have multiple micro-frontends that should implement similar logic. Instead of implementing inside the client-side code, consider moving some configurations on the server and implementing the logic for reacting to the server response. In this way, with a simple and strategic decision we will be able to solve many headaches that may happen in production and affect our users.

Summary

We have covered how micro-frontends can be integrated with multiple API layers. Micro-frontends are suitable for not only microservices but also monolith architecture. There may be strong reasons why we cannot change the monolithic architecture on the backend, but we want to create a new interface with multiple teams. Micro-frontends may be the solution to this challenge. We discussed the service dictionary approach that could help with cross-platform applications and with the previous layer for reducing the need for a shared client-side library that gathers all the endpoints.

We also discussed how BFF can be implemented with micro-frontends and a different twist on BFF using API gateways. In the last part of this chapter, we reviewed how to implement GraphQL with micro-frontends, discovering that the implementation overlaps quite nicely with the one described in the API gateway and BFF patterns. Finally, we closed the chapter with some best practices, like approaching API design with an API-first approach, leveraging DDD at the infrastructure level for using the right technical approach for a subdomain, and designing APIs for cross-platform applications by moving some logic to the backend instead of replicating into multiple frontend applications.

As we have seen, micro-frontends have different implementation models based on the backend architecture we choose. The quickest approach for starting the integration in a new micro-frontends project is the service dictionary that can evolve over time to more sophisticated solutions like BFF, or BFF with GraphQL. Remember that every solution shared in this chapter brings a fair amount of complexity if not analyzed and contextualized inside the organization structure and communication flow. Don't focus your attention only on the technical implementation but move a step further by looking into the governance for future APIs' integration or breaking changes of an API.

CHAPTER 9

From Monolith to Micro-Frontends: A Case Study

Let's say that in the last few weeks, you've researched and reviewed articles, books, and case studies and completed several proofs of concept. You've spoken with your managers to find the best people for the project, and you've even prepared a presentation for the CTO explaining the benefits you can get from introducing micro-frontends in your platform. At last, you've received confirmation that you have been granted the resources to prepare a plan and start migrating your legacy platform to micro-frontends. Great job! It's been a long few weeks, and you've done an amazing job, but this is only the start of a large project.

Next, you will need to prepare an overall strategy, one that's not too detailed but not too loose. Too detailed, and you'll spend months just trying to nail everything down. Too loose, and you won't have enough guidance. You need enough of a strategy to get started and a North Star to follow during the journey whenever you discover—and, trust me, you will—new challenges and details you didn't think about until that point. Meanwhile, you also have a platform to maintain in production, which the product team would like to evolve because the replatforming to micro-frontends shouldn't block the business. The situation is not the simplest ever, but you can mitigate these challenges and find the right trade-off to make everyone happy and the business successful while the tech teams are migrating to the new architecture.

We have learned a lot about how to design and implement micro-frontends, but I feel this book would not be complete without looking at migration from a monolithic application to a micro-frontend one—by far, the most common use case of this architecture. I believe any project should start simple. Then, over the course of months or years, when the business and the organization are growing, the architecture should evolve accordingly to support the evolving needs of the business. There may be some scenarios where starting a new application with micro-frontends may help the business move in the right direction, such as when you have an application that is composed of several modules that you can ship all together along with some customization for every customer. But the classic use case of micro-frontends is the migration from a legacy frontend application to this new approach. In this chapter, I will share a case study example that stitches together all the information we have discussed in this book.

The Context

ACME Inc. is a fairly new organization that, in only a few years, has gained popularity for its video-streaming service across several countries around the world. The company is growing fast. In the last couple of years, it has moved from hundreds of employees to thousands, located all across the globe, and the tech department is no exception.

The streaming platform is currently available on desktop and mobile browsers, and on some living-room devices such as smart TVs and consoles. Currently the company is onboarding many developers in different locations across Europe. Having all the developers in Europe was a strategic decision to avoid slowing down the development across distributed teams while having some hours of overlap for meetings and coordination.

Due to the tech department's incredible growth from tens to hundreds of people, tech leadership reviewed and analyzed the work done so far, finally embracing a plan to adapt their architecture to the new phase of the business. Leadership acknowledged that maintaining the current architecture would slow down the entire department and wouldn't allow the agility required for the current expansion the business is going through.

Technology Stack

The current platform uses a three-tier application deployed in the cloud, composed of a single database with read replicas (they have more reads than writes in their platform), a monolithic API layer with auto-scaling for the backend that scales horizontally when traffic increases, and a single-page application (SPA) for the frontend, as shown in Figure 9-1.

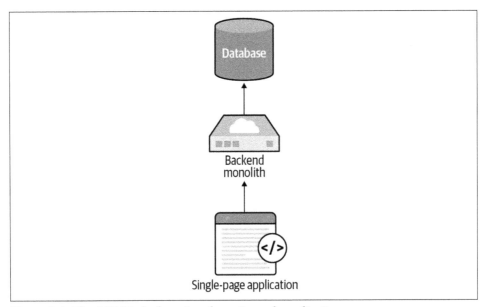

Figure 9-1. The ACME platform is a three-tier web application

A three-tier application allows the layers to be independently scaled and developed. However, ACME is scaling and increasing in complexity, as well as increasing the teams working on the same project. This architecture is now impacting the day-to-day throughput and generating communications overhead across teams that may lead to more complexity and coordination despite not being necessary in other solutions.

As the tech leadership team rightly points out, in this new phase of the business, the tech department needs to scale with more developers and with more features than before. A task force with different skill sets reviews how the architectures—frontend and backend—should evolve in order to unblock the teams and allow the company to scale in relation to business needs.

After several weeks, the task force proposed migrating the backend layer to microservices and the frontend to micro-frontends. This decision was based on the capabilities and principles of these architectures. They will allow teams to be independent, moving at their own speed, scaling the organization as requested by the business, choosing the right solution for each domain, and scaling the platform according to the traffic on a service-by-service basis by leveraging the power of cloud vendors.

From here, we'll focus our discussion on the frontend part. There will be some references on how the frontend layer is decoupled from the backend using the service dictionary approach discussed in Chapter 8.

Platform and Main User Flows

The frontend is composed of the following views:

- Landing page
- Sign-in
- Sign-up
- Payment
- Forgot email
- Forgot password
- Redeem gift code
- Catalog (with video player)
- Schedule
- Search
- Help
- My account

To provide us enough information to understand how the migration to micro-frontends will work, we will analyze the authentication flow for existing customers, the creation of a subscription flow for new customers, and the experience inside the platform for authenticated customers. Many of these suggestions can be replicated for other areas of the application or applied with small tweaks.

When a new user wants to subscribe to the video-streaming platform, they follow these steps (see also Figure 9-2):

1. The user arrives on the landing page, which explains the value proposition.
2. The user then moves to the sign-up page, where they create an account.
3. On the next page, the user adds their payment information.
4. The user can then access the video platform.

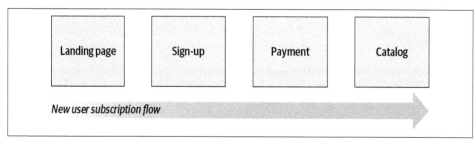

Figure 9-2. New user subscription flow

When an existing user wants to sign in on a new platform (browser or mobile device, for instance) to watch some content, they will do the following (see also Figure 9-3):

1. Access the platform in the landing page view
2. Select the sign-in button, which redirects them to the sign-in view
3. Insert their credentials
4. Access the authenticated area and explore the catalog

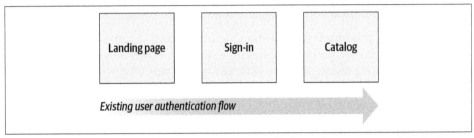

Figure 9-3. Existing user authenticating on a new platform (browser or mobile device, for instance)

Once a user is authenticated, they can watch video content and explore the catalog following these steps (see also Figure 9-4):

1. They start at the catalog to choose the content to view.
2. When content is selected, the user sees more details related to the content and the possibility to search for similar content or just play the content.
3. When the user chooses to play the content, they are redirected to a view with only the video player.
4. When the user wants to search for specific content not available in the catalog view, they can choose to use the search functionality.

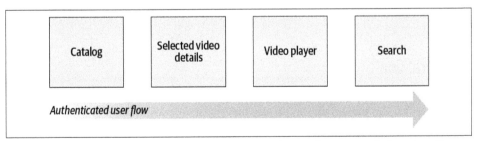

Figure 9-4. Existing users can navigate content via the catalog or search functionality and then play any content after discovering the details of what they are about to watch

These are the main flows, which should be enough to explore how to migrate to micro-frontends. Obviously, there are always more edge cases to cover, especially when we implement errors management, but we won't cover those in this chapter.

The application is written with Angular, with a continuous integration pipeline and a deployment that happens twice a month because it is strictly coupled with the back-end layer. In fact, the static files are served by the application servers where the APIs live, so therefore, every time there is a new frontend version, the teams have to wait for the release of a new application server version. The release doesn't happen very often due to the organization's slow release cycle process.

The final artifact produced by the automation pipeline is a series of JavaScript and CSS files with an HTML entry point. In the continuous integration process, the application has some unit testing, but the code coverage is fairly low (roughly 30%), and the automation process takes about 15 minutes to execute end to end to create an artifact ready to be deployed in production.

The organization is using a three-environment strategy: testing, staging, and production. As a result, the final manual testing happens in the staging environment before being pushed into production, another reason why deployments can't happen too often. The user acceptance testing department (UAT) does not have enough resources, compared to the developers who handle platform enhancement. Due to the simple automation process put in place, some developers on different teams are responsible for maintaining the automation pipelines; however, it's more of an additional task to shoehorn into their busy schedules than an official role assigned to them. This sometimes causes problems because resolving issues or adding new functionalities in the continuous integration process may require weeks instead of days or hours.

Finally, the platform was developed with observability in mind, not only on the back-end but also on the frontend. In fact, both the product team and the developers have access to different metrics to understand how users interact with the platform so they can make better decisions for enhancing the platform's capabilities. They are also using an observability tool for tracking JavaScript runtime errors inside their frontend stack.

Technical Goals

After deciding to move their frontend platform to micro-frontends, the tech leadership identified the goals they should aim for with this investment.

The first goal is maintaining a seamless experience for developers despite the architectural changes. Degrading a frictionless developer experience, available with the SPA, could lead to a slower feedback loop and decrease the software quality. Moreover, the leadership decided that it doesn't want to reinvent the wheel either, so it will be acceptable to create some tools for filling certain gaps but not a complete custom developer experience that may prevent new tools from being embraced in the future. It's important to fix the automation strategy for reducing the feedback loop that now takes too long.

Another key project goal is to decouple the micro-frontends and allow independent evolution and deployment. Micro-frontends that are tightly coupled together must be released all together. Every micro-frontend should be an independent artifact deployable in any environment.

Moreover, tech leadership wants to reduce the risk of introducing bugs or defects in production, easing the traffic toward new micro-frontend versions. This way, developers can test with real data in production but not affect the entire user base.

An additional goal is to generate value as soon as possible to demonstrate to the business the return of value of their investment. Therefore, a strategy for transitioning the SPA to micro-frontends has to be defined in a way that when a micro-frontend is available, it will initially work alongside the monolith.

The tech leadership has also requested tracking the onboarding time for new joiners in order to understand whether this approach extends developer onboarding time. The team will need to figure out a way to reduce this period, perhaps by creating more documentation or using different approaches.

The last goal for this project is finding the right organization setup for reducing external dependencies between teams and reducing the communication overhead that could increase due to the company's massive growth.

Migration Strategy

Based on tech leadership's requirements and goals, the ACME teams started to work on a plan for migrating the entire platform to micro-frontends. The first step was embracing the micro-frontend decisions framework, as outlined in Chapter 2. The first four decisions—defining what a micro-frontend is in your architecture, composing micro-frontends, routing micro-frontends, and communicating between micro-frontends—will lead the entire migration toward the right architecture for the context.

As discussed in several chapters of this book, the micro-frontend decisions framework gives us a skeleton to architect a micro-frontend project onto. All the other decisions will build on top of this frame, creating a reliable structure.

Micro-Frontend Decisions Framework Applied

The first decision of the framework is how a micro-frontend will look. The ACME teams decided on a *vertical split*, where micro-frontends represent a subdomain of the entire application (see Figure 9-5).

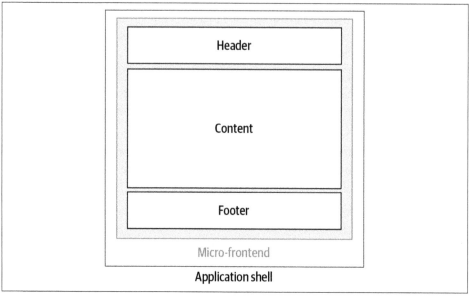

Figure 9-5. A vertical-split micro-frontend, where the application shell loads only one micro-frontend at a time

The teams took into account the following characteristics for their context before deciding to use a vertical split:

Similar developer experience
  Because the current platform is an SPA, a vertical split allows developers to work like they have so far but with a smaller context and less code to be responsible for.

Low component reusability
  The teams have identified that not many components are similar across the different subdomains. This clearly indicates that the reusability of micro-frontends, a plus of a horizontal-split approach, is not needed. A light design system will ensure consistency across micro-frontends and reduce overhead.

Better integration with current automation strategy
  The vertical split fits very well with the current automation strategy, considering right now ACME is building an SPA. The teams have enhanced their automation pipelines for building multiple SPAs without the need to create custom tools for embracing this architecture style. They will need to use infrastructure as code for

automating the process of building their pipelines and replicating them without human intervention.

No risk of dependency clashes

In a vertical split, the application shell always loads one micro-frontend at a time, due to its nature. As a result, the teams won't have to deal with dependency clashes, like different versions of the same library, because there will be dependencies of just one micro-frontend, reducing the possibility of runtime errors and bugs in production. There also won't be any CSS style clash because only one stylesheet per micro-frontend will load.

A consistent user experience

Creating a consistent user experience is easier with a vertical split because the same team is working on one or multiple views inside the same SPA. Obviously, a level of coordination is required for maintaining consistency across micro-frontends, but it's definitely less prone to errors than having multiple micro-frontends in the same view developed by multiple teams.

Reduction of cognitive load

For ACME, a vertical split will decrease its developers' cognitive load, because they'll only have to master and maintain a part of the platform. This choice also won't dilute the decisions made by developers inside their business subdomain. However, every developer should have an overall understanding of the platform architecture so that when they're on call, they can understand the touch points of their business domain and recognize where a bug may appear despite not being inside their domain.

Faster onboarding process

As the tech leadership requested, using this approach will lead to a faster onboarding process because the teams can use well-known, standard tools and won't need to create their own to build, test, and deploy micro-frontends. Also, because teams will be responsible for only a part of the platform, less coordination with other teams will be required. New joiners can hit the ground faster, with less information needed to start. Finally, every team will be encouraged to create a starter kit and induction for every new joiner to speed up the learning process and make a person capable of contributing to the base code in the fastest way possible.

The second decision of the framework is related to the composition of the micro-frontends. In this case, the best approach is composing them on the client side considering they are using a vertical-split approach. This means that the teams will have to create an *application shell* that is responsible for mounting and unmounting micro-frontends, exposing some APIs to allow communication between micro-frontends and ensuring it will always be available during the user session (see Figure 9-6). A server-side composition was rejected immediately due to the traffic spikes, which required more effort to support and maintain than the simple infrastructure they would like to use for this project.

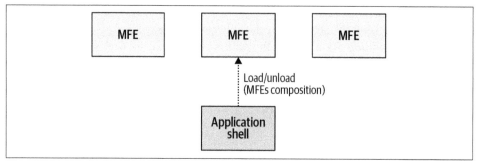

Figure 9-6. Client-side composition, where the application shell is responsible for loading and unloading one micro-frontend at a time

The third decision is the routing of micro-frontends, that is, how to map the different application paths to micro-frontends. Because ACME will use a vertical split and is composing on the client side, the routing must happen on the client side, where the application shell knows which micro-frontend to load based on the path selected by the user. This mechanism also has to handle the deep-linking functionality; if a user shares a movie's URL with someone else, the application shell should load the application in exactly that state (see Figure 9-7).

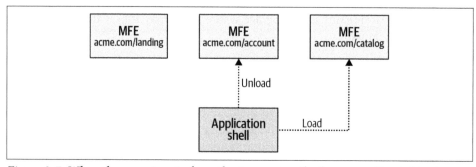

Figure 9-7. When the user signs in from the /account path, they are redirected to the authenticated area (/catalog). The application shell owns the logic for unloading the current micro-frontend and loading the next one based on the URL.

When an unauthorized user tries to access an authenticated part of the system via deep linking, the application shell should validate *only* if the user has a valid token. If the user doesn't have a valid token, it should load the landing page so the user can decide to sign in or subscribe to the service.

Last but not least, ACME teams have to decide how micro-frontends communicate with each other. With a vertical split, communication can happen only via a query string or using web storage. ACME decided to mainly leverage the web storage and use the application shell as a proxy for storing the data. In this way, the application shell can verify the space available and make sure data won't be overridden by other micro-frontends (see Figure 9-8).

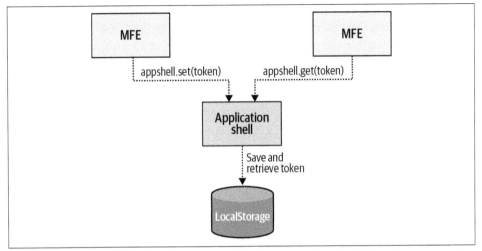

Figure 9-8. The application shell is responsible for storing data in the local storage and exposing several APIs to the micro-frontends for storing and retrieving data

Let's summarize the decisions made by the teams in Table 9-1.

Table 9-1. Summary of ACME architectural decisions

Micro-frontend decisions framework	
Defining micro-frontends	Vertical split
Composing micro-frontends	Client side via application shell
Routing micro-frontends	Client side via application shell
Communication between micro-frontends	Using web storage via application shell

Splitting the SPA in Multiple Subdomains

After creating their micro-frontend framework, the ACME tech teams analyzed the current application's user data to understand how the users were interacting with the platform. This is another fundamental step that provides a reality check to the teams. Often what tech and product people envision for platform usage is very different from what users actually do.

The SPA was released with a Google Analytics integration, and the teams were able to gather several custom data points on user behavior for developing or tweaking features inside the platform. These data are extremely valuable in the context ACME operates because they help identify how to slice the monolith into micro-frontends.

Looking at user behaviors, the teams discover the following:

New users

Users who are discovering the platform for the first time follow the sign-up journey as expected. However, there are significant drops in visualization from one view to the next. As we can see in Table 9-2, all the new users access the landing page, but only 70% of that traffic moves to the next step, where the account is created. At the third step (payment), there is a drop of an additional 10%. At the last step, only 30% of the initial traffic has converted to customer.

Table 9-2. New user traffic per view on ACME platform

View	Traffic
Landing page	100%
Sign-up	70%
Payment	60%
Catalog	30%

Unauthenticated existing users

Existing users who want to authenticate on a new browser or another platform, such as a mobile device, usually skip the landing page, going straight to the sign-in URL. After signing in, they have full access to the video catalog, as seen in Table 9-3.

Table 9-3. Unauthenticated existing user traffic per view for accessing ACME platform

View	Traffic
Landing page (as entry point)	25%
Sign-in (as entry point)	70%

Authenticated existing users

Probably the most interesting result is that authenticated users are not signing out. As a result, they won't see the landing page or sign-in/sign-up flows anymore. They occasionally explore their account page or the help page. But a vast majority of the time, authenticated users are staying in the authenticated area and not navigating outside of it (see Table 9-4).

Table 9-4. Authenticated existing user traffic per view for accessing ACME platform

View	Traffic
Landing page	0%
Sign-in	1%
Sign-up	0%
Catalog	92%

View	Traffic
My account	4%
Help	2%

This is extremely valuable information for identifying micro-frontends. In fact, ACME developers can assert the following:

- The landing page should immediately load for new users, giving them the opportunity to understand the value proposition.
- Landing page, sign-in, and sign-up flows should be decoupled from the catalog since authenticated users only occasionally navigated to other parts of the application.
- "My account" and Help don't receive much traffic.
- There is a considerable drop of new users between landing page and sign-up flows, and we can expect the product team would like to make multiple changes for reducing this drop.

Another important aspect is understanding how the current architecture can be split into multiple subdomains following domain-driven design practices. Taking into consideration the whole platform—not only the client-side part—the teams identified some subdomains and relative bounded context.

For the frontend part, the subdomains that the teams took into consideration for their final decisions are:

Value proposition
    A subdomain for sharing all the information needed to make a decision for subscribing to the platform.

Onboarding
    A subdomain focused on subscribing new users and granting access to the platform for existing users. In the future, should complexities arise, this may be split into smaller subdomains, such as payment methods, user creation, and user authentication, but for now they will be one subdomain.

Catalog
    A core subdomain where ACME gathers the essential part of its business proposition, such as the catalog, video player, and all the controls for allowing users to consume content respecting the rights holders' agreements.

User management
    A subdomain where the user can change account preferences, payment methods, and other personal information.

Customer support
> A subdomain for helping new and existing users to solve their problems in any part of the platform.

With this information in mind and the decisions made for approaching this project using the micro-frontend decisions framework, the teams identified the migration path with the following micro-frontends (see also Figure 9-9):

Landing page
> Considering that the landing page is viewed by all new users, the teams want to have a super-fast experience where the page is rendered in a blink of an eye. It needs its own micro-frontend so all the technical best practices for a highly cacheable micro-frontend with a small size to download can be applied.

Authentication
> This micro-frontend is composed of all the actions an unauthenticated user should perform before accessing the catalog, such as moving from sign-in to sign-up view, retrieving their credentials, and so on.

Catalog
> This is an authenticated area frequently viewed by authenticated users. The teams want to expedite the experience for these users when they return to the platform, so they encapsulate it in a single micro-frontend.

My account
> This micro-frontend is a combination of information available in different domains of the backend, allowing users to manage their account preferences. It is available only for authenticated users. Because of the small traffic and the cross-cutting nature of this domain, ACME decided to encapsulate it in a micro-frontend.

Help
> Like the "My account" micro-frontends, Help has low traffic, a different use case from other micro-frontends, and highly cacheable content (because Help pages are not updated very often). Encapsulating this subdomain in a micro-frontend allows ACME to use the right infrastructure for optimizing this part of the platform.

Application shell
> This is the micro-frontend orchestrator. Because ACME decided to use a vertical split with a client composition, this element is mandatory to build. The main caveat is trying to keep it light and as decoupled as possible from the rest of the application so that all the other micro-frontends can be independent and evolve without any dependency on the application shell.

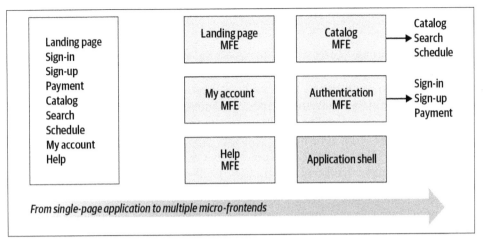

Figure 9-9. Migration path: from SPA to micro-frontends

Technology Choice

Because the Angular SPA was developed some years ago with patterns and assumptions that were best practices at that time, ACME tech teams investigated their relevance, as well as new practices that might make developers' lives easier and more productive. The teams agreed to use React, and they have discovered in the reactive programming paradigm a development boost during their proof of concepts.

Although Redux allows them to embrace this paradigm using libraries such as redux-observable (*https://redux-observable.js.org*), they found in MobX-State-Tree (*https://oreil.ly/nzsXI*) an opinionated and well-documented reactive state management that works perfectly with React and allows state composition so they can reuse states across multiple views of the same micro-frontend. This will enhance the reusability of their code inside the same bounded context.

Thanks to the nature of the vertical-split micro-frontends, which loads only one micro-frontend at a time, there is no need to coordinate naming conventions or similar agreements across multiple teams. The teams will mainly share best development practices and approaches to make the micro-frontends similar and allow team members to understand the codebase of other micro-frontends or even join a different team.

The micro-frontends will be static artifacts and therefore highly cacheable through a content delivery network (CDN), so there's no need for runtime composition on the server side. The delivery strategy will need to change, however, because of this aspect. Currently, ACME is serving all the static assets directly from the application server layer. Because the API integrations are happening on the client side, there will be no need to continue maintaining the application servers for serving static contents but only for exposing the backend API.

ACME decided to use object storage like AWS S3, storing all the artifacts to serve in production in a regional bucket and enhancing the distribution across all the countries they need to serve using a CDN such as Amazon CloudFront. This will simplify the infrastructure layer, reducing the possible issues happening in production due to misconfiguration or scalability. Additionally, the frontend has a different infrastructure than the API layer, allowing the frontend developers to evolve their infrastructure as needed. This new infrastructure allows every team to independently deploy their micro-frontend artifacts (HTML, CSS, JS files) in a S3 bucket and have them automatically available for the application shell to load them.

Another goal for this migration is to reduce the risk of bugs in production when a new micro-frontend version is deployed while immediately creating value for the users and the company without waiting for the entire application to be rewritten with the new architecture. Considering the simple frontend infrastructure adopted for the project, the ACME teams decided to leverage Lambda@Edge, a serverless computation layer offered by AWS (see Chapters 7 and 8), for analyzing the incoming traffic and serving a specific artifact to the application shell, implementing a de facto frontend canary release mechanism at the infrastructure level that won't impact the application code but will run in the cloud (see Figure 9-10).

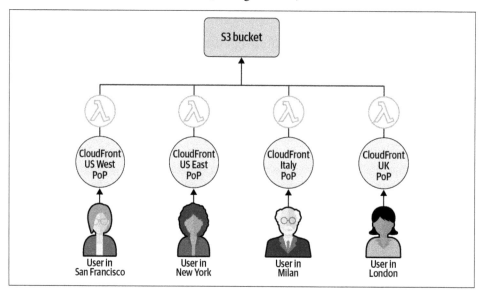

Figure 9-10. Simple infrastructure based on S3 bucket, Lambda@Edge, and a CDN like Amazon CloudFront distribution, with point of presence (PoP) available all over the world

Thanks to this implementation, ACME can also apply the strangler pattern (see Chapter 7) for gradually moving to micro-frontends while maintaining the legacy application. In fact, they can use the application URL to trigger the Lambda@Edge that will serve the legacy or application shell to the user (see Figure 9-11).

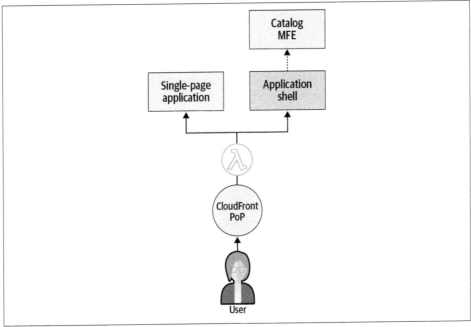

Figure 9-11. Strangler pattern applied at the infrastructure level using Lambda@Edge for funneling the traffic toward either the legacy or micro-frontend application

In the configuration file loaded by the Lambda@Edge at the initialization phase, developers mapped the URLs belonging to the legacy application and the ones to the micro-frontend application. Let's clarify this with an example. Imagine that the catalog micro-frontend is released first, because at this stage you want all or part of the traffic going toward the micro-frontend branch (see Figure 9-11). The authentication remains inside the legacy application, so after the user signs in or signs up, the SPA will load the absolute URL for the catalog (e.g., www.acme.com/catalog). This request will be picked up by Amazon CloudFront, which will trigger the Lambda@Edge and serve the application shell instead of the SPA artifact.

This plan acknowledges that during the transition phase, a user will download more library code than before because they're downloading two applications at the end. However, this won't happen for existing users; they will always download the micro-frontend implementation, not the legacy one.

As you can see, there is always a trade-off to make. Because ACME's goal was finding a way to mitigate bugs in production and generate value immediately, these were the points they have to optimize for, especially if this is just a temporary phase until the entire application is switched to the new architecture. At this stage, ACME teams have made enough decisions to start the project. They decide to create a new team to take care of the catalog micro-frontend, which will be the first to be deployed into production when ready.

The teams know that the first micro-frontend will take longer to be ready because on top of migrating the business logic toward this new architecture style, the new team has to define the best practices for developing a micro-frontend that other teams will follow. For this reason, the catalog team starts with some proofs of concept to nail down a few details, such as how to share the authentication token between the SPA and the micro-frontend initially and then between micro-frontends when the application is fully ported to this pattern, or how to integrate with the backend APIs with consideration for the migration on that side as well as the potential impact to API endpoints, contracts, and so on.

Initially, the team splits the work in two parts. Half of the team works on the automation pipeline for the application shell and the catalog micro-frontends. The other half focuses on building the application shell. The shell should be a simple layer that initializes the application retrieving the configuration for a specific country and orchestrates the micro-frontend life cycle, such as loading and unloading micro-frontends or exposing some functions for notifying when a micro-frontend is fully loaded or about to be unloaded.

The first iteration of this process will be reviewed and optimized when more teams join the project. The automation and application shell will be enhanced as new requirements arise or new ideas to improve the application are applied.

Implementation Details

After identifying the next steps for the architecture migration, ACME has to solve a few additional challenges along the migration journey. These challenges, such as authentication and dependencies management, are common in any frontend project. Implementing the following features in a micro-frontend architecture may have some caveats that are not similar in other architectures. The topics we'll dive deeply into include:

- Application shell responsibilities
- Integration with the APIs that takes into account the migration to microservices happening in parallel

- Implementation of an authentication mechanism
- Dependencies management between micro-frontends
- Components sharing across multiple micro-frontends
- Introduction of design consistency in the user experience
- Canary releases for frontend
- Localization

In this way, we cover the most critical aspects of a migration from SPA to micro-frontends. This doesn't mean there aren't other important considerations, but these topics are usually the most common ones for a frontend application, and applying them at scale is not always as easy as we think.

Application Shell Responsibilities

The application shell is a key part of this architecture. It's responsible for mounting and unmounting micro-frontends, initializing the application. It's also responsible for sharing an API layer for the micro-frontends to store and retrieve data from the web storage and triggering life cycle methods. Finally, the application shell knows how to route between micro-frontends based on a given URL.

Application Initialization

The first thing the application shell does is consume an API for retrieving the platform configuration stored in the cloud. It consumes an API and returns feature flags, a services dictionary with a few endpoints used for validating tokens before granting the access to an authenticated area, and a list of micro-frontends available to mount.

After consuming the configuration from the backend, the application shell performs several actions:

1. Exposes the relevant part of the configuration to any micro-frontends and appends it to a window object so that every mounted micro-frontend will have access to it.

2. Checks business logic: if there is a token in web storage, validates it with the API layer. Routes the user to the authenticated area if they're entitled or to the landing page if they're not.

3. Mounts the right micro-frontend based on the user's state (whether they're authenticated).

Communication Bridge

The application shell offers a tiny set of APIs that every micro-frontend will find useful for storing or retrieving data or for dealing with life cycle methods. There are three important goals addressed by the application shell exposing these APIs:

- Exposing the life cycle methods for micro-frontends frees up memory before it is unmounted or removes listeners and starts the micro-frontend initialization when all the resources are loaded.

- Being the gatekeeper for managing access for the web storage in this way, the underlying storage for a micro-frontend won't matter. The application shell will decide the best way to store data based on the device or browser it is running on. Remember that this application runs on web, mobile, and living room devices, so there is a huge fragmentation of storage to take care of. It can also perform checks on memory availability and return consistent messages to the user in case all the permissions aren't available in a browser.

- Allow micro-frontends to share tokens or other data using in-memory or web storage APIs.

All the APIs exposed to micro-frontends will be available at the window object in conjunction with the configurations retrieved consuming the related API.

Mounting and unmounting micro-frontends

Since ACME's micro-frontends will have HTML files as an entry point, the application shell needs to parse the HTML file and append inside itself the related tags. For instance, any tag available in the body element of the HTML file will be appended inside the application shell body. In this way, the moment an external file tag is appended inside the application shell Document Object Model (DOM), such as JavaScript or a CSS file, the browser fetches it in the background. There is no need to create custom code for handling something that is already available at the browser level.

To facilitate this mechanism, the teams decided to add an attribute in the HTML elements of every micro-frontend for signaling which tags should be appended and which should be ignored by the application shell.

Sharing state

A key decision made by ACME was that the sharing state between micro-frontends has to be as lightweight as possible. Thus, no domain logic should be shared with the application shell that should be only used for storing and retrieving data from web storage. Because the vertical split architecture means only one micro-frontend can load at a time in the application shell, the state is very well encapsulated inside the micro-frontend. Only a few things are shared with other micro-frontends, such as access tokens and temporary settings that should expire after a user ends the session. Some components will be shared across multiple micro-frontends, but in this case there won't be any shared states, just well-defined APIs for the integration and a strong encapsulation for hiding the implementation details behind the contract.

Global and local routing

Last but not least, the application shell knows which micro-frontend to load based on the configuration loaded at runtime, where a list of micro-frontends and their associated paths is available. In this configuration, every micro-frontend has a global path that should be linked to it. For example, the authentication micro-frontend is associated with *acme.com/account*, which will load when a user types the exact URL or selects a link to that URL.

When a micro-frontend is an SPA, it can manage a local route for navigating through different views. For instance, in the authentication micro-frontend, the user can retrieve a password or sign up to the service. These actions have different URLs available, so that the logic will be handled at the micro-frontend level. The application shell is completely unaware, then, of how many URLs are handled inside the micro-frontend logic.

In fact, the micro-frontend appends a parameter belonging to a view to the path. The sign-up view, for instance, will have the following URL: *acme.com/account/signup*. The first part of the URL is owned by the application shell (global routing), while the *signup* part is owned by the micro-frontend. In this way, the application shell will have a high-level logic for handling a global routing for the application, and the micro-frontend will be responsible for knowing how to manage the local routing and evolving, avoiding the need to change anything in the application shell codebase.

Migration strategy

During the migration period, the application shell will live alongside the SPA. In this way, ACME can deliver incremental value to their user, testing that everything works as expected and redirecting traffic to the SPA if it finds some bugs or unexpected behavior in the new codebase. The trade-off will be in the platform performances because the user will download more code than formerly. However, this method will enable one of the key business requirements: reduce the risk of introducing the micro-frontend architecture. In combination with the canary release, this will make the migration bulletproof to massive issues, thanks to several levers the teams can pull if any inconveniences are found during the migration journey.

Backend Integration

Because ACME is migrating the backend layer from a monolith to microservices, the first step will be a lift and shift, in which they will migrate endpoint after endpoint from the monolith to microservices. Using a strangler fig pattern (*https://oreil.ly/cCGmk*), they will redirect traffic to either the monolith or a new microservice. This means the API contract between frontend and backend will remain the same in the first release. There may be some changes, but they will be the exception rather than the rule.

This approach allows ACME to work in parallel at different speeds between the two layers. However, it may also create a suboptimal solution for data modeling. The drastic changes required to accommodate microservices' distributed nature means some services may not be as well designed as they can be. For the ACME teams, though, this is an acceptable trade-off, considering there are a lot of moving parts to define and learn on this journey. The tech teams agreed to revisit their decisions and design after the first releases to improve the data modeling and APIs' contracts.

Based on this context, the development and platform teams agreed to use load balancers to funnel the traffic to the monolithic or microservices layer, so that the client won't need to change much. Every change will remain at the infrastructure level. Deciding the best way to roll out a new API version can be done without making the client aware of all these changes. The client will fetch the list of endpoints at runtime via the configuration retrieved initially by the application shell, eliminating the need to hardcode the endpoints in the JavaScript codebase.

Integrating Authentication in Micro-Frontends

One of the main challenges of implementing micro-frontend architecture is dealing with authentication, especially with a shared state across multiple micro-frontends. The ACME teams decided to ensure that the application shell is not involved in the domain logic, keeping every micro-frontend as independent as possible. Thanks to the vertical-split approach, sharing data between micro-frontends is a trivial action because they can use web storage or query string for passing persistent data (e.g., simple user preferences) or volatile data (e.g., product ID).

ACME uses the local storage in its monolithic SPA for storing basic user preferences that don't require synchronization across devices, such as the video player's volume level and the JSON web token (JWT) used for authenticating the user. Because the developers want to generate immediate value for their users and company, they decided to stick with this model and deliver the authenticated area of the catalog alongside the SPA. When a user signs up or signs in within the SPA, the JWT will be placed in the local storage. When the application shell loads the catalog micro-frontend, the micro-frontend will then request the token through the application shell and validate it against the backend (see Figure 9-12).

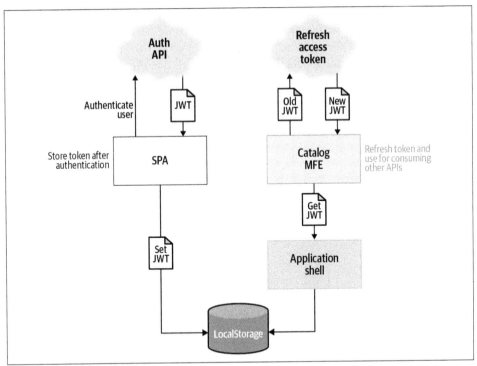

Figure 9-12. During the migration, the SPA authenticates a user and stores the token in the local storage, which the authenticated micro-frontend retrieves once loaded

Due to the local storage security model, the SPA, the application shell, and all the micro-frontends have to live in the same subdomain because the local storage is accessible only from the same subdomain. Therefore, the SPA will have to be moved from being served by an application server to the S3 bucket, where the new architecture will be served from.

Local Storage Security Model

The data processed using the local storage object persists through browser shutdowns, while data created using the session storage object will be cleared after the current browsing session. It's important to note that this storage is origin specific. This means that a site from a different origin cannot access the data stored in an application's local database. For instance, if we store some website data in the local storage on the main domain *www.mysite.com*, the data stored won't be accessible by any other subdomain of *mysite.com* (e.g., *auth.mysite.com*).

Thanks to this approach, ACME can treat the SPA as another micro-frontend with some caveats. When it finally replaces the authentication part and finishes porting to this new architecture, every micro-frontend will have its own responsibility to store or fetch from the local storage via the application shell (see Figure 9-13).

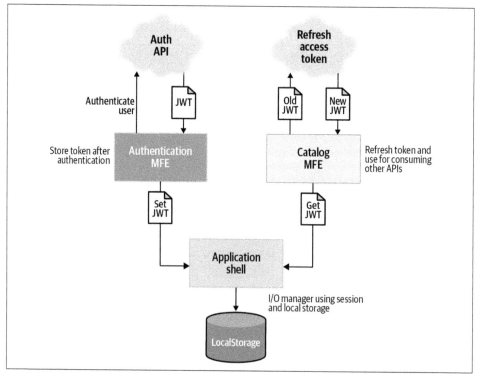

Figure 9-13. When the frontend platform is fully migrated to micro-frontends, every micro-frontend will be responsible for managing part of the users' authentication

After the architecture migration, ACME will revisit where to store the JWT. The usage of local storage exposes the application to cross-site scripting (XSS) attacks, which may become a risk in the long run when the business becomes more popular and more hackers would be interested in attacking the platform.

Cross-Site Scripting

Cross-site scripting (XSS) attacks are a type of injection in which malicious scripts are injected into otherwise benign and trusted websites. XSS attacks occur when an attacker uses a web application to send malicious code, generally in the form of a browser-side script, to a different end user. Flaws that allow these attacks to succeed are widespread and occur anywhere a web application uses input from a user within the output it generates without validating or encoding it.

An attacker can use XSS to send a malicious script to an unsuspecting user. The end user's browser has no way of knowing that the script should not be trusted and will execute it. Because the browser thinks the script came from a trusted source, the malicious script can access any cookies, session tokens, or other sensitive information the browser retains and uses with that site. These scripts can even rewrite the content of the HTML page.

Dependencies Management

ACME decided to share the same versions of React and MobX with all the micro-frontends, reducing the code the user has to download. However, the teams want to be able to test new versions on limited areas of the application so they can test new functionalities before applying them to the entire project. They decided to bundle the common libraries and deploy to the S3 bucket used for all the artifacts. This bundle doesn't change often and therefore is highly cacheable at the CDN level (see Figure 9-14).

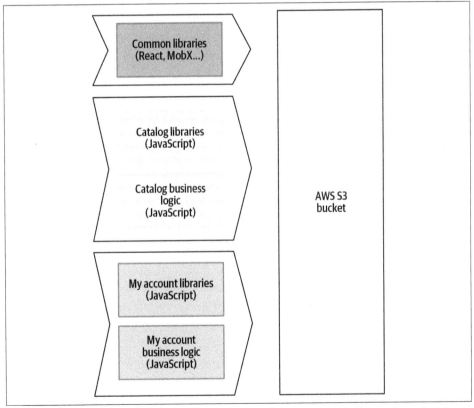

Figure 9-14. Every micro-frontend builds and deploys its own JavaScript dependencies, apart from the common libraries, which have a separate automation strategy

Other teams that want to experiment with new common library versions can easily deploy a custom bundle for their micro-frontend alongside the other final artifact files and use that version instead of the common one.

In the future, ACME's teams are planning to enforce bundle size budgets in the automation pipelines for every micro-frontend to ensure there won't be an exploit of libraries bundled together, which increases the bundle size and the time to render the whole application. This way, ACME aims to keep the application size under control while keeping an eye on the platform evolution, allowing the tech teams to innovate in a frictionless manner.

Integrating a Design System

To maintain UI consistency across all micro-frontends, the tech teams and the UX department decided to revamp the design system available for the SPA using web components instead of Angular. Migrating to web components allows ACME to use the design system during the transition from monolith to distributed architecture, maintaining the same look and feel for the users. The first iteration would just migrate the components from Angular to web components maintaining the same UI. Once the transition is completed, there will be a second iteration where the web components will evolve with the new guidelines chosen by the UX department.

The initial design system was extremely modular, so developers can pick basic components to create more complex ones. The modularity also means the design system library will not be a huge effort to migrate and the implementation will be as quick as it was before.

Due to the distributed nature of the new architecture, ACME decided to enforce at the automation pipeline level using a fitness function for checking that every micro-frontend should use the latest version of the design system library. In this way, they will avoid potential discrepancies across micro-frontends and force all the teams to be up to date with the latest version of the design system. The fitness function will control the existence of the design system in every micro-frontend's *package.json* and then validate the version against the most up-to-date version in case the design system version is older than the current one. The build automation will be blocked and return a message in the logs, so the team responsible for the micro-frontend will know the reason why their artifact wasn't created.

Sharing Components

ACME wants a fast turnaround on new features and technical improvements to reduce external dependencies between teams. At the same time, it wants to maintain design consistency and application performance, so it will share some components across micro-frontends. The guidelines for deciding whether a component may be shared is based on complexity and the evolution, or enhancement, of a component.

For example, the footer and header formerly changed once a year. Now, however, these components will change based on user status and the area a user is navigating. The solution applied for the header and footer will be created with the different modular elements exposed by the design system library. These two elements won't be abstracted inside a component, since the effort to maintain this duplication is negligible and there are only a few micro-frontends to deal with. These decisions may be reverted quickly, however, if the context changes and there are strong reasons for abstracting duplicated parts into a components library.

To avoid external dependencies for releasing a new version or bug fix inside a component, the teams decided to load components owned by a single specialized team, like the video player components, at runtime. A key component of this platform, the video player evolves and improves constantly, so it's assigned to a single team that specializes in video players for different platforms. The team optimizes the end-to-end solution, from encoders and packagers to the playback experience. Because the header and footer will load at runtime, they won't need to wait until every micro-frontend updates the video player library. The video player team will be responsible for avoiding contract-breaking changes without the need to notify all the teams consuming the component.

ACME will make an exception for the design system. Although it's built by a team focused only on the consistency of the user experience, the design system will be integrated at development time to allow developers to control the use of different basic components and to create something more sophisticated inside their micro-frontends. All the other components will be embedded inside a micro-frontend at development time, like any other library such as React or MobX (see Figure 9-15).

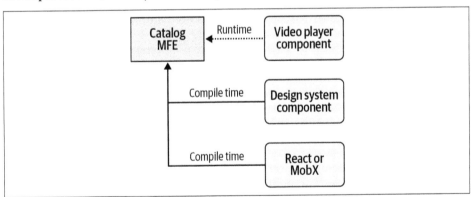

Figure 9-15. In a micro-frontend, complex components owned by a single team are loaded at runtime, while all the others are embedded at compile time. The only exception is the design system due to its modular nature.

None of the components created inside each team will be shared among multiple micro-frontends. If there are components that might simplify multiple teams' work if shared, a committee of senior developers, tech leads, and architects will review the request and challenge the proposal according to the principle defined at the beginning of the project. These principles will be reviewed every quarter to make sure they are still aligned with the platform evolution and business road map.

Implementing Canary Releases

Another goal of this project is being able to release often in production and gather real data directly from the users. It's a great target to aim for, but it's not as easy to reach as we may think.

Based on its infrastructure for serving frontend artifacts, ACME decided to implement a canary release mechanism at the edge, so that it can extend the logic of its Lambda@Edge once the migration is completed, adding logic to manage the micro-frontend releases.

ACME will also need to modify the application shell to request specific micro-frontend versions and delegate retrieving the exact artifact version to the Lambda@Edge. The tech teams decided to identify every micro-frontend release using semantic versioning (semver) (*https://semver.org*). This allows them to create unique artifacts, appending the semver in the filename and easily avoid caching problems when they release new versions.

Semantic Versioning

Given a version number MAJOR.MINOR.PATCH like 1.1.0, increment the:

- MAJOR version when you make incompatible API changes
- MINOR version when you add functionality in a backward-compatible manner
- PATCH version when you make backward-compatible bug fixes

Additional labels for prerelease and build metadata are available as extensions to the MAJOR.MINOR.PATCH format.

As we can see in Figure 9-16, first the application shell retrieves a configuration from the APIs. The configuration contains a map of available micro-frontends versions where only the major version is specified (e.g., 1.x.x). This allows the teams to upgrade the application while maintaining backward compatibility. They also only need to upgrade the major version when an API breaking change updates the configuration file served by the backend.

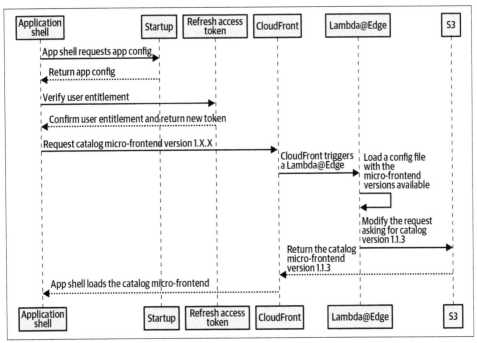

Figure 9-16. Sequence diagram describing how ACME implements canary releases for micro-frontends

When the artifact request hits Amazon CloudFront, a Lambda@Edge that retrieves a list of versions available for the micro-frontends is triggered; the traffic should then be redirected to a specific version. The logic inside the Lambda will associate a random number—from 1 to 100—to every user. If a user is associated with 20% and 30% of the traffic should be redirected to a new version of the requested micro-frontend, that user will see the new version. All the users with a value higher than 30 will see the previous version.

The Lambda returns the selected artifact and generates a cookie where the random value associated with the user is stored. If the user comes back to the platform, the logic running in the Lambda will validate just the rule applied to the micro-frontend requested and evaluate whether the user should be served the same version or a different one based on the traffic patterns defined in the configuration. As a result, both authenticated and unauthenticated traffic will have a seamless experience during the canary exploration of an artifact.

Using this mechanism, ACME can reduce the risk of new releases without compromising fast deployment because they can easily move users from newer versions to an older one simply by modifying the configuration retrieved by the Lambda@Edge.

Localization

The ACME application has to render in different languages based on the user's country. By default, the application will render in English, but the product team wants the user to be able to change the language in the application and have the choice to persist for authenticated users inside their profile settings, creating a seamless experience for the user across all their devices.

In this new architecture, ACME tech teams have to consider two forces:

- Every micro-frontend has a set of labels to display in the UI, some of which may overlap with other micro-frontends, such as common error messages.
- Every micro-frontend represents a business subdomain, so the service has to return just enough labels to display for that specific subdomain and not much more; otherwise, resources will be wasted.

ACME tech teams decided to modify the dictionary API available in the monolith to return only the labels needed inside a micro-frontend. In this way, the SPA can still receive all the labels available for a given language, and the micro-frontend will only receive the label needed for its subdomain during the transition (see Figure 9-17). At migration completion, all the micro-frontends will consume the microservices API instead of the legacy backend, and there won't be a way to retrieve all the labels available in the application through the legacy backend.

When a micro-frontend consumes the dictionary API, it has to pass the subdomain as well as the language and country related to the labels in the request body in order to display them in the user interface. When it receives the request, the microservice will fetch the labels from a database based on the user's country, favorite language, and the micro-frontend subdomain.

Because micro-frontends are not infinite and the platform supports less than a dozen languages, having a CDN distribution in front of the microservice will allow it to cache the response and absorb the requests coming from the same geographical area.

Being able to rely on the monolith via a different endpoint during micro-frontend development creates a potential fallback, if needed. It allows older versions of native applications on mobile devices to continue working without any hiccups.

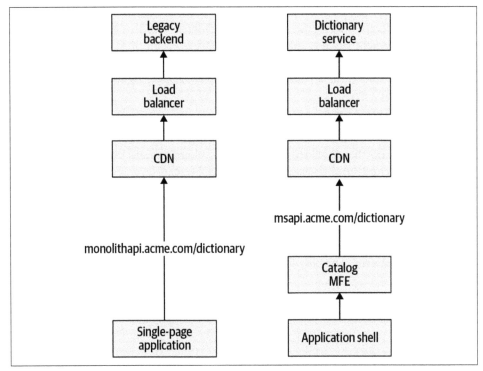

Figure 9-17. The micro-frontend consumes a new API for fetching the labels to display in the interface through a new microservice. The SPA will consume the API from the legacy backend.

Summary

In this chapter, we have gathered all the insights and suggestions shared across the book and demonstrated how they play out in a real-world example. Sharing the reasoning behind certain decisions—the *why*—is fundamental for finding the right trade-off in architecture and, really, in any software project. When you don't know the reasons for certain decisions inside your organization, I encourage you to find someone who can explain them to you. You will be amazed to discover how much effort is spent before finding the right trade-offs between architecture, business outcomes, and timing.

You will see in your career that what works in one context won't work in another because there are so many factors stitching the success of the project together, such as people skills, environment, and culture. Common obstacles include the seniority of the engineers, company culture, communication flows not mapping team interactions, dysfunctional teams, and many more.

When we develop any software project at scale, there are several aspects we need to take into consideration as architects and tech leaders. With this chapter, I wanted to highlight the thought process that moved ACME from an SPA to micro-frontends because these are decisions and challenges you may face in the real world. Some of the reasoning shared in these pages may help you to take the right direction to project success.

One thing that I deeply like about micro-frontends is that we finally have a strong say about how to architect our frontend applications. With SPAs, we followed well-known frameworks that provided us speed of development and delivery because they solved many architectural decisions for us. Now we can leverage these frameworks and contextualize them using their strengths in relevant parts of our projects.

We still have a lot to explore with micro-frontends, including finding the right balance of both technology and people. I find this aspect both extremely challenging and fascinating. Nowadays, we have the opportunity to shape this ecosystem with tools, practices, and patterns. The only limit is our imagination.

CHAPTER 10

Introducing Micro-Frontends in Your Organization

You've arrived at the last chapter of this book and have learned a lot about how to create micro-frontends, the best architectural approach for your project, and all the best practices to follow to make your project successful. It's time to start your project and write a few lines of code, right?

Not quite. There are still some key topics related to the human aspect that we must take into consideration when we introduce this architecture, just as we do whenever we revisit our architecture or introduce a new one. When making significant changes to architecture, we need to think about how to organize the communication flows, how to avoid siloed groups, and how to empower the developers to make the right decisions inside a business domain. These are just some of many important considerations related to the human side of the project we need to think about at the beginning and during the entire life cycle. Micro-frontends may help you mitigate some of these considerations, but they can make others more complex if not approached properly. Therefore, it's crucial for you to invest the time needed to analyze your current organization structure and see how it would fit inside your new architecture.

Why Should We Use Micro-Frontends?

Tech leaders and CTOs often ask this question when someone introduces the idea of micro-frontends inside an organization. It's a valid question, and the best way to answer it is to use a common language to evaluate the benefits of this architecture paradigm. Micro-frontends bring several benefits to the table, such as team independence, riskless deployment, reduction of cognitive load for developers, fast iterations, and innovation. Despite all of that, they also bring challenges, such as a risk of creating silos inside the organization, higher investment in automation pipelines, and risk of user interface discrepancies. When you introduce the idea of micro-frontends to your organization, focus your presentation on not only the technical benefits but also the organizational benefits. Let me provide some food for thought to help you prepare an impactful presentation for your stakeholders:

- Point out that micro-frontends allow faster feature iterations and reduce the risk of introducing bugs into the entire application.
- Research and describe the context you operate in daily and why micro-frontends may help you to achieve business goals.
- List the problems you are trying to solve with this paradigm.
- Ponder the best way to implement micro-frontends in your context.
- Analyze the impact this architecture may have on team communication.
- Identify the ideal governance for managing such an architecture.
- Retrieve metrics from your automation pipeline, like time to deployment and testing, and think how you would be able to improve them.

These are just some topics that are relevant to your organization's tech leaders or clients.

Remember to present not just a technical solution, which can leave many organizational challenges to overcome. Instead, think about an end-to-end transformation that brings value to the company as well as to your customers. To discover the best technical solution for your context, I strongly encourage you to first run a proof of concept (PoC) to understand the challenges and benefits of this approach better; what works for one team or organization doesn't always work for another. Be mindful and share the insights that will work best for your organization with your peers and tech leaders. Try to involve the right people up front, because understanding the context in which you operate may result in a nontrivial activity, especially in midsize to large organizations, where you may be dealing with distributed teams whose culture and context change office by office. In the following sections, you'll discover some insights on how to manage the governance, documentation, organization setup, and communication flows for a micro-frontend project.

The Link Between Organizations and Software Architecture

What sort of software architecture should you be implementing? You'd be forgiven for wanting to copy others' success. But there is no perfect architecture, only good and bad fits for a context. Everything is a set of trade-offs. Perfection is unavailable, unfortunately. What we need to create is an architecture that fits our organization's needs and, especially, the context we operate in.

We often hear conference talks that explain a specific use case. The ideas and solutions the speaker brings up feel like a perfect fit for what we are trying to solve in our organization. Unfortunately, it's not often the case. In any talk or book, the solution to a problem is given from the perspective of just one person, who may represent only part of the organization. Often the speaker or writer focuses more on the how and less on the context where their specific solution was successful. There's little on *why* this solution worked for this context. But that context provides us with the information we need to make the right trade-offs for our architectures.

What software architecture should you be implementing? The answer is "It depends." There is no single architecture that works well in all cases and at all times. You have to customize your architecture for your needs, applying the patterns that solve your problems and fit your situation best. Bear in mind that the business evolves over time and, therefore, a good trade-off today may not be a good one tomorrow.

Modularity is the key for moving in the direction the business wants to go, allowing it to arrive faster and with minimal complexity. At the same time, modularity is far from a trivial task. It requires discipline, analysis, and a lot of work from everyone involved in the project. Micro-frontends are no exception to this. They're definitely not suitable for all projects. But they may be useful when you work in a midsize to large environment, with three or more teams working exclusively on the frontend side of a project. They may also be really helpful when scaling the organization is a requirement, when an application's success depends on time to market, when we are transitioning from a legacy application to a new one and want to generate immediate value for our users instead of waiting several months before the application is finished, and in many other scenarios.

You may want to embrace a micro-frontends implementation different from the approaches described in this book or even try new approaches for solving specific problems inside your organization. This is absolutely fine, as long as there are strong reasons for doing so and the new trade-off will benefit a team, the entire organization, or a process.

How Do Committees Invent?

In the first chapter, I briefly introduced Conway's law: "Any organization that designs a system (defined more broadly here than just information systems) will inevitably produce a design whose structure is a copy of the organization's communication structure." This law is from the 1968 paper "How Do Committees Invent?" (*https://oreil.ly/v5WM0*) by Melvin Conway. In his paper, Conway explains how software architecture is usually designed alongside the company structure. But this is not always the case. Sometimes we want to focus on a high-level architecture that is the best trade-off for designing a platform and then restructure our teams around that architecture. In these situations, we are applying the opposite technique, called the "inverse Conway maneuver." In the "Stages of Design" section of the paper where he describes the steps for designing software architectures, Conway recommends the following:

- Understanding of the boundaries, both on the design activity and on the system to be designed, placed by the sponsor and by the world's realities

- Achievement of a preliminary notion of the system's organization so that design task groups can be meaningfully assigned

Though these principles are half a century old, they feel more relevant than ever. In the book *Accelerate*, authors Nicole Forsgren, Jez Humble, and Gene Kim share incredible research on the best practices of high-performance organizations from across multiple industries. The inverse Conway maneuver plays an important part in the social-technical aspect of every high-performance organization the authors study.

Architecture and team communication are strongly linked. It's crucial to understand and internalize this, because it will greatly influence which micro-frontend architecture we decide to use. Ideally, we would design the best architecture possible for a given context and then assign teams to fulfill the design, but that's not always possible. In fact, in my experience, it's rarely possible, but it could happen sometimes. In cases where we need to respect the current organization structure, we need to take into consideration teams' current communication flows, daily interactions, and the organization structure during our architecture design process in order to design an architecture suitable for our teams. Realizing that communication flow and architecture are linked together allows you to aim for the best architecture for the context you operate within.

When considering communication flows, we need to distinguish between collocated and distributed teams. Sam Newman shared a very valid point in an article about Conway's law (*https://oreil.ly/Uoa6j*): "The communication pathways that Conway refers to are in contrast to the code itself, *where a single codebase requires fine-grained communication, but a distributed team is only capable of coarse-grained communication.* Where such tensions emerge, looking for opportunities to split monolithic systems up around organizational boundaries will often yield significant advantages" (my emphasis).

The communication type, coarse or fine, is another essential consideration when we design our architecture. In a distributed company, the best way to achieve fine-grained communication across teams is to have a fully remote organization so that there isn't any difference between teams. However, the moment an organization has multiple developer centers in multiple locations, the communication flow changes again, and having multiple teams working on the same area of the codebase in different offices may be more of an issue than a benefit. A good way to mitigate this problem is by assigning all the subdomains that intersect and share similarities to a colocated team instead of distributing them. For example, imagine a video-streaming platform composed of the following areas:

- Landing page
- Movies catalog
- Playback
- Search
- Personalization
- Sign-in
- Sign-up
- Payment
- Remember email
- Remember password
- Help
- My account

When we group subdomains that intersect and share similarities, we can group subdomains related to new-user onboarding:

- Landing page
- Sign-up
- Payment

Then we can group subdomains related to existing users who may or may not already have authenticated inside our platform:

- Sign-in
- Remember email
- Remember password
- My account

Finally, we can group subdomains related to existing users who have authenticated:

- Movies catalog
- Playback
- Search
- Personalization

What we've done is group subdomains by user journey, that is, subdomains that intersect. The playback experience, for instance, certainly has more in common with the movies catalog than with the Help pages. Did you notice that the Help domain wasn't in any of the previous groups? That's because the Help section may be useful for authenticated and nonauthenticated users alike.

It's very hard to have a perfect split between the user journeys. This is also true when we identify the different subdomains available in these user journeys. In this example, we ended up with several buckets of user journeys, with one or more subdomains within each bucket. However, the moment we are able to identify these subdomains, we can determine how to map the development of our micro-frontends inside a company. This exercise may force us to swap some domains from one office to another one, although it provides great long-term benefits reducing external dependencies across offices and keeping them in the same one, maintaining a fine-grained communication where subdomains work together and a coarse-grained communication across offices where the need of synchronization happens less often and with fewer touching points. Yet, as stated before, it's very unlikely to have this perfect split, so don't be surprised if you end up with some subdomains developed by different offices. Just be sure to constantly review the performance and bottlenecks created inside the organization and adjust your decisions accordingly. When done right, microarchitectures are great because they can follow a business's evolution and, thanks to their modular nature, provide the tech department a great degree of flexibility.

Features Versus Components Teams

Nowadays, many companies are debating which team structure they should use to enable developers to work on their tasks without impediments or external dependencies. Usually agile methodologies suggest one of two structures: features teams and components teams. Features teams, also known as cross-functional teams, are organized with all the skills needed for delivering a specific feature. When we are developing a web application, for instance, a cross-functional team is organized to deliver user value around a specific feature. Let's imagine that we have a cross-functional team that will create the credit card payment feature inside an ecommerce store. The team will have both frontend and backend (a.k.a. full-stack) developers who will develop, test, and deploy the feature end to end. Figure 10-1 depicts this example with Team Burrito, which is responsible for delivering the product details micro-frontend.

In this case, Team Burrito will be composed of full-stack developers working on the APIs, as well as the frontend that will consume these APIs.

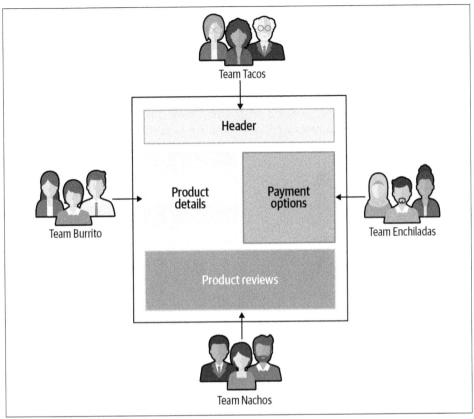

Figure 10-1. This diagram depicts the responsibilities of the features teams working on a horizontal-split architecture, where every team is responsible end to end for a micro-frontend and the APIs that it consumes

Features teams are recommended when you can organize the architecture using a horizontal split, and every team is responsible for one or more micro-frontends. With this approach, the teams can focus solely on their features with an end-to-end approach, taking care of the entire feature life cycle. The cognitive load of a features team is more manageable than any other team's structure because every person responsible for generating value for the user is part of the same team. Usually, features teams are highly focused on the user, iterating constantly to enhance the user experience and the value created by their development effort.

One challenge with this approach is that we will need to assign page composition to an external team or, more likely, to one of the teams developing a feature. The team responsible for composing the page must ensure the final result for the user is the one expected, without any logical or cosmetic bugs. We can mitigate this challenge by standardizing the page composition with templates and conventions. In this case, it would be easier to manage but will offer a lot less flexibility across page layouts. Another option would be working with component teams, where every team is responsible for a specific component of a platform (a vertical split), as we can see in Figure 10-2.

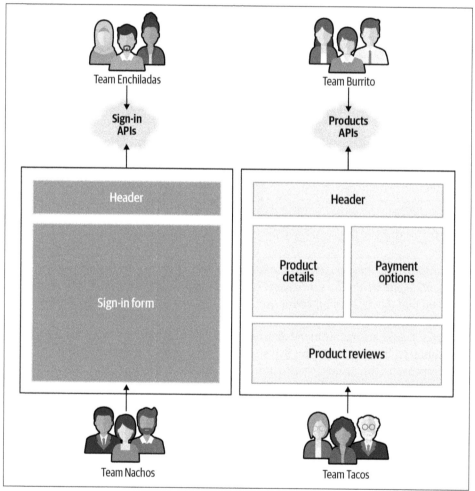

Figure 10-2. In this example, components teams are each responsible for a specific part of a platform

With a vertical-split architecture, Teams Burrito and Enchiladas are responsible for the backend services, and Teams Nachos and Tacos are responsible for the frontend. This way of organizing teams works better when we are dealing with cross-platform applications in midsize to large organizations, where we usually develop at least a web application in conjunction with a native mobile application each for Android and iOS. In this instance, when the APIs are consumed by several client applications (mobile, web, and maybe other devices), a backend team responsible for creating an API takes into consideration all the needs of the consumer (frontend teams) instead of features teams optimizing the APIs for just one platform and treating the other clients' teams as second-class citizens. When we are working with cross-platform applications and hybrid technologies like Flutter, Ionic, or React Native, cross-platform teams are a more viable option than component teams. The codebase between frontend projects may be shared across targets, so organizing teams around features becomes the better choice. If you want to pursue the native option, however, think twice about how to organize your teams because switching from one native language to another and finally to web and backend languages is challenging and increases the cognitive load.

It's important to recognize that different stages of the business life cycle require different team structures. In the case of growth, you will encounter a moment where the organization requires some structural changes. These changes will lead you to reassess the teams around the architecture in order to reduce the friction for delivering a feature or any other stream of work. Invest time analyzing the communication flows and potential patterns established across teams, like constant external dependencies or slow stories throughput due to distributed teams in multiple time zones.

Domain-driven design (DDD) is helpful when we are organizing our team structure, because it helps to consider the direct connection between architecture and team structure. Not only does DDD help identify the boundaries between subdomains, but we can follow these boundaries for structuring our teams as well. For instance, with a small company, it's very likely that a team would be responsible for a specific business subdomain end to end; however, within a larger organization, a multitude of teams create a subdomain, working together due to the work's inherent complexity and scope. It's not always possible to create the perfect structure, and often we need to make some trade-offs to create a model that almost fits everywhere. This is not necessarily a roadblock for your strategy, but do understand that trade-offs could happen. When trade-offs become a constant across the entire organization, we need to step back and review our team structure and architecture.

The structure of our teams—whether organized around features or components—and how we structure our micro-frontend applications will impact the communication flow inside the organization. There are certain practices that may help us achieve an efficient spread of information across teams, enhancing the governance for developing new features and capabilities inside our platform. Let's analyze some of them in the next section.

Implementing Governance for Easing the Communication Flows

Working for midsize to large organizations means defining communication flows that work; otherwise, we risk slowing down development or creating too many external dependencies across teams. An investment worth making is governance. This is not just an upfront investment; it has to be a constant review and optimization of the practices and documents needed for scaling an organization. There are some simple wins for allowing our developers to scale their communication, especially for the future. We should remember that there will always be new employees at our company; the best way for them to fill their knowledge gaps would be to understand the context in which certain decisions were made. Without that context, they won't have enough information to fully understand the situation. Architecturally speaking, there are two practices that can spread the information and track why certain decisions were or were not made: the request for comments (RFC) and the architecture decision record (ADR).

Requests for Comments

RFCs are an established way to gauge the interest in a change in a technical approach or a new technology or practice inside an organization. Usually RFCs are kicked off by developers or tech leads who see some gaps or potential improvement in the organization and want to understand if there is room for a change. RFCs are often available in the version control system (GitHub, for example), so every technical person has access to them. RFCs are timeboxed and are a short markdown document composed of the following sections:[1]

Feature name
    The name of the feature or practice to introduce or change

Summary
    One-paragraph explanation of the feature or practice

Motivation
    Usually the *why* of making a change

---

[1] This list is just a suggestion. Not all of the items may be present in your RFC template, but it's a good starting point.

Description of the change
    Detailed analysis of the change or new feature

Drawbacks
    All the potential issues identified by the proposal submitter

Alternatives
    Potential alternatives to achieve the goals with pros and cons

Unresolved questions
    Any blind spots in the proposal

Additional resources
    A list of resources related to the RFC

After filing an RFC, the submitter shares the link with the interested parties inside the organization. Then the dialogue starts to flow, with people sharing ideas, asking questions, and trying to understand whether the proposal has any potential for being introduced inside the company. Despite its simplicity, this document is important in the present because it may improve current software development or practices. Moreover, the RFC has a fundamental benefit for the future as well. In fact, this document tracks the discussion happening among all the developers, architects, and tech leads, recording the full discussion and approaches. This history will give new employees a clear context that describes the reasons behind certain decisions. RFCs are great for proposing not only new features but also changes. For instance, when we need to update an API contract, using an RFC allows us to gather our consumers' thoughts, ideas, and concerns, allowing us to shape the best way to achieve the goal. This scenario often happens when we work with component teams, and the backend team comprises multiple teams that consume their APIs.

With an RFC, the team that owns the API contract can propose changes and collect the feedback from the other teams, gathering the evolution of the API and the reasons behind them. This practice becomes even more important when we work with distributed teams across multiple time zones, because we can share all the information needed without remote meetings, closing the feedback loop in a reasonable time.

Architectural Decision Records

Another useful document for sharing decision context for current and future developers is the ADR, in which architects or tech leads gather the decisions behind a specific architecture implementation. ADRs are focused solely on architecture, but they are still useful for providing for future readers a context and a snapshot in time of your organization. In fact, an ADR specifically describes the company context when the ADR is first written. ADRs also differ from RFCs in that they provide the context of why an architecture change is needed and explain why a specific decision was made. Architecture is always about finding the balance between long-term and short-term wins. These trade-offs are defined in the company context we operate within. With ADR, we want to create a snapshot of the company context and provide a description about why we pick one direction over another. An ADR structure is composed of the following sections:

Status
> The status of an ADR (e.g., draft, agreed)

Stakeholders
> People behind the ADR, usually architects and tech leads

Outcome
> The final decision made

Due date
> The date for when the decision has to be made

Owners
> Document's owners

Introduction
> A paragraph describing the company context and the problem the ADR is trying to solve

Forces
> The parallel or overlapping streams of work that are pushing toward an architecture change

Options
> List of potential solutions with business and technical details and the pros and cons for every proposal

Final decision and rationale
> A summary of the final decision explaining the reasons behind choosing a proposal listed in the options paragraph

Appendix
> Additional resources needed for providing more context to the readers

As with RFCs, not all these parts are mandatory, but they are highly recommended. Remember, ADRs have to provide the context for everyone interested in why an architectural decision was made, so the reader needs to have clarity on the technical and business context when the ADR was created. When we design our micro-frontends, we may change the framework or design patterns implemented inside the architecture. By using ADRs, we can provide the context that existed before the architecture decision and why we now want to change it. This way, everyone will be on the same page, despite not being physically present in the meetings.

Techniques for Enhancing the Communication Flow

When first approaching micro-frontends, many people think this architectural pattern may result in organizational silos due to its intrinsic characteristics, such as independency and decentralization. Although micro-frontends enable teams to work in parallel and release artifacts independently, there is no excuse for not creating a collaborative environment inside the tech department. We cannot embrace distributed systems without establishing mechanisms for teams to come together on a regular basis for sharing knowledge, solutions, and challenges. It's essential to curate the technical as well as the social aspect for guaranteeing the right flow of information inside an organization. Everything should start from the feature's specifications.

Working Backward

Famous for its customer-centric approach, Amazon often works backward when considering product ideas. Simply put, they start with the customer and work backward to the product rather than starting with a product idea and bolting customers onto it. It's a method for creating a customer-focused vision of your product. A working-backward document, called a PR/FAQ, is up to six pages long: a one-page press release (PR) and up to five pages of frequently asked questions (FAQs). An appendix section is also included. While working backward can be applied to any specific product decision, using this approach is especially important when developing new products or features.

Because it starts with where you want to be 12 months in the future, the working-backward method forces you to think big, focusing on big goals and the changes you need to achieve. A well-crafted press release is a great use of storytelling. It gets the team excited and focused before any lines of code are written.

The FAQ section is composed of two subsections. The first one is based on the public questions a customer might have about the product or feature, written as if it is public product documentation that is released at the same time as the press release. The second subsection consists of questions internal stakeholders might have asked during the product development process.

The PR/FAQs focus effort on how a specific feature benefits the customer and why the company should invest in a product or feature like that in its system. After a PR/FAQs is written, a meeting is scheduled with the main stakeholders, including developers, QAs, tech leads, architects, and other product people. In general, though, any stakeholder who may help improve the decision process is invited. This may seem like overkill, but one hour of socializing requirements can allow techies to raise questions and become familiar with the feature. It's a first step for having multiple teams understand the initial requirements of a new feature and aligning it with the business goals to reach. When we work with micro-frontends, a PR/FAQs can bridge the teams that will collaborate in the implementation phase.

Two extremely valuable benefits of the PR/FAQs process are the resulting concise documentation and initial collaboration phase before the implementation phase. Usually a PR/FAQs document is a good starting point for architects to think about the high-level design, including the challenges and the architecture characteristics needed for implementing a feature.

This is also true for micro-frontends when a new requirement arises and it has to be implemented across multiple domains. Having this kind of document can facilitate the discussion between teams via the requirements socialization between engineers and product teams.

If you are interested in knowing more, I recommend reading Chris Vander Mey's *Shipping Greatness* (O'Reilly), a book that provides more information on how to write PR/FAQs, following Amazon learnings and suggestions. If you prefer a short document about PR/FAQs instead, check out "PR FAQs for Product Documents" (*https://oreil.ly/6xuxA*), a blog post by Robert (Munro) Monarch that offers a great summary of this topic.

Community of Practice and Town Halls

The community of practice and town halls are two more important practices for facilitating the communication flows across the organization. With both cross-functional and components teams, there is a need to spread knowledge among developers of the same discipline (frontend developers in the micro-frontend world). Usually communities of practice are biweekly or monthly meetings scheduled by engineer managers or tech leads to facilitate discussions across team members responsible for the same discipline. In these meetings, the developers share best practices, how they have solved specific problems, new findings, or topics they've recently been exposed to inside their domain. Communities of practice are useful for introducing new practices across the organization, discussing automation pipelines improvements, or even hosting mob programming (*https://oreil.ly/DLkbs*) events, which has engineers collaboratively implementing a new feature or discussing a specific programming approach all together. While usually restricted to a team, I've experienced some mob programming sessions during a community of practice that have worked well.

Mob Programming

Mob programming is a software development approach in which a whole team works on the same project as a group, working on the same computer at the same time. This is similar to pair programming, in which two people work on the same code together at one computer. Mob programming just extends the collaboration to everyone on the team. This technique is typically used when a team is implementing an important but complex feature or during a community of practice where a vertical inside an organization wants to introduce new practices across the tech department.

Town halls are events organized across the tech department that provide a general knowledge of what's happening across teams, such as a team's recent achievements or new practices to introduce inside the organization. Town halls work especially well when an organization works with distributed teams and developers cannot engage with all the teams on a daily basis. During these events, the tech leadership facilitates the knowledge to be shared through short presentations covering the key initiatives brought up by different teams. Considering the large audience attending these events, any questions or deep dives should be taken up at a separate time by the interested people and the team or person involved in a given initiative.

Town halls are very useful when a team would like to share a new library they have developed that may be used by different teams, new practices introduced by a team and the results after embracing it, or more general topics like new joiners or shared goals across the department.

Depending on the company's size, town halls may not be the right choice for some companies. A good alternative for spreading these initiatives and communications could be an internal newsletter for the tech department. We may decide to split the newsletter by topics and allow developers to pick their favorite information, but this will depend on the organization's size and structure.

Managing External Dependencies

Sometimes during a sprint (*https://oreil.ly/cjONE*), external dependencies may impede the delivery of a task or story. While this is not usually a problem, when distributed teams work on microarchitectures, it can slow down feature delivery, creating frustration and frictions across teams. When a team is hampered by too many external dependencies, it may be time to revisit our decisions and review the boundaries of a micro-frontend. Frequently occurring external dependencies is one of the strongest signs that something is not working as expected. But fear not: it's a fixable problem! As long as the information bubbles up from the teams to the tech leadership, leadership may decide to rearrange the organization, reducing communication friction and improving the throughput.

With micro-frontends, this situation can occur when we share libraries across micro-frontends or when we compose multiple micro-frontends in the same view, if we don't pay enough attention to how to decouple them. With a horizontal-split architecture, we need to invest time reviewing the communication flows, especially at the beginning of the project. A classic example is when we are porting a frontend project from a monolith, single-page application or from a server-side-rendering one to micro-frontends. When we embrace the horizontal-split architecture, we need to assign ownership of the view composition process. In fact, despite having multiple teams contributing with their micro-frontends to the final result, we need to identify the owner of the composition stage (either client or server side). This team should be responsible for not only composing the view but also understanding potential scenarios where a micro-frontend could cause other micro-frontends problems due to CSS style issues or events dispatched but not properly handled by other micro-frontends.

It's true that this architecture style provides more flexibility on reusing micro-frontends across a project, but at the same time, we need to make sure the final result is what the user expects to have. Another challenge in the communication flow for the horizontal split architecture may happen when a micro-frontend is reused in different views of one or more applications. In this case, the team responsible for the micro-frontend should create strong relationships with all the other teams that may asynchronously interact with the micro-frontend and have regular catchups to make sure the touching points within a view are respected.

The problem of too many external dependencies may happen in very limited cases with a vertical-split architecture, especially if we are using an application shell that orchestrates the micro-frontend life cycle. For example, let's say we want to add a new route inside our application. The application shell will need to be aware that a new micro-frontend needs to be loaded and that it will have to manage the new route. When well designed, the application shell loads an external configuration retrieved from a static file served by a content delivery network (CDN) or as a response of an endpoint. In this case, the effort to coordinate with the team that owns the application shell would be minimal because all that's required is changing the configuration, adding new automation tests, and following the testing life cycle implemented inside the organization.

Another potential activity slowdown can occur when you need to make changes across multiple micro-frontends. This usually happens once or twice a year; if it occurs more often, that's another sign we should review the division of our micro-frontends. However, with a vertical split, teams have more autonomy. If we are able to review the communication flows iteratively, we shouldn't have many surprises or external issues.

For all these situations, reviewing the communication flows with the right cadence, and making sure the assumptions made during the architecture design process are still valid, are good practices. Another way to ensure the communication is flowing across teams is by having ad hoc meetings for the teams that have to work together for the final-view result, especially for a horizontal-split architecture. Using agile ceremonies like Scrum of Scrums or less informal catch-ups on a regular cadence result in a better understanding of the overall system, as well as better bounding between team members.

Finally, agile practices provide some tools that may be used either ad hoc or on a case-by-case basis to solve specific challenges we face with our teams. One tool that I have personally experienced in multiple companies I've worked for is big room planning, where we gather an entire department for one or two days inside a room and we map the activities for the next few months. In this way, we can immediately spot external dependencies and potential bottlenecks due to a wrong sequence of deliverables. There are many techniques available for solving specific challenges. I recommend first gaining an understanding of the problem you need to solve and then finding the right approach for that problem.

A Decentralized Organization

A key advantage of working with micro-frontends specifically, and with microarchitectures in general, is the possibility of empowering the teams to own a business domain end to end. As we have seen throughout this book, micro-frontends are not for all organizations. They work well for midsize to large ones, where insight on the intrinsic complexity the company is working on is needed. Complexity is not necessarily a negative attribute; it can allow us to move from a centralized approach to a decentralized one.

Every company moves through different phases. In the startup phase, a company usually has a small tech team capable of working on a project end to end. The communication flow in the startup phase is straightforward because all the developers are aware of the goals to achieve, and the number of connections needed for a correct communication flow is manageable. When the startup grows larger, it's usually structured around business function hierarchies, introducing roles like head of engineering, engineer manager, tech leader, and many other well-known titles in the tech ecosystem. Usually these organization layers provide directions to coordinate teams, defining the communication flows. In an ideal scenario, the teams may have the level of autonomy needed to do their jobs and to experiment with new practices and technologies at the same time, but this doesn't always happen. The reality will depend on the company culture, as well the leadership style of every individual.

When the organization moves from hundreds to thousands of employees, we need to look again at how to organize our teams. A natural evolution from the hierarchical structure would be aligning teams around value streams instead of following a centralizing hierarchy. Decentralizing the decision-making and allowing an independent path for the teams inside a value stream will empower the technical teams to express themselves in the best way in the large, complex context where they operate. These three types of structure are visually represented in Figure 10-3.

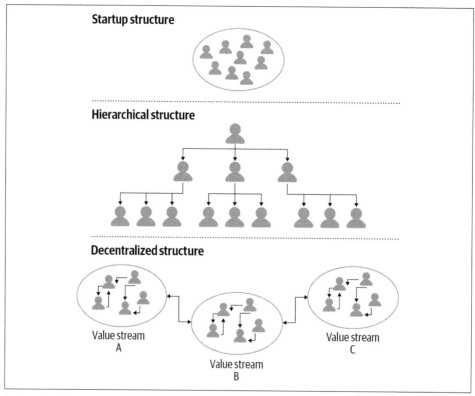

Figure 10-3. Different organizational structures are usually implemented in different stages of a company life cycle

An interesting point highlighted in Figure 10-3 is that, with the decentralized structure, teams must coordinate among themselves when needed. Empowering these teams means giving not only technical freedom but also organizational duties. Technical leaders then become a support function that should facilitate the streams of work inside the teams, providing context or technical direction when a team requests it and driving and aligning the technical boundaries with the business results so that the team knows how to achieve these goals.

Another great achievement of decentralization is error mitigation. In this structure, it's unlikely that only one or a few people are capable of making every decision for every team, especially because the leadership is not always involved in the day-to-day conversations. Therefore, the role of an architect or a tech lead would include posing the right questions and becoming a servant-leader for the team, creating solutions hand in hand with the team rather than in isolation.

Organize for Complexity

Many of the concepts of decentralization that I've described are part of a great book called *Organize for Complexity* by Niels Pflaeging (BetaCodex Publishing). This short, straightforward book provides many insights on how to decentralize an organization handling complexity. I was lucky enough to meet Niels during an agile retreat and received a complimentary copy of his book. It changed the way I thought about tech organizations, opening several doors in my mind. The book doesn't focus on tech organizations but more generally on any organization. That's the reason I shared these insights, contextualizing the core concepts in the tech context. I found these concepts extremely valid for microarchitectures.

Decentralization Implications with Micro-Frontends

The first step in decentralizing decision making and empowering the teams that are closer to the business domain is identifying the subdomains available in an application. As we have seen so far, DDD helps us identify the business subdomains where we create a common language (ubiquitous language), we introduce patterns for communicating across subdomains for decoupling them, and we allow them to evolve at their own pace. Another important aspect to take into consideration is user behavior, especially when we are porting an existing application to micro-frontends. These two metrics allow us to identify the different pieces of a complex puzzle and assign every piece to a specific team.

I highly recommend basing the micro-frontends split on data, because this can really save you a lot of aggravation in the long run. Starting with incorrect assumptions creates friction across teams and release cycles. Data can help prevent those incorrect assumptions.

Another important thing to consider is balancing complexity when we assign a team to a subdomain. When a team is assigned to multiple complex subdomains, there is a high risk of resource burnout and intrinsic maintenance complexity. There are several situations we need to be aware of:

High-complexity subdomain
This type of subdomain usually doesn't manifest at the beginning of the project. They're created when we underestimate a subdomain's complexity in terms of the business logic and permutations that a micro-frontend needs. Usually a micro-frontend becomes complex over time because new features are added to it. A good practice, therefore, is to understand the cognitive load of every team member working on that subdomain and determine whether they can handle the

situation properly. The main struggle is often in maintenance and support, especially when the team deals with projects that have to be live 24/7 and where bugs have to be fixed as quickly as possible. High complexity is difficult to handle in general, and it's even more difficult when a developer is under pressure because a live bug is found in the middle of the night and requires a quick fix.

In these cases, remember to review the boundaries of your subdomain and see if it can be split in a more sensible manner, especially when you work with a vertical-split architecture. Consider, for instance, when you have an authentication micro-frontend containing the sign-in and sign-up flows in a vertical-split architecture. If you are working on a global platform, you may have to support multiple payment methods, which adds a lot of information to remember and own. Splitting the authentication micro-frontends into sign-in and sign-up micro-frontends would maintain a frictionless user experience while reducing the cognitive load on the team, as described in Figure 10-4.

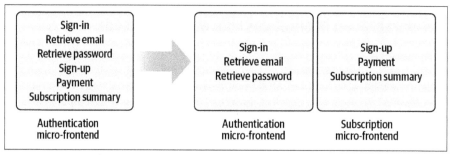

Figure 10-4. Another option is to split the micro-frontend to reduce the team's cognitive load without impacting the user's experience

Now we have a team dedicated to new users who want to sign up and another dedicated to existing users who have to sign in or retrieve their email or password. In this way, we simplify the logic and code and can have quicker fixes when bugs are discovered.

High initial-effort subdomain
Sometimes we may have micro-frontends that require a high effort to create them, but then they don't evolve very often in the application life cycle. In this case, we can afford to have a team with multiple micro-frontends, bearing in mind we need to balance the micro-frontends' complexity to avoid drowning the team in work.

Normal-complexity subdomain
When considering a single team, these are the subdomains we should aim for. Sometimes when we have high-complexity subdomains, we may decide that splitting the micro-frontend representing that subdomain would not help much.

However, we can componentize a specific complex part of the micro-frontend and assign the component to another team, as we can see in Figure 10-5.

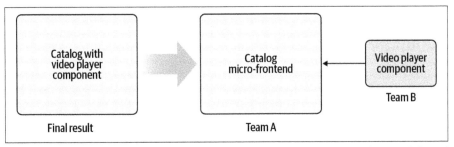

Figure 10-5. This example shows a project with high complexity but the possibility of extracting a component to another team to spread the cognitive load

In this case, we have a vertical-split architecture with a micro-frontend with multiple views and a complex business logic to implement for the video player that should play video, advertising, and so on. The video player can be peeled off from the micro-frontend. This self-contained component may be reused in other micro-frontends and has an intrinsic complexity, making it a good choice to be handled by a different team, reducing the cognitive load of both the micro-frontend and the video player. The teams can collaborate when new versions of the video players version are available. In this case, working with an API contract and scheduling regular touch points between teams is sufficient to coordinate the integration, new releases, and breaking changes.

Low-complexity subdomain
Finally, some micro-frontends are easy to build and maintain so one team can own a multitude of them. As with the previous cases, make sure to regularly rebalance the complexity assigned to these teams because, while the complexity may be low in this case, having dozens of low-complexity micro-frontends may cause high-context switching, reducing the team's productivity.

Decentralizing decision-making and empowering teams doesn't mean we need to create chaos inside the organization. In fact, some decisions should remain centralized and made by the teams across all of an organization's domains, such as a platform or developer experience team, or by tech leadership, like head or vice president of engineering, providing a framework for the teams to operate with. We mentioned such decisions in previous chapters, like the platform to run the automation strategy; programming languages or frameworks available for the teams to use guidelines on when to abstract and when to duplicate code; and architecture characteristics, such as performance metrics, code coverage and complexity, setting up the observability of the entire platform (frontend and backend), and support governance when the application fails in production. All these decisions provide a concrete framework for the teams to operate on. They don't affect the teams' freedom, and they align the company behind some guidelines that should allow your technical teams to achieve business goals.

Summary

In this chapter, we learned that we cannot design a software architecture without taking into consideration the human factor. Architecture and organization structure go hand in hand when we want any project to succeed. We need to be aware that these two forces are part of a project's success and they cannot be decoupled. They must be looked at together and revised often. Any business can evolve over time, and the same is true for software architecture and communication flows inside a company. The communication flow can be enhanced by spreading information across the teams, but it has to be thought through and designed carefully, and we need to iterate to find the right balance. What works in one company will not necessarily work in others, so carefully analyze your context and apply the best practices for your organization.

Finally, we looked at how decentralization helps the implementation of any micro-architecture, whether microservices or micro-frontends. It's important to highlight that the micro-frontends architecture we chose should influence the way we structure our teams. It's very unlikely that when we move from a monolith architecture to a microarchitecture the organization can remain the same. The communication flow changes with the new architecture, and we need to at least review the flow so that we don't create bottlenecks inside the teams due to the wrong setup.

What Does the Community Think About Micro-Frontends?

Throughout this book, we have discussed what micro-frontends are, how we can create a micro-frontend architecture, and what the socio-technical impact of this paradigm is. As explained in Chapter 1, many companies have implemented micro-frontends in production in many different ways.

I interviewed several industry professionals who are embracing micro-frontends in their organizations to share the breadth of uses. The following are interviews with tech leads, architects, and developers sharing their development challenges with micro-frontend projects.

Enjoy the interviews!

Nimisha Asthagiri, Chief Architect at edX

Please introduce yourself.

Nimisha Asthagiri is chief architect at edX, where she actively drives strategic initiatives to implement an intentional architecture for the next generation of large-scale online learning. Since joining edX in 2014, she spent countless hours tackling problems of distributed computing and scalability. Now, she focuses on taming a monolithic architecture, redesigning the platform for the future of learning, and aligning the edX development community on sound design principles and practices.

Nimisha is passionate about education as an avenue to inspire and improve the lives of many. edX is a global nonprofit, open source platform for education and learning.

What is your experience with micro-frontends?

Two years ago, we began replatforming our architecture so the frontend is decoupled from the backend. We embarked upon this journey since frontend development was too painful and too slow in our platform.

We use Django as our web framework, where our frontend views are implemented in Django templates and served from the backend, in a Python-based development environment. Imagine the developer experience of JavaScript-focused frontend developers who were constantly blocked and impaired in a monolithic backend environment! (Note there are 1.5 million lines of code in the monolith and 4.5 million lines of code in the platform.)

We formed a team of three that grew to six to tackle this problem and establish the basic foundation and initial architectural principles for micro-frontends (MFEs) in the platform. Inspired by Tech Radar's note on MFEs (*https://oreil.ly/lC4eO*) and other MFE experiences (*https://micro-frontends.org*), I proposed a capabilities model (*https://oreil.ly/vFzEV*) that provided a direction for us to move from our monolith to a domain-driven decoupled architecture.

What benefits and pitfalls did you encounter in your journey with micro-frontends?

The benefits were tremendous in developer productivity. The developer experience dramatically improved with frontend developers using frontend-familiar technologies such as npm and webpack. The time-to-deploy of frontend changes were remarkably reduced to 10 minutes (as opposed to multiple hours for the monolith). The frontend code was now reasonably sized for cognitive comprehension and decoupled from the accumulated complexity of the backend.

One of the major pitfalls was not a factor of MFEs themselves as a technique but the high cost of replatforming eight-year-old features that didn't have defined APIs in place (since the UI was server-rendered) and our goal to achieve feature parity. We chose to retain parity with the old implementation in order to avoid making multiple changes at once (technology plus features) that could result in inadvertent business performance issues. We also chose to cease the replatforming team after rewriting only some high-value pages. As a result, the replatforming effort is still not complete. We are thus in a non-ideal state, with some of our frontends as MFEs and others still stuck within Django. For the rest, we plan to have feature teams rewrite along with UX-product and not necessarily with feature parity but using the strangler design pattern.

Another pitfall we faced is in supporting small operators in our open source community. These smaller establishments do not have as much experience with management of cloud infrastructure, and so introducing new deployment pipelines to a previously single-step monolithic deployment introduced additional challenges for us to address.

Did you contribute to any OSS project related to micro-frontends? If so, which one?

We have open sourced our own MFE libraries. The following may be useful to others:

Frontend-platform (*https://oreil.ly/ujlM6*) is an application framework for microfrontend applications with APIs for logging, analytics, authentication, and internationalization.

Frontend-build (*https://oreil.ly/3CX8q*) is a library that provides a foundation for linting (eslint), testing (jest), building (webpack), and creating a development server (webpack-dev-server).

Also, not necessarily MFE-related, but an OS resource for React development: Paragon (*https://oreil.ly/6uyip*) is a pattern library containing accessible (a11y) React components and a SCSS foundation built on Twitter Bootstrap.

When would you suggest using micro-frontends, and when should we avoid them?

MFEs are a good technique for scaling frontend development in a large codebase and across multiple teams. Each MFE has its own boundary, which naturally lends itself to team autonomy and smaller cognitive load.

MFEs are too heavy-handed for initial prototypes and smaller implementations. In this phase, a simple web framework is easier to manage with less infrastructure.

At the end of your last micro-frontend project, what worked and what didn't?

What worked: the new MFE technique and framework were readily adopted by development teams throughout the organization. The significant increase in frontend developer velocity and the newly found satisfaction of frontend developers were easy to observe and thus advocated for by both the technical and business function in the organization.

What didn't work: the lack of preexisting backend APIs for MFEs to use slowed down development. We considered investing in GraphQL to alleviate this issue so MFE developers can more easily ask for the data they need without being blocked by updating or creating RESTful APIs.

What are the must-have tools for developers to have an efficient experience with micro-frontends?

A deployment infrastructure that scales with the number of MFEs with the ability to distinguish between MFE code versions.

A local development environment that is easy to use and develop in.

A testing strategy with appropriate tools for unit testing and API contract testing. The latter is needed to catch contract failures by the backend.

What would you suggest for a person who wants to embrace this architecture?

A similar decision process to whether your company is mature and capable to implement microservices holds for micro-frontends as well. Even with MFEs, there is both a common infrastructure and a common framework that the company needs to invest in.

What was the impact of introducing micro-frontends to developers who didn't know about them? What challenges have you faced?

Overall, we had a pretty smooth transition and adoption of MFEs in the organization since we had early support from our leadership team—they were onboard early since they knew how painful frontend development was prior to this shift.

To help developers, we held hopes-and-fears workshops, training workshops, and now have a regular frontend study group to educate and communicate cross-team pro tips.

What was the developer experience like in your last project?

Our investment in developing the frontend-platform and frontend-build libraries [described earlier in this interview] now drastically simplifies the creation of a new MFE. Unfortunately, there's still some one-time manual effort whenever a new MFE is created to integrate it with our infrastructure: GoCD, Terraform, Travis, Analytics, APM, i18n.

Many developers are concerned about performance and design consistency with micro-frontends. What are your suggestions for overcoming these challenges?

For performance, we have invested in SpeedCurve and use it as a tool to discover performance-impacting user experience. We take deliberate steps to design a progressive rendering experience so the immediate initial render of the page is speedy with adequate information before further data is accessed from the server. Also, we decide what data remains in the browser for ready use in subsequent MFE loads. The data may remain in localStorage or in a cookie.

For design consistency, we are investing in Paragon (linked above) as our design library of reusable components.

What are the first steps for working with micro-frontends?

First, ensure this is a path you need to travel since there is upfront investment.

Then, choose a small page with very few UI elements to get started. Beyond the elements on the page itself, there is a lot of technology, framework, and infrastructure that you'll need to figure out.

For us, in our replatforming effort, we iterated on the framework as we implemented new pages. We initially worked on supporting authentication and build/deploy of MFEs. Then, we supported i18n and error logging and monitoring. Later, we added support for analytics and A/B tests.

Can you share the main thing to avoid when working with micro-frontends?

Haphazardly creating MFEs without consideration of their granularity and boundaries. Use domain-driven design practices to consider MFE context boundaries and names.

What are the main challenges in embracing this architecture from your perspective?

The custom creation and maintenance of the build-and-deployment infrastructure are challenges until cloud vendors provide them out of the box.

Would you like to share some useful resources about micro-frontends?

http://thoughtworks.libsyn.com/whats-so-cool-about-micro-frontends

Micro-frontends in three words…

Delightful Frontend Development.

Felipe Guizar, Senior Software Engineer at Wizeline

Please introduce yourself.

I'm Felipe Guizar, a senior software engineer at Wizeline. I have more than five years of experience working mainly with content publishing platforms for big media companies.

What is your experience with micro-frontends?

I haven't yet had the opportunity to implement micro-frontends in a greenfield project. However, I've worked on several projects that migrated websites to new technologies.

On those projects, we agreed that migrating from scratch was not a good business approach because we can't deliver new features until we finish the migration. Instead, we decided to look for an approach to gradually migrate the websites and set the basis for integrating new features easily, introducing micro-frontends to our solutions.

What benefits and pitfalls did you encounter in your journey with micro-frontends?

Context

Frontend technologies (FE) evolve very fast. For instance, I've seen companies that started developing their applications using old frameworks/libraries (AngularJS, BackboneJS) years ago. At some point, new frameworks were introduced in the FE world (React, VueJs), and then developers started learning and choosing those as their main tech stack.

For those companies, it's difficult to keep developers engaged and hire developers who are glad to maintain applications using old technologies.

Benefits

Micro-frontends help to evolve applications along with the technologies. However, it's not only about bringing the application up to date in terms of technology; it's also about aligning the company tech stack with the developer's expertise.

Pitfalls

This architecture adds more complexity for managing different pipelines, versioning and integrating the micro-frontends in the host application. Additionally, managing authentication is one of the trickier parts.

Did you contribute to any OSS project related to micro-frontends? If so, which one?

Yes, I'm the creator of Ara Framework.

Ara Framework makes developing micro-frontends easier by integrating any view library (React, VueJS, Svelte) on any web technology/framework, such as NuxtJS, GatsbyJS, WordPress, Flask, and more.

When would you suggest using micro-frontends, and when should we avoid them?

I believe having good knowledge of the business domains is necessary to identify each micro-frontend's boundaries; otherwise, it leads to bad abstractions that can introduce more complexity for integrating and communicating them.

At the end of your last micro-frontends project, what worked and what didn't?

Server-side includes using a proxy server work well for integrating nonauthenticated micro-frontends in non-JavaScript frameworks. This approach helps us to migrate partial views from WordPress to React along with the content necessary to render those views.

In the early days of the project, we tried to use authenticated micro-frontends using server-side rendering through the SSL proxy server (Nova Proxy). We faced issues forwarding the authentication header, but we realized we could just render those views from the client side using a kind of client-side include (Nova Bridge). Here are a few relevant resources:

- *https://ara-framework.github.io/website/docs/nova-architecture*
- *https://ara-framework.github.io/website/docs/nova-bridge*

Also, centralizing the SSL proxy server created the main point of failure. We tackled it by using the server as a sidecar proxy (*https://oreil.ly/XV4b2*).

What are the must-have tools for developers to have an efficient experience with micro-frontends?

A command-line interface (CLI) for scaffolding, running services locally, and easily deploying micro-frontends.

For example, Ara Framework has a CLI to create new micro-frontends for different view libraries, and commands to run Nova Proxy and Nova Cluster locally.

What would you suggest for a person who wants to embrace this architecture?

Evaluate the problems you're trying to solve against the challenges you'll face implementing this architecture.

What was the impact of introducing micro-frontends to developers who didn't know about them? What challenges have you faced?

It encouraged developers to be more involved in the business side, promoting a common language that improves communication. It also encouraged developers to be more involved in making architectural decisions.

However, when micro-frontends were announced in 2019 in the ThoughtWorks Radar as an "adopt technique" in the social networks, there were some misunderstandings about the main goal of micro-frontends. It's still challenging to introduce the architecture to developers biased by those comments.

What was the developer experience like in your last project?

As I mentioned before, a CLI tool significantly improves the developer experiences. However, we needed to extend the Ara CLI to automate deployments and provisioning infrastructure necessary to run the application.

Many developers are concerned about performance and design consistency with micro-frontends. What are your suggestions for overcoming these challenges?

I believe performance issues related to loading several micro-frontend views on the same page is a sign that micro-frontend boundaries are not well defined. A user flow can involve several subdomains, but the user only interacts with one at a time. For example, when a user navigates to the product listing page (product subdomain) and chooses a product, they finally go to the payment page (payment subdomain).

I recommend lazy-loading each micro-frontend entry point based on routing (routes usually represent a subdomain involved in a user flow).

Obviously, there are cases when we have several subdomains on the same page. For example, in an article page, we have the content itself (content subdomain) and the comments and rating section (content feedback subdomain). Users mainly view an article to read the content. Micro-frontends give us the flexibility to server-side render the content and make it available as soon the user opens the page, and we can let the browser client-side render the other sections on demand (lazy-loading based on scrolling).

Regarding design consistency, I suggest using design systems with reusable components that are domain agnostic. Atomic design is a good methodology for implementing design systems in micro-frontends.

What are the first steps for working with micro-frontends?

Define the micro-frontends' boundaries based on the business subdomains, and identify subdomains that interact together in the user flows.

Can you share the main thing to avoid when working with micro-frontends?

Avoid thinking of micro-frontends as components we can deploy and integrate independently (we can use Module Federation instead). Micro-frontends are views that represent a business subdomain.

What are the main challenges of embracing this architecture from your perspective?

Identifying the business subdomains and defining the micro-frontend boundaries.

Looking for an approach to aggregate them in the host application.

Handling authentication and authorization.

Would you like to share some useful resources about micro-frontends?

- Luca's resources on Medium (*https://oreil.ly/PeGl7*)
- Ara's articles (*https://oreil.ly/tGYD2*)
- My articles:
  - "Micro-Frontends Using Vue.js, React.js, and Hypernova" (*https://oreil.ly/oFY3R*)
  - "Serverless Micro-Frontends Using Vue.js, AWS Lambda, and Hypernova" (*https://oreil.ly/7WLtF*)
  - "Strangling a Monolith Application with Micro Frontends Using Server Side Includes" (*https://oreil.ly/LDYED*)
- This curated list of resources on GitHub (*https://oreil.ly/lJvk6*)

Micro-frontends in three words…

Evolutionary, resilient, agile.

Anthony Frehner, Frontend Architect

Please introduce yourself.

I'm Anthony Frehner. I currently work as a frontend architect, which means I have the privilege of working on just about anything related to the frontend. I've spoken at React Rally, I'm helping drive the W3C CSS proposal for "vhc" units (name subject to change), and I'm a core team member of single-spa. You can find me on GitHub at *https://github.com/frehner*.

What is your experience with micro-frontends?

I was introduced to micro-frontends (MFEs) when I joined CanopyTax, which is the company where Joel Denning and Bret Little (the creators of single-spa and related tools) worked. It was an amazing transition to be in a place where anywhere from 6 to 12—depending on the situation—squads were able to work autonomously. (*Squads* is a term that was taken from the Spotify model, but essentially they're full teams that are centered around a feature instead of being organized by role.)

I left Canopy because another company was interested in setting single-spa up for two reasons: 1) to enable future growth and scale, and 2) to help gradually sunset their legacy application and write new code, while running both side by side. I like to think we were successful at both, and the company was later acquired.

I think that was one of the first implementations of single-spa that used SystemJS 3.0 with import maps, so it was fun to see how these new standards greatly simplified the infrastructure required for single-spa. That infrastructure would also later help form the foundation for single-spa's "recommended setup."

My current company is currently investigating using single-spa because it acquired a company that built a tool in a different frontend framework than the one we use, and we would like to potentially integrate the two without having to do a major rewrite of either.

What benefits and pitfalls did you encounter in your journey with micro-frontends?

You've heard this a thousand times, but MFEs aren't a silver bullet. That being said, they have some great pros and a couple of cons to be aware of.

Here are the pros:

- Team/squad independence. No release trains, code freezes, merge conflicts, long-lived feature branches, QA frustration with testing environments changing/not changing, etc.

- A shared infrastructure that means that everyone is always on the latest version of a library. For example, designers love it because changes to your style guide go out instantly to the whole app.

- A (variable) amount of freedom to experiment and let the best technologies rise out of those experiments, instead of being stuck on the legacy technology because of either the fear of trying something and it failing or not wanting to rework your whole app.

- Lazy-loading built-in, which means a better and faster user experience.

- Bundle sizes and speeds comparable to a monolithic app. There's a misconception that MFEs are significantly bigger and slower than a monolith, and that's simply not true.

- Ability to seamlessly combine legacy software with new software and to integrate software that may have come through an acquisition with in-house software.

- An amazing developer experience. You only have to run a single MFE locally at a time, while all the others can just run their production code. Nearly every single developer that I've worked with has mentioned how much better the DX is for them over a monolithic setup.

- For single-spa at least, it's based on web standards: ES modules, import maps, etc.

- Teams that are focused on vertical slices of the app translate into teams that are specialized and know their feature set really well.

However, there are some cons as well:

- On rare occasions, you will need to do an update on all your MFEs, which is a monotonous task.

- The shared infrastructure can be a double-edged sword. For example, it's great to have your style guide update for everyone at the same time, until you accidentally break something and now it's broken everywhere.

- This is minor, but you need to ensure that your CSS is scoped so that one MFE's CSS doesn't conflict with another's.

- The infrastructure takes a bit more work than just building a monolith. However, to put it into perspective, in my experience, the vast majority (~90%) of DevOp's time was spent working on the backend's microservices infrastructure.

Did you contribute to any OSS projects related to micro-frontends? If so, which one?

I'm a core-team member of single-spa, so I've worked on the library itself as well as the documentation, browser plug-in, example repos, and so on, and I am active in the Slack channel. I've been a participant in other projects related to MFEs, namely SystemJS, the Import Map specification, and webpack's Module Federation plug-in.

When would you suggest using micro-frontends, and when should we avoid them?

I generally don't recommend them for small teams of one to five developers. That being said, there are still situations where that can make sense. Beyond that, it really comes down to how comfortable (or willing to learn) you are with frontend architecture, such as CI/CD pipelines and webpack/rollup configurations.

At the end of your last micro-frontend project, what worked and what didn't?

Almost everything went well, except for one thing: the decision to support multiple frameworks by using web components. In practice, that turned into everyone still only using one framework, but at the cost of additional time and overhead to support web components instead of using framework-specific components. My recommendation is to stick to just one framework when at all possible.

What are the must-have tools for developers to have an efficient experience with micro-frontends?

With single-spa, it's really just about getting the infrastructure up and running; after that, the tools used on a day-to-day basis are exactly the same as a monolith. For the infrastructure, you need to understand import maps and webpack/rollup configuration and have a way to scope your CSS. It's also important to understand coupling and cohesion and how they relate to microservices. You want MFEs that are highly cohesive and have low coupling in order to succeed.

What would you suggest for a person who wants to embrace this architecture?

Ask yourself for what purpose do you want this infrastructure? If you're doing it because you're a small team but you want independent deploys, it may not be worth the effort.

What was the impact of introducing micro-frontends to developers who didn't know about them? What challenges have you faced?

When I've had genuine conversations with developers about it, they generally are open to the idea but don't know how to set it all up in practice. After helping them out, they're almost always excited about it all and love it.

I've had conversations with people who are very hesitant about certain aspects (e.g., "the infrastructure is difficult" or "what about consistent styles?"), and the conversations generally go well, even if they still decide to not implement them. That's OK! Not everyone is up to the task of spending a couple days to work on infrastructure, but at least some misconceptions were dispelled.

And then there's been conversations with people who are completely unwilling to listen and just want to make memes about MFEs. In those situations, there hasn't been much I could say that would help them understand.

What was the developer experience on your last project?

Excellent. There are open source tools for doing MFE overrides with single-spa, so that makes working on an MFE easy. Additionally, running only a portion of your whole app locally means that when you hit the save button, webpack takes only a fraction of a second to update instead of multiple seconds to recompile.

Many developers are concerned about performance and design consistency with micro-frontends. What are your suggestions for overcoming these challenges?

Regarding performance, you mainly just need to put constraints on your team, such as saying, "We'll only support Vue, not any other framework." Just doing that will take care of 90% of your performance issues; the other 10% is no different than taking care of performance for a monolith.

As far as design consistency goes, that's actually a straw man put up by people who haven't used modern MFEs. You'll find that your designs will actually be *more* consistent when you only have to deploy your style guide once and it's updated for all apps everywhere, instead of needing to `npm install` your style guide in each app.

What are the first steps for working with micro-frontends?

Go to one of the example websites that exist for single-spa and set up an override for one MFE. Try it out and see what you like and don't like. Then find us on GitHub, Twitter, or on Slack and ask questions.

Can you share the main thing to avoid when working with micro-frontends?

Just because you can have multiple frameworks doesn't mean you should. It's still recommended to try and stick to one framework if at all possible.

What are the main challenges in embracing this architecture from your perspective?

Your willingness to be open to new ideas and to work on infrastructure such as CI/CD pipelines and webpack/rollup. You also need to understand when you should create a new MFE versus adding to an existing one.

Would you like to share some useful resources about micro-frontends?

We try to keep the single-spa website up to date. Also, the single-spa Slack channel is open to anyone, and we frequently talk about tech-related things besides single-spa in the #randomstuff channel. The book *Building Microservices* is a good reference, even though it's very backend focused.

Micro-frontends in three words…

Enables team independence.

Joel Denning, Frontend Software Dev and Independent Consultant

Please introduce yourself.

Joel Denning, frontend software dev and independent consultant. I've authored single-spa and maintain a lot of other open source, too. I made more than 4,000 GitHub contributions in the last year.

What is your experience with micro-frontends?

I've implemented micro-frontends at five companies and consulted with several dozen more. I created several example repositories: e.g., for Vue micro-frontends (*https://oreil.ly/0674J*), React micro-frontends (*https://oreil.ly/rV0gW*), and polyglot micro-frontends (*https://oreil.ly/zUobJ*). I talk to people every day in the single-spa Slack workspace and GitHub issue queues about implementing micro-frontends.

Which benefits and pitfalls did you encounter in your journey with micro-frontends?

Pros:

- Independently deployed micro-frontends are a huge organizational win. This is the primary benefit in my opinion.
- Incremental migration between frameworks, with "strangler pattern." If you can convert your existing app into a micro-frontend, you can start adding new micro-frontends without rewriting the old one. This lets you introduce the new framework without the cost of rewriting everything.
- Ability to hire developers with a larger range of talents, since they can work in more technologies rather than living with the one set chosen for a monolith.
- Ability to use the "best tool for the job." Does that React library solve everything? Use it. Does that Vue library solve everything? Use it.

Cons:

- Conceptual complexity. It takes a while to explain what's going on to everyone.
- Technical complexity. Separate CI processes, in-browser module loader, Module Federation, and so on.
- Possibility for duplicated dependencies between micro-frontends, which is worse for performance than a single monolithic build. There are solutions to this, but they are often not implemented perfectly.
- Deployment dependencies between micro-frontends are a new thing to consider that don't exist if you have a single deployable.

Did you contribute to any OSS project related to micro-frontends? If so, which one?

Yes, single-spa and all its helper projects (single-spa-react, single-spa-vue, single-spa-angular, import-map-deployer, import-map-overrides, SystemJs, etc.).

When would you suggest using micro-frontends, and when should we avoid them?

Use micro-frontends when:

- You're trying to migrate away from an old framework or monolith.
- You want independent deploys for separate dev teams.

- You want some level of independent technical decision making for separate dev teams (which date formatting lib to install, which React CSS lib, or perhaps even which UI framework).
- You want to split your UI into highly cohesive, loosely coupled sections. This comes from the *Building Microservices* O'Reilly book.

Avoid micro-frontends when:

- You don't want to do micro-frontends.
- Your monolith is working well for you.
- There is only one dev on the project.
- Separate deployments cause more pain than benefit due to deployment dependencies. This occurs especially when you have very few developers.
- Your micro-frontends regularly engage in heavy, chatty communication. If the micro-frontends are talking to each other all the time, perhaps you should not be using micro-frontends.
- Your dev team does not have the technical expertise, time, or desire to manage a more complex system.

At the end of your last micro-frontends project, what worked and what didn't?

What worked:

- We created a separately deployable project with its own *package.json*, build, and CI process. This was a huge win over our PHP/Laravel monolith that built React with an old version of node and gulp.
- We were able to free ourselves from many of the technical decisions of the past.
- We were able to create a style guide / component library that lets us collaborate with UX a lot easier.

What didn't work:

- DevOps was very resistant and took a lot of convincing. The new CI pipelines and infrastructure took a long time to build.
- Some devs confuse micro-frontends with React. They were new to it and couldn't tell what things came from what.

What are the must-have tools for developers to have an efficient experience with micro-frontends?

import-map-overrides
>   They allow you to develop one micro-frontend at a time instead of running all of them locally.

single-spa
>   The most popular open source framework for micro-frontends that I'm aware of.

import-map-deployer
>   A clear way to achieve independent deployments for your separate projects.

Import maps
>   A separate name of the micro-frontend from its URL. This is important for independent deploys.

SystemJs
>   For in-browser module and import maps polyfill support.

What would you suggest for a person who wants to embrace this architecture?

Look at your backend code's architecture and evaluate whether it is working for you. It often makes sense for your backend and frontend architecture to match. If one is a monolith, the other should be. If one is microservices, the other should also be microservices.

Look at how your organization gets things done. If your organization's culture is geared toward product ownership, team autonomy, and distributed decision making, then micro-frontends might make sense. If it's more of a centralized decision-making process, then it might not make sense.

What was the impact of introducing micro-frontends to developers who didn't know about them? What challenges have you faced?

Where are the lines between micro-frontends and a UI framework? What is doing what? How do the pieces fit together? What does this repo (or that repo) do? What's the mental model for the whole system?

What was the developer experience on your last project?

See *https://github.com/joeldenning/import-map-overrides*. You do `npm install` and `npm start`. Then you go to a deployed environment and set up an override so that it uses your local version of the micro-frontend instead of the deployed version.

Many developers are concerned about performance and design consistency with micro-frontends. What are your suggestions for overcoming these challenges?

For shared dependencies, see *https://oreil.ly/w2LFu*.

For design consistency, create a shared style guide module and/or choose a design system such as bootstrap. See *https://oreil.ly/YZyB6* and *https://oreil.ly/UdK5G*.

What are the first steps for working with micro-frontends?

1. Create a PoC to help you decide whether you want to do it.
2. Convert your existing app to a single micro-frontend. Release it to production.
3. Pull out shared navigation into its own micro-frontend. Release it to production.
4. Implement your next new feature as its own micro-frontend. Release that to production.
5. Pull out a small part of your monolithic app into its own micro-frontend. Release that to production.

Can you share the main thing to avoid when working with micro-frontends?

- Splitting them up too much or incorrectly, such that they're all highly coupled
- Shared, single deployment for all your micro-frontends

What are the main challenges in embracing this architecture from your perspective?

- Converting your existing code into a micro-frontend, so that future code can be split into separate micro-frontends
- Setting up CI/CD
- Organizational buy-in, trust, and training

Would you like to share some useful resources about micro-frontends?

This YouTube playlist is great:

https://oreil.ly/Okqtm

Micro-frontends in three words…

Microservices for frontends.

Zack Jackson, Principal Engineer of Lululemon

Please introduce yourself.

Zack Jackson, principal engineer of Lululemon. I focus on distributed JavaScript application architecture and how to scale a company's codebase, teams, and platforms. I'm passionately involved in open source! I created the first code-split SSR system for React, and I'm the creator of webpack 5's flagship feature Module Federation.

What is your experience with micro-frontends?

I have exclusively built micro-frontend stacks for companies since 2015. The largest stack I've built consisted of 150 separate micro-frontends. It consisted of a shared component library; feature-based components used the component library, but most features were deployed independently as micro-frontends. The range of what the micro-frontends were made of was pretty wide. Some were single components, some were full features, and others were whole pages or user flows.

I designed the Starbucks inventory management platform, used by all its stores. This stack consisted of six separate micro-frontend applications with helper services for authentication.

At Lululemon, I am building a powerful stack that leverages an AppShell and Module Federation and that enables drag-and-drop refactors as features or code that can be moved between servers with no need for regression or extra engineering time. I've extended Module Federation beyond managing seamless micro-frontend experiences, into analytics, A/B testing, and configuration management—all while remaining standalone and independently deployable at any time, providing evergreen code to consumers.

What benefits and pitfalls did you encounter in your journey with micro-frontends?

One pitfall was poor code sharing. Sharing vendor code is manual and primitive, causing centralized dependency on an external set of vendors, and upgrading package versions is complex as breaking changes would require all micro-frontends to be prepared for the upgrade of a shared vendor.

Another was poor UX. When moving between micro-frontends, a page will reload. There are very few solutions to sharing global state or making micro-frontends work as well as a monolithic SPA. Huge amounts of time can go into improving the UX.

The benefits of micro-frontends outweigh the pitfalls at scale. Code can be deployed independently, builds are faster, regressions are easier to run, and the blast radius of a critical failure is well contained. It saves engineering time and company money, as features can be delivered at a fast rate, unlike in a monolith, where the rate of delivery slowly degrades as the codebase increases in size and complexity. Micro-frontends remove the harsh requirement of communication and coordination overhead between teams. They are also cheaper to run and scale because you can use cheaper, less-powerful servers. Unlike a monolith, you can scale per page or per component on cheaper hardware instead of scaling expensive and powerful hardware to meet the base demands and memory consumption of the entire monolith.

Micro-frontends are far more agile, and they safeguard companies against site-wide critical failures. Redundancy layers can be built easier, and teams can model a platform to fit their needs instead of using a one-size-fits-all model that monolithic platforms enforce.

Did you contribute to any OSS project related to micro-frontends? If so, which one?

Next.js, webpack 5 core, single-spa, React Static, and Module Federation extensions and enhancements.

When would you suggest using micro-frontends, and when should we avoid them?

Small companies will likely not benefit from the engineering overhead. Larger companies with challenges at scale or companies with multiple teams who rapidly deploy are likely best suited to benefit from distributed JavaScript applications.

Regardless of use case and scale, it's very important to design your platform from the ground up to handle scale. If you foresee rapid scale in the future, designing a system that can be migrated into a distributed application model is key. You'll save time and money by avoiding a full-scale rewrite.

At the end of your last micro-frontend project, what worked and what didn't?

Automatic vendor sharing was challenging, routing between the separate apps and making that route transition seamless were a major challenge, and maintaining authentication sessions and sharing state were very challenging as well. My current micro-frontend project has been designed to avoid these issues by rethinking how applications interface with each other and are designed in general.

What are the must-have tools for developers to have an efficient experience with micro-frontends?

Webpack 5 Module Federation is a massive unlock, single-spa provides a strong orchestration layer, Next.js with a custom AppShell, and yarn workspaces that serve as sub-apps is a robust design pattern, which can enable scale and can integrate with Module Federation if or when needed. Micro is another fantastic tool for creating an ingress to route a user to the correct micro-frontend. Leveraging monorepos keeps code organized but will still have the pitfall of having only one master branch, bottlenecking deployments. Semantic-release is vital for micro-frontend architecture, where semver plays an important role in the scalability and reliable code distribution.

What would you suggest for a person who wants to embrace this architecture?

Give Module Federation a try. Most importantly, design a system that supports scale. Think about monorepos, feature binding, how bound a page or feature is to a specific server, and how hard it would be to split some of the app into another micro-frontend at a later point in time. Avoid hard binding to a server; build software that can be easily migrated to a new stack. Globals like shared state should encapsulate a page or feature, keeping it independent and unbound to the server. Moving a page or feature to another server instance should be built in a way that will provide any globals needed out the box, not involve multiple copy-pastes of various parts of the application. GitLab CI is powerful and a strong contender for sophisticated infrastructure requirements.

What was the impact of introducing micro-frontends to developers who didn't know about them? What challenges have you faced?

Development time decreases and efficiency usually quadruples. Introducing the pattern has given development teams a better experience and the ability to move more code through the pipeline at a faster rate. Challenges revolved around performance concerns from SRE and getting developers used to working in more than one repo at the same time. In highly granular MFE stacks, it can be a learning curve to run multiple MFEs locally and to get used to having several IDEs open, depending on what feature is being developed.

What was the developer experience on your last project?

Kubernetes, custom router and auth layers, shared global packages, and special script to boot and run all MFEs in one place for full workflow use.

Many developers are concerned about performance and design consistency with micro-frontends. What are your suggestions for overcoming these challenges?

Webpack 5 Module Federation is the best solution to this problem. There are no performance concerns or design consistency issues. Code is shared at runtime; it's evergreen.

A non-webpack-5 solution would be to use *renovate bot* and depend on abstraction for distribution or have the micro-frontends supply a render API to allow other applications to retrieve HTML and other resources over a network call. Ultimately, these are better ways to share feature and vendor code along with automation around upgrading dependencies.

What are the first steps for working with micro-frontends?

Figure out how it's going to scale. Centralize shared code, utilities, and data calls. Make sure the platform layer does not become fragmented when managing several independent servers. Think about routing and how you will map various routes to their MFEs.

Can you share the main thing to avoid when working with micro-frontends?

Not abstracting core code to npm. Copy-pasting server infrastructure, which leads to maintenance challenges and fragmentation at the platform level. Either an application shell or server shell should exist, which holds high-level aspects, like auth, user state, tooling, and translation configurations.

What are the main challenges in embracing this architecture from your perspective?

Avoiding UX degradation in favor of DX improvement; neither should be compromised. Thinking out how your MFE stack is going to look and work in one year's time with over 10 stacks: does it architecturally scale?

Would you like to share some useful resources about micro-frontends?

Here is a good resource: "Webpack 5 Module Federation: A Game-Changer in JavaScript Architecture" (*https://oreil.ly/0ny3I*)

Micro-frontends in three words...

Cheap, flexible, scalable.

Erik Grijzen, Software Engineer

Please introduce yourself.

My name is Erik Grijzen. I'm from the Netherlands but currently living in Barcelona, Spain, where I work for New Relic, a company that has an observability platform that gives its customers insights on how their systems and software are running in real time.

About three years ago, shortly after I joined the company, I began working on a new project to build a completely new platform UI, using a micro-frontend architecture. As of today, I'm still working and evolving this project as a lead software engineer on the team and the technical product manager for the UI of the platform.

I've worked as a software engineer for many years in a variety of different companies throughout my career. My focus has always been more on the frontend side of things, which is what I'm most passionate about.

What is your experience with micro-frontends?

My experience with micro-frontends has been solely working on this new platform within New Relic over the last three years. Let me give you some context on how we ended up deciding to use this architecture, because I think this is quite interesting and I believe many other companies find themselves in a similar position.

New Relic is a fast-growing company, and in the last 10 years, it has built many different products. All these products were built separately as monolithic single-page applications that were linked together through one common navigation. This approach was very successful until more or less three years ago, when we discovered that we had several problems related to the consistency of our user experience, extensibility of our UI, and the way we did UI development within our company. Let me go over each one of these problems to explain them a bit more in depth.

Many of our customers were starting to have more and more complex systems because they were adapting to a microservices architecture and moving towards the cloud. As a result of this, our users were forced to switch constantly between our separate applications to troubleshoot problems in their systems. Despite all the best efforts of our UI engineers, our products were all working and looking slightly different (in some cases very different), which led to undesirable user experiences. On top of that, switching between applications also caused our users to lose the context of the issues that they were troubleshooting, which was an even bigger problem.

The landscape of technology (software, tools, programming languages, integrations, open source, etc.) that our customers wanted to instrument and observe was (and still is) exploding. It's almost impossible to keep up, so it was clear that we wanted a new approach where we could provide new functionality for our users in an easy and fast manner. Besides that, we also noticed that some customers had very specific use cases that only applied to them. To also cover these cases, we wanted to provide a way to make our user interfaces programmable so that they could extend the platform for their specific needs.

We also saw that inside our company, many UI engineers were doing a lot of duplicate efforts regarding project setup, tooling, configuration, etc. We wanted to reduce the toil and boilerplate that each team has to go through to build new features so that they could spend more time on building innovative and creative product solutions for our users.

It turned out that a micro-frontends architecture was a perfect fit for us to tackle these problems. Users are demanding more unified product experiences, but it's not easy to build a product with hundreds of UI engineers at the same time, especially when they are located in different offices around the world and in different time zones. And in our case, allowing customers to build on top of the platform as well made the problem even more difficult. In the end, we decided that a micro-frontend architecture was how we wanted to scale our UI development within our organization.

What benefits and pitfalls did you encounter in your journey with micro-frontends?

In our experience, this architecture has very similar benefits and downsides that you can expect from using a microservices architecture on the backend. However, there are a few exceptions to this due to the nature of how browsers work.

Let's start with the benefits. I believe the main topics that we should cover where we noticed the biggest differences are the following:

- Team autonomy
- Small and decoupled codebases
- Modeled around a business domain
- Automation and standardization

To scale the UI development inside our organization, the most important thing we wanted to achieve was for teams to work autonomously. They should be able to deploy new code whenever and as many times as they want without depending on any other team. Each team should be cross-functional, meaning they have every role (designer, frontend engineer, backend engineer, QA engineer, etc.) on the team to build the functionality they want, so that they can do a complete end-to-end implementation. This means they have full ownership and can take all the responsibility for one or more related micro-frontends that are part of a specific business domain. This is important because this allows parallel development without slowing down when more and more teams are working on our platform.

To achieve this autonomy from a technical point of view, the micro-frontends must be loosely coupled, so that they don't depend on each other, and whenever they interact they should have clear contracts. Each micro-frontend is also small in size so that they are easier to reason about (you don't need to know the whole system), easier to test, and you can easily add, change, or remove them over time.

Our micro-frontends are modeled around a business domain or subdomain, because this aligns better with the structure of our business. It creates fewer team dependencies, gives teams more autonomy, and improves the communication to make quick decisions so that teams can iterate over features faster. To give a more concrete example, one team could be organized around the domain of NodeJS application monitoring. They are highly specialized and are subject-matter experts on that topic, which typically results in higher-quality code and better solutions for our end users.

With our micro-frontend architecture setup, we moved from several monolithic single-page applications to many small micro-frontends that are composed at runtime into one unified platform. This resulted in an explosion of a lot of small codebases, which are each owned by separate teams. It was very important to be prepared for this because this architecture introduces a lot of repetitive work and duplication. That's why it's very important to have the proper infrastructure, tools, and standardization in place. We automated every step in the development process, from project creation and pipeline build to continuous integration and continuous deployment, basically providing everything that the team needs, so they can focus on building functionality that our users love.

Let's move now to some of the pitfalls we encountered using micro-frontends. In our journey, the two hardest parts were:

- UX consistency
- Performance

Every architecture comes with trade-offs. I don't think we have a perfect solution to make the UI always consistent and performant, but we try to mitigate the downsides as much as we can. In most cases, this means putting certain constraints in place and reducing the autonomy of teams. For example, we have a constraint in place that every team should use a specific version of the ReactJS library to build their user interfaces. This obviously limits the teams from using any technology they want, but we think it's worth it because this constraint reduces the performance costs a lot for our users. We don't want to limit innovation in the organization, but when we try out new technologies and we carefully evaluate the impact it has on the system, we then update the organization standards and move this innovation to the platform level, so that everyone can benefit from it.

When you have many teams working on the same platform, the consistency of the UI is at risk. To reduce this downside as much as possible, we think it's critical to at least have a design system in place. This won't magically make everything consistent, but I think without it, you will definitely be in a world of trouble. In our experience, this design system is best owned and maintained by one team. This doesn't mean others cannot contribute, but there's one team making sure it aligns with the bigger picture.

We've tried an open source model where everyone could contribute to the design system, but this didn't work out for us, because when everyone is responsible for it, nobody is responsible for it. Maintenance work, bug fixes, and keeping everything aligned with the bigger picture are especially hard to do in this setup. To further improve consistency, we also implemented an SDK that all micro-frontends have access to. This SDK has all the UI components from our design system and provides several APIs to standardize certain patterns such as navigating around the platform.

To make sure our platform stays as performant as possible, we have several things in place. First of all, the platform is built with the application shell model, which makes it very minimal and fast-loading to achieve a good initial perceived performance for the users. When the platform is loaded, we lazy-load the micro-frontends based on the client-side routing, which allows us to only load the minimal JavaScript and CSS necessary to render the screen. To reduce the payload size of the assets we load and memory consumption of the application, we think it's necessary to deduplicate the frontend dependencies as much as possible. On the platform level, we provide some dependencies (i.e., ReactJS) that we are sure every micro-frontend is going to need. We do that by defining those dependencies as webpack externals so that these don't get bundled up for each micro-frontend. This alone reduces the bundle sizes by an incredible amount. For each repository that contains micro-frontends, we are code-splitting the bundles so that we can lazy-load them incrementally at runtime inside the platform. The last thing we do is provide the previously mentioned SDK on the platform level by injecting it in each micro-frontend. This reduces the need to use other npm dependencies, which should decrease bundle sizes even more.

Did you contribute to any OSS project related to micro-frontends? If so, which one?

No, I'm not contributing to any open source projects at the moment. I looked into several of the bigger micro-frontend frameworks and libraries a while back, but none of them really matched with how we wanted this architecture to look for our platform.

I've been asked several times if we will open source what we've built at New Relic. Unfortunately, we don't have any plans to do so. I think that what we have right now is too tailored for our needs, and we would have to change it quite a bit before it would make sense to release it to the public.

When would you suggest using micro-frontends, and when should we avoid them?

Using an architecture like this comes with a lot of trade-offs that have to be evaluated carefully and need to make sense for your project and company. Typically, the benefits outweigh the downsides when you need to scale your UI development to a lot of teams, which normally only happens for midsize to large companies. So my recommendation is to not use this architecture for small projects or companies. If you're not sure you need micro-frontends, you most likely don't need them. Just start simple; you can always slowly migrate to micro-frontends over time when there's a need for them.

At the end of your last micro-frontend project, what worked and what didn't?

I never officially completed a project using micro-frontends. We are continuing to evolve the architecture of the platform as the product and organization change over time. I consider it nearly impossible to get the architecture right from the start, so you are guaranteed to encounter things that are not working as you might expect. Our current architecture is very different than the one we started with three years ago.

What really worked well for us was to set up some ways to regularly communicate and get feedback from other teams. This was crucial in adjusting over time and refining the balance on several architectural topics. I think we have been too restrictive in some areas, and we had to put some more restrictions in other places to get the results that we wanted. We try to keep a close eye on what's not working for us and adjust over time to improve the situation.

What are the must-have tools for developers to have an efficient experience with micro-frontends?

This depends on a lot of things, because there are many ways you could implement micro-frontends based on the requirements of the project, its business requirements, and how your company is organized. But generally speaking, you want to make it as easy as possible for teams to be successful, whatever that implies in your context.

At New Relic, we've built a command-line interface that utilizes our internal infrastructure and tools to provide teams with everything they need to develop features fast. Almost everything you can think of is automated, from project creation to the final deployment to production. We are in a very competitive market, so for us, it's vital to have a fast time to market, be able to quickly iterate on features based on the feedback from the user and spend as little time as possible on technical configuration, setup, and other repetitive boilerplate.

What would you suggest for a person who wants to embrace this architecture?

Micro-frontends are not a silver bullet. Just like with any architecture, there are many trade-offs to be made. You have to find the right balance between those trade-offs that works best for your project, company culture, and organization. What typically happens is that you go from one or several big codebases to many small codebases. That's why I think it's important as a company to make sure you first have the necessary infrastructure, tooling, and standardization in place to support this architecture before you make the change.

What was the impact of introducing micro-frontends to developers who didn't know about them? What challenges have you faced?

I think people don't talk about this a lot, but introducing micro-frontends can be quite a cultural and organizational change that requires kind of a shift in the way you work. This might come as a surprise sometimes to developers who never worked with such an architecture. For us, this was a change that happened slowly over time, so as more and more teams onboarded to work on top of the new platform, the company and the people slowly transitioned to this new way of working.

Especially for the teams that were building micro-frontends on top of the platform in the early stages, it was not always easy. They didn't always have everything they needed and there were still dependencies and things that were blocking them from completing their work. This has improved a lot over time, with better communication, documentation, resources, and better tooling in place to support developers from day one.

What was the developer experience on your last project?

To build micro-frontends on top of our platform, you have to use a command-line interface. Both our customers and internal teams can use this to extend the platform with all different kinds of micro-frontends. This CLI automatically takes care of the project setup, pipeline build, continuous integration, and continuous delivery. This allows for rapid feature development; you can go from idea to production within hours.

When you create a new project, it automatically scaffolds the repository with all the required dependencies, structure, configuration, version control, and integration with internal tools. By default, there are many npm scripts configured to take care of typical developer experience, such as local development, linting, prettifying, bundling, testing, and other automated tasks to make sure that what you build will work within the platform. When we do pull requests, we automatically generate URLs to test the changes against the platform, which makes code review much smoother. Finally, when a pull request gets merged, we automatically create a release for our continuous delivery system, which makes it easy to deploy a specific version to any environment, do rollbacks, and so forth.

Many developers are concerned about performance and design consistency with micro-frontends. What are your suggestions for overcoming these challenges?

As I mentioned, we don't have a perfect solution, but we try to reduce the downsides as much as we possibly can in the context of how we implement micro-frontends in New Relic.

My suggestion would be to carefully evaluate the importance of these topics; based on that, you can define the appropriate constraints on the autonomy of the teams that are building micro-frontends. The more constraints you put in place, the more you can reduce the downsides. You will probably end up with a middle-ground solution that is best suited for your project and organization.

What are the first steps for working with micro-frontends?

It's hard to give specific recommendations on how to start working with micro-frontends because this depends so much on the type of project, culture, organization, and the size of the company. The way we have organized, set up, and architectured our UI development with micro-frontends might be a complete disaster for another company.

Some general recommendations for when you get started:

- Make sure you find the right balance of trade-offs that work for you.
- Make sure to communicate and get feedback, so you can adjust architectural decisions to overcome challenges.
- Make sure you have enough infrastructure, tooling, and standardization in place that support this architecture.

Can you share the main thing to avoid when working with micro-frontends?

The main goal of micro-frontends is to scale the UI development within the organization. So the main thing to avoid is creating dependencies between teams or blocking the development of teams in any way.

What are the main challenges in embracing this architecture from your perspective?

I think the main challenge is to tackle some difficult trade-off decisions, where you are forced to choose between the autonomy of teams and the user experience of the end users. This is not always easy, but I think with time, you will always find a good middle ground for each of these trade-offs.

Would you like to share some useful resources about micro-frontends?

If you are reading this, you already have the best resource at hand. I would also recommend your YouTube talks (*https://oreil.ly/AdyzO*), especially for those who are new to micro-frontends.

Micro-frontends in three words...

Scaling UI development.

David Leitner, Cofounder of SQUER Solutions

Please introduce yourself.

David Leitner is cofounder of SQUER Solutions, a Viennese software company, and describes himself as an enthusiastic software professional who works on various projects using a bunch of different stacks and environments. He spends much of his time on the frontlines tackling the challenges of scaling software and complex domains. A software engineer with more than 10 years' experience, David prefers his code simple and small instead of clever and edgy. David enjoys sharing his knowledge as speaker at conferences, as a podcast cohost, and as a lecturer for his post-diploma courses at the University of Applied Sciences Technikum Vienna.

In 2016, David was one of the first who dealt with the topic of micro-frontends intensively and proposed his ideas to international conferences.

What is your experience with micro-frontends?

When consulting with our customers, we always stress that microservices are about end-to-end verticals that enable independent deployments of autonomous parts of an application at a high pace. Following this idea, it was clear from the very beginning that we had to somehow make this possibility on the frontend parts of these architectures as well. We experimented in a dozen projects with different approaches, including simple ones, like linked applications, but also more sophisticated ideas, like the integration on the client side with web components.

What benefits and pitfalls did you encounter in your journey with micro-frontends?

One big lesson was the impact on the look and feel of huge frontend applications. Thus, a micro-frontend architecture must go hand in hand with a strong understanding and maturity in design systems. In addition, you also have to deal with the classical issues of distributed systems, like performance and latency. For example, over the years we discovered that a shared caching layer on the frontend is a good idea; it was a game changer for how we designed our micro-frontend architectures. And last but not least, it's nearly always a wise decision to start with a monolith-first approach.

Did you contribute to any OSS project related to micro-frontends? If so, which one?

Unfortunately, I have not actively contributed to one of them so far, mainly because we almost never use off-the-shelf frameworks for our micro-frontend architectures. We try to keep the dependencies small and stuck to basic web standards, like web components, to build micro-frontends.

When would you suggest using micro-frontends, and when should we avoid them?

It's really hard to answer this question without any further context, but I think it is important that, as with every new architecture or technology, micro-frontends should not be an end in itself. Still, in our experience at SQUER Solutions, it shows its benefits mainly when the team size gets too big to work on one codebase in the frontend, when resilience issues start to erase, or when the time to market is below expectations.

At the end of your last micro-frontends project, what worked and what didn't?

I think we started to have the maturity that allowed us to spot the right points where the frontend should be split up. But especially for client-side integration, it's a daily challenge to let the integration module of your micro-frontend architecture not sprawl too big and become a bottleneck.

What are the must-have tools for developers to have an efficient experience with micro-frontends?

In most cases, the concept of monorepo makes a lot of sense: a single repo for all the micro-frontend projects, especially to share and ensure consistency for commonly used UI components. Besides this, each module that is used inside the micro-frontend architecture should, of course, strictly follow semantic versioning, and the team should have a common understanding about breaking changes.

What would you suggest for a person who wants to embrace this architecture?

As mentioned before, start with a monolith-first approach. Only start to use micro-frontends once you understand the domain well enough to split them up reasonably.

What was the impact of introducing micro-frontends to developers who didn't know about them? Which challenges have you faced?

I have seen similarities to the introduction of microservices a few years ago, which makes total sense, as in both cases distributed architectures are introduced. The new challenges are therefore to design micro-frontends to be backward compatible and to enforce asynchronous over synchronous communication.

What was the developer experience on your last project?

I think a solid CI/CD pipeline is essential. In a micro-fronted architecture, most of the complexity moves from a developer's machine to the build-and-deployment process. Thus, a feature in such an architecture is delivered once it's deployed to production, not once it's committed to the version-control system. All the tooling should support and align with this thinking.

Many developers are concerned about performance and design consistency with micro-frontends. What are your suggestions for overcoming these challenges?

Basically, it can be said that these concerns are absolutely justified. The question should be whether other advantages of micro-frontends outweigh these problems for a specific use case. My rule of thumb for performance is the more we strive for performance in a micro-frontend architecture, the more we must move the integration to the client. For design consistency, a mature design system can usually overcome most of the challenges.

What are the first steps for working with micro-frontends?

Don't be too opinionated, search for diverse resources that will help you make decisions. In addition, conference talks are a good source for practitioners' reports and learning from the mistakes others have already made.

Would you like to share some useful resources about micro-frontends?

As mentioned before, I usually like to listen and learn from the experiences of others; conference videos on YouTube are a good way to get those insights. In addition, the micro-frontend introduction on Martin Fowler's blog (*https://martinfowler.com*) is a good jump start to this topic. Well, and of course, the book readers are holding in their hands!

Micro-frontends in three words…

Go for it!

Philipp Pracht, Architect and Product Owner at SAP

Please introduce yourself.

My name is Philipp Pracht. I work as an architect and product owner at SAP, located in Munich, and I'm a proud father and husband.

What is your experience with micro-frontends?

I'm currently working on project Luigi (*https://luigi-project.io*), a technology-agnostic micro-frontend framework for admin and business UIs. Before that, I was working on the user interface part of YaaS (a microservice-centric platform and commerce-as-a-service solution), where we successfully established a micro-frontend architecture back in 2014, before the term "micro-frontends" even existed.

What benefits and pitfalls did you encounter in your journey with micro-frontends?

The main benefit is the efficiency boost for any large-scale UI development landscape with multiple teams. In my previous project, I was part of the team responsible for the UI. There were more than 20 teams developing microservices. After we established a micro-frontend architecture (again, it wasn't called that back then) and asked the service teams to take ownership of their UI parts, I was extremely impressed and surprised by how well it worked out. After a short technical introduction, all teams were able to develop and release completely independently, and we never heard back from most of them. It just worked.

The main pitfalls were not on a technical level but rather with some people who did not really stick to the philosophy of micro-frontends or even of independent, self-empowered teams in general. Sometimes this led to long-lasting and unproductive discussions.

Did you contribute to any OSS project related to micro-frontends? If so, which one?

Apart from Luigi, which is open source, I contributed to Kyma (*https://kyma-project.io*), a platform based on Kubernetes for extending applications with serverless functions and microservices. Luigi started out as a Kyma side project, with the goal of extracting the micro-frontend architecture of Kyma's admin console into a framework so that it can be reused in other applications. Of course, Kyma is now using Luigi.

When would you suggest using micro-frontends, and when should we avoid them?

In general, there is a correlation between the (predicted) functional scope and the benefits of using a micro-frontend architecture. If you are certain your UI will have a fixed set of UI components and will be developed by only one team, then you should go with a conventional approach. For all other scenarios, you should check if there is a micro-frontend framework out there that can help you. Even small projects can benefit from something like Luigi, as it offers some extra features that go beyond a pure micro-frontend framework.

At the end of your last micro-frontend project, what worked and what didn't?

On a technical level, everything worked and there were no major issues.

What are the must-have tools for developers to have an efficient experience with micro-frontends?

Tools for reliable development and testing environments are key. Developers should feel confident at all times that what they are currently implementing will work in the bigger context. For example, in my previous project, we offered a CLI tool with which developers could run an emulated main application with their micro-frontend included.

An excellent IDE is also a must.

What would you suggest for a person who wants to embrace this architecture?

As with any trend, read about the topic first, then lean back and think about it from different angles. Think about the possible impact for people in different roles and try to come to a good understanding of where micro-frontends would be a good fit—not only from a technical point of view but also when it comes to organization structures and people.

What was the impact of introducing micro-frontends to developers who didn't know about them? What challenges have you faced?

From my experience with introducing Luigi, developers were happy with it in general, probably because Luigi helps where help is needed but doesn't impose anything —developers still had full freedom within their boundaries. In my previous project, though, there were situations where developers had problems focusing only on their part.

What was the developer experience on your last project?

In project Luigi, we created a tool called Luigi Fiddle (*https://fiddle.luigi-project.io*), a playground where you could try out most of our core functionality. It turned out to be pretty helpful, especially for onboarding new developers.

Many developers are concerned about performance and design consistency with micro-frontends. What are your suggestions for overcoming these challenges?

This depends heavily on the approach you choose, especially the performance topic. For example, Luigi has various mechanisms (like the "viewgroups" concept, caching, preloading) to mitigate performance issues for the end user. With concerns about design consistency, I was a bit surprised when I found out people consider this an issue. I usually ask them how they ensure design consistency in an app that doesn't use micro-frontends, and the answer is something like "This is not a problem, because we have the same CSS." Eventually, most of them realize that you can also share CSSs across different applications. You could also develop Angular components that are not consistent with the rest of the app, so it is the developer who ensures consistency, because they want their piece of UI looking good in its context.

What are the first steps for working with micro-frontends?

Think about how you want to subdivide your UI, then have a look at Luca Mezzalira's micro-frontend decision framework. Also, check if there is already a framework out there that fits your requirements.

Can you share the main thing to avoid when working with micro-frontends?

Avoid introducing a monolithic layer somewhere else in your stack, because you lose most of the benefits from micro-frontends. Micro-frontends work best with microservices.

From your perspective, what are the main challenges in embracing this architecture?

The main challenge would be if your organization structure isn't a good fit. Your management has to set up a structure where dedicated units (a single dev team in the easiest case) can independently deliver end-to-end features.

Would you like to share some useful resources about micro-frontends?

All publications from Luca Mezzalira, of course. There is also a good explanation of micro-frontends on Martin Fowler's website (*https://martinfowler.com*). And, of course, you can look at the project Luigi website (*https://luigi-project.io*) and our YouTube channel, where you can find Luigi-specific content, as well as some general information about micro-frontends.

Micro-frontends in three words...

Divide and conquer!

Index

micro-frontend architectures developed using web components, 97

micro-frontends developed using webpack with Module Federation, 87

micro-frontends with edge-side includes, 112

core subdomains, 25

costs of detecting and fixing defects, 177

crawler-user-agents library, 59

cross-origin resource sharing (CORS) authentication, 49

cross-site scripting (XSS), 238

CSS

    clashes with CSS classes in horizontal-split architecture, 74

    overlaps in CSS classes in server-side architectures, 106

    prefixing class names using seed value, 128

custom elements (web components), 94

custom events, 43

    using for communication between micro-frontends, 34

    using in horizontal-split architecture with client-side composition, 72

cyclomatic complexity (CYC), 179

D

databases

    in microservices architecture, 12

    for monolithic applications, 11

DDD (see domain-driven design)

decentralization

    decentralized organization, 263-265

    implications for micro-frontends, 265-268

decisions framework, 23-36, 115

    application to migration case study, 222-225

    composition of micro-frontends, 29-31

    defining a bounded context, 28

    defining micro-frontends, 24-25

    domain-driven design with micro-frontends, 25-28

    micro-frontends communication, 33-36

    routing micro-frontends, 31-33

    use in ecommerce website project, 117

defects in software, costs for, 177

DefinePlugin (webpack), 120

dependencies

    dependency management in migration case study, 239

external, 56

installing and hoisting across packages using Lerna, 154

loading synchronously or asynchronously with Module Federation, 126

managing external dependencies, 261

sharing across micro-frontends using Module Federation, 85

simplified management in monorepo, 153

deployability, 43

    horizontal-split micro-frontends with server-side composition, 106

    micro-frontend architecture developed using web components, 96

    micro-frontends developed using horizontal split and iframes, 92

    micro-frontends using webpack with Module Federation, 86

    micro-frontends with edge-side includes, 111

    vertical-split architectures, 63

deployment strategies, 167-173

    blue-green deployment versus canary releases, 167

    canary releases in migration case study, 242-244

    observability, 172

    strangler pattern, 170

    talk on, AWS re:Invent 2019, 170

deployments

    independent deployment of micro-frontends, 19

    independent deployment of microservices, 17

    micro-frontend, in automation pipeline case study, 182

depth command for retrieving last commit, 178

design system, implementing, 55-62

    developer experience, 57

    Material-UI framework, 128

    in migration case study, 240

    search engine optimization, 58

design teams, structure of, 57

design tokens, 55

developer experience (DX), 44, 148-151

    automating infrastructure configurations, 183

    defined, 149

    with edge-side includes, 111, 112

in SPA development, 5
organizations and software architecture, link
   between, 248-256

P

package.json file, 166, 180, 240
performance, 44
   achieving good performance with micro-
      frontends, 59
   benefits of server-side composition, 42
   better performance by bunding shared
      libraries in vertical-split architectures, 61
   effects of iframes on, 88
   horizontal-split micro-frontends with
      server-side composition, 107
   improvement using webpack with Module
      Federation, 83
   metrics for, 165
   micro-frontend architectures developed
      using web components, 97
   micro-frontend architectures with edge-side
      includes, 112
   micro-frontends developed using iframes,
      92
   micro-frontends developed using webpack
      with Module Federation, 86
   performance checks in automation pipeline
      case study, 182
   score for vertical-split micro-frontends, 64
   time to display final result to user, 61
performance budget for micro-frontends, 60
persistence layer
   in microservices architecture, 12
   monolithic applications, 11
polyfills, 95
polyrepo strategy, 155-158
   benefits of, 156
   caveats, 157
   combining with monorepo, 158
post-build review, 181
Poster library, 89
postMessage method, 88
PR/FAQs, 259
progressive web apps, 4
proxy servers with ESI implementations, 108
publish/subscribe (pub/sub) pattern, 74
   using between iframes and host page, 89
   using for communication between micro-
      frontends, 43

Q

qiankun framework, 62
query strings or URL, micro-frontend communication via, 35, 132

R

rate-limiting, 187
React, 6, 50
   unidirectional data flow, 84
   use in migration case study, 239
React Router, 126, 131
React Suspense, 127, 135
reactive programming, 229
reactive streams, using for communication
   between micro-frontends, 43, 72
Redux library, 103
refactoring code
   incremental code refactoring with micro-
      frontends, 141
   large-scale, advantages of monorepo for,
      153
   refactoring micro-frontends, 77
registration of micro-frontends, 62
remotes (Module Federation), 119
   configuring remote authentication micro-
      frontend, 129
   implementing dynamic remotes containers,
      140
   listing remotes to load in ecommerce web-
      site project, 124
   loading remote micro-frontends, 123, 127
   specifying in webpack configuration and
      loading them, 120
repositories, 151
   (see also version control)
   artifacts repository, 181
   hybrid approach combining monorepo and
      polyrepo, 158
   monorepo strategy, 152-155
   polyrepo strategy, 155-158
requests for comments (RFCs), 79
   content and structure of, 256
response time, 99
REST, 185
routing micro-frontends, 31-33
   in application shell, 127
   client-side routing in swag ecommerce web-
      site project, 117
   deciding on routing strategy, 42

About the Author

Luca Mezzalira (*https://www.linkedin.com/in/lucamezzalira*) is principal solutions architect at AWS, an international speaker, and an author. Over the past 18 years, he's mastered software architectures from frontend to the cloud, providing the right solution for the context of the job at hand.

Colophon

The animal on the cover of *Building Micro-Frontends* is the Jamaican tody (*Todus todus*). It is one of five species making up the *Todus* genus of birds, which are endemic to the Greater Antilles in the Caribbean. The Jamaican tody can only be found on the island of Jamaica, where it is commonly known as the rasta bird, the robin, and the robin red breast. It lives primarily in forested areas across the island.

The Jamaican tody is small and vibrantly colored, with a green head, red throat and bill, and green-white or yellow-white breast. It is about 4.25 inches (9 cm) in size, with an average weight of 6.4 grams and a wingspan of around 1.8 inches (4.6 cm).

Jamaican todies typically travel in pairs and are most conspicuous in the spring and summer breeding months, when they may be spotted performing wing-rattling or courtship feeding behaviors. Their characteristic vocalizations include a loud beep sound and throat-rattle. Jamaican todies nest and lay their eggs in burrows dug in the soil. They feed almost entirely on insects and their larvae but occasionally consume fruit as well.

The current conservation status of the Jamaican tody is "Least Concern." Many of the animals on O'Reilly covers are endangered; all of them are important to the world.

The cover illustration is by Karen Montgomery, based on a black and white engraving from Lydekker's *Royal Natural History*. The cover fonts are Gilroy Semibold and Guardian Sans. The text font is Adobe Minion Pro; the heading font is Adobe Myriad Condensed; and the code font is Dalton Maag's Ubuntu Mono.

O'REILLY®

There's much more where this came from.

Experience books, videos, live online training courses, and more from O'Reilly and our 200+ partners—all in one place.

Learn more at oreilly.com/online-learning

Milton Keynes UK
Ingram Content Group UK Ltd.
UKHW050046230924
448644UK00004B/15